THE

HIPPOLYTUS OF EURIPIDES.

𝔓𝔦𝔱𝔱 𝔓𝔯𝔢𝔰𝔰 𝔖𝔢𝔯𝔦𝔢𝔰.

ΕΥΡΙΠΙΔΟΥ ΙΠΠΟΛΥΤΟΣ

THE

HIPPOLYTUS OF EURIPIDES

WITH INTRODUCTION AND NOTES

BY

W. S. HADLEY M.A.

FELLOW OF PEMBROKE COLLEGE, CAMBRIDGE

EDITED FOR THE SYNDICS OF THE UNIVERSITY PRESS.

CAMBRIDGE:
AT THE UNIVERSITY PRESS.
1889

CAMBRIDGE UNIVERSITY PRESS
Cambridge, New York, Melbourne, Madrid, Cape Town,
Singapore, São Paulo, Delhi, Tokyo, Mexico City

Cambridge University Press
The Edinburgh Building, Cambridge CB2 8RU, UK

Published in the United States of America by
Cambridge University Press, New York

www.cambridge.org
Information on this title: www.cambridge.org/9781107601390

First published 1889
First paperback edition 2011

A catalogue record for this publication is available from the British Library

ISBN 978-1-107-60139-0 Paperback

PREFACE.

IN preparing the text of this Edition, it has been my aim to adhere closely to the readings of the MSS as recorded by Kirchhoff (1867), and only in cases where they are contradictory or untranslatable have I felt at liberty to admit any save trifling alterations. This principle appears sound as a general law of criticism, and is of special importance in dealing with the text of the Hippolytus, which, over and above the ravages of the ordinary emender, has suffered many things at the hands of editors who endeavour to account for difficult lines of the Ἱππόλυτος στεφανηφόρος by branding them as interpolations from the Ἱππόλυτος καλυπτόμενος, and would purify the text by wholesale banishment of offending passages. That there are such interpolations it would be as useless to deny, as it is impossible (or well-nigh) to demonstrate: but even assuming the probability of their presence, it seems dangerous to use this probability as a weapon, wherewith to excise wholesale lines which incur the displeasure of a critic or an editor, in whose case perchance vastness of learning may not be directed by infallibility of taste. The authority of the MSS is surely of some weight; of more, it may be thought, than the conflicting theories of rival emenders. The following quotation is taken from Barthold's preface to his edition of the Hippolytus (1885); "omnium autem codicum Euripidis cum mihi persuaserim auctoritatem admodum infirmam esse, non dubitavi multis locis omnium auctoritate neglecta ea recipere, quae vel ab aliis vel a me excogitata, *poeta videbantur digna esse*". Such subjective criticism is surely a source of real danger.

In writing the notes I have derived most assistance from the editions of Valckenaer, Monk (1840) and Wecklein (1885), though I am also under obligations to Paley, Weil, Hartung and many others too numerous to particularize, and whose help I acknowledge as occasion arises in the notes. I have also derived great benefit from Dr Verrall's admirable edition of the Medea. The grammars to which I have referred are those of Goodwin, Hadley (Macmillan, 1884) and Madvig (*Greek Syntax*).

In conclusion I wish to tender my heartiest thanks to Mr R. A. Neil, who has revised the proof-sheets and given me most valuable advice and help throughout, and to Mr L. Whibley, to whose kindness I am indebted for the index.

INTRODUCTION.

LIFE OF EURIPIDES.

EURIPIDES was born at Salamis in B.C. 480, the year of the battle which takes its name from that island. His parents Mnesarchus and Clito were prosperous people, who gave their son a liberal education, and left him ample means at their death. He studied painting in his youth, was a friend of Anaxagoras the philosopher, and became deeply imbued with the new learning which was beginning to be diffused through Greece. He published his first play (the Peliades) in 455, the year of the death of Aeschylus, and 13 years after the first victory of Sophocles; it gained the third prize: in 441 he secured the first prize, though with what plays we do not know: in 438 the Alcestis appeared, in 431 the Medea, in 428 the Hippolytus. With the Hippolytus he won the first prize, a distinction which in his long career fell to him only four times. He was twice married, and was father of three sons, one of whom, also named Euripides, followed in his father's steps as a tragedian. He removed towards the close of his life to the court of Archelaus of Macedon, where he lived as an honoured guest, and wrote the Bacchae. He died aged 74 at Pella in 406; the following year witnessed the death of Sophocles. Euripides took no share in public affairs, but lived the retired life of a student, and was reputed to be morose. His domestic life was not happy; it is said to have been embittered by the misconduct of his wives.

That he was a misogynist has been stated on the ground of the abuse of women which is found in his plays: this deduction however is disproved by the portraits of true and noble womanhood which he has left us. Eighteen of his plays are extant.

EURIPIDES IN RELATION TO HIS TIMES.

The youth and early manhood of Euripides had been passed amid the stirring life which accompanied the making of Athens: his full manhood and age witnessed her empire and the beginning of her fall: death saved him from the sight of Lysander in possession of his native city. The marvellous expansion of Athens in literature and art, to find a parallel to which we must look forward 2000 years to our own Elizabethan era, was due to the stirring of men's hearts which a period of national crisis, followed by the glorious victory of few over many, almost inevitably produces. Brilliantly endowed by nature, the citizens of Athens were roused to a consciousness of their power, and their awakened interests were stimulated by the mutual contact and debate, which freedom from home cares, the one great advantage conferred by slave-employment, made possible. Their real education was carried on in the agora and the law-courts, an education open to or rather imposed on rich and poor alike: when every citizen was a critic if not a creator, rapid progress was assured: arts indeed may flourish under an enlightened despotism, but the natural growth which the educated encouragement of the people fosters, could alone produce the marvels of the Attic and Elizabethan drama. This activity however brings with it its own danger: soon nothing escapes challenge: political institutions, religious beliefs, time-honoured methods of education and life, all have to make good their pretensions, or fall before innovations, some wise, some hasty and prejudicial. So it was at Athens: the democracy became more impatient of control, and when Pericles' firm hand was removed, Cleon and Hyperbolus succeeded: Zeus and the Olympians had to endure the rivalry of the *νοῦς* of Anaxagoras: Homer and the gymnasium made way for rhetoric and the Sophists. It was a time of questioning, and its representative is Euripides. Naturally these changes and tendencies were viewed by lovers of the good old times with great suspicion and alarm: unable, perhaps unwilling, to discriminate, they involved in the same condemnation the honest friends of progress and the selfish traders in new things. Were the plays of Aristophanes, the uncompromising champion of the old order, our only means of judging Socrates and Euripides, we should be led to regard them as dangerous subverters of religion and morality. Socrates at least has been vindicated by time: but Euripides has his detractors still: the reason perhaps is that the latter did not know his own mind, had nothing definite and systematized to announce, no gospel save the gospel of doubt, and thus inspired suspicions, which a frank avowal of opinion, had he been in a position to make one, could not have increased, and which hesitation was certain to confirm. Socrates too in many cases left the final decision of a question open, yet he spoke with no faltering tone on what he conceived it to be his mission to proclaim.

In the case of a dramatic poet it must from the nature of things be hard to separate the poet's own views from the sentiments which he regards as appropriate to the particular character speaking: in Euripides the task is still harder, from the apparent contradictions so often met with. If anywhere it is in the choral odes, which, as we shall see, are in Euripides tending to become separable poems, that we may look for the expression of the poet's own ideas: and in the chorus of the Hippolytus 1102 sq. I think we may find the key to his position—keen sympathy with human sorrow, leading to a mistrust of the gods who permit it to fall upon the innocent. The problem is insoluble, but his is a mental attitude which would welcome the searchings of Anaxagoras, would be hopeful that from the new methods of enquiry brought into vogue by the Sophists, some light might be shed

on the dark places, which the old beliefs tended rather to
obscure than to illumine.   Such a man could not speak out.
So in Politics he was the champion of liberty and progress,
though therein he saw and deplored the germs of license and
decay: again and again he raises his voice against the ἀκοῆς
ἡδονή, the pleasure which his fellow-citizens felt in listening
to the rhetoric of the selfish intriguers, who could by skilful
flattery and seeming honesty raise themselves from the degra-
dation to which their counsels were hurrying their native
land.   It would seem that individual freedom guided by a
strong wise leader realised his political ideal: such a leader
had been Pericles, and Pericles had been his friend. Towards
the close of his life we may imagine that the rising monarchy
of Macedonia would in his eyes be preferable to the dema-
gogism of Athens.

In any estimate of his works, it must be borne in mind
that he was first of all a poet, the most tragic of poets, as
Aristotle calls him : his character was deeply tinged by a
melancholy which shows itself in the selection and the treatment of his themes : human troubles, the troubles of the
individual man or woman, occupy him : not the divine law of
retribution visiting generation after generation of a guilty
house, not transgression working itself out in the offender
through suffering to forgiveness and peace, but sorrow and
affliction in themselves, not as the penalty or expiation of
previous sin, find in him their poet: not principles but
persons fill his canvas.   In the second place he was a philosopher: not in the sense of the teacher of a system, but as
being in sympathy with all that tended to knowledge : a
friend of the 'new learning', he had to encounter the hatred
of the Scotists of his day, and doubtless of many an honest
man besides, who feared what he could not understand, or
ascribed to education the evils which really arose from its
abuse.

Lastly, he was a citizen of Athens, having in common with
that marvellous 'nation of jurymen' the keen admiration for
skill in debate, for adroitness in argument, for subtlety of

thought, which hurried him into as many errors of style, as them into errors of policy. Indeed speech after speech in his plays reads like a pattern pleading of Antiphon done into metre.

It has been not uncommon to decry Euripides as lacking in originality, and endeavouring to catch popular favour by vulgar appeals to the eye and ear, introducing for instance on the stage princes in rags or demigods in distress, to the neglect of more legitimate and artistic methods. Euripides we may admit makes a more liberal use of such expedients than his predecessors: with his view of tragedy they may perhaps have appeared indispensable, but still we must not refuse to him the credit of being practically the founder of the drama of incident: his sympathy with the individual naturally led him in this direction, but he was hampered by the conventional necessity of selecting his subjects from a mythology, the recognised incidents of which he was bound however unwillingly to follow: had tragedy after him developed on his lines, while allowing itself a freer range of subjects (as did comedy in the hands of Menander), Aristotle would not perhaps have insisted on the right of princes only to be miserable, and the moderns might have had fewer Rodogunes and more Romeos.

The consideration of Euripides as the introducer of a new idea in tragedy may serve as some excuse for other defects in his work; the too frequent solution of a situation by the deus ex machina, for example: the poet had not attained sufficient mastery of the technique of the new variety of drama to enable him to bring about a natural denouement by mutual play of characters and circumstances, and criticism directed against him on this ground is in a way similar to criticism of Aeschylus for occasional bombast.

Again, in a play where the interest centres round the person of the hero, while but little attempt is made to show the connection between the fate of the individual and the great moral law or divine ordinance of which that fate is the application, there is small scope for the chorus. In the dramas of Aeschylus and Sophocles, it had had the high function of tracing the finger of God in the fates of men, or of expounding the inevitable workings of the moral law: in Euripides it sinks to the position of the idle and undignified onlooker at the changing fortunes of the characters, marring by its presence and its platitudes situations of intense dramatic interest, though bursting at times, as though to justify its existence, into lyrics of the most perfect grace, which in their pathos and appreciation of the beauties of nature transport us into the modern world of romance. We have only to consider the position and behaviour of the chorus in the Hippolytus, knowing all but able to reveal nothing, to feel how burdensome to the poet must have been the necessity for their perpetual presence, spoiling as they do the verisimilitude of admirable scenes, though we must be grateful to the agency, be it what it may, that gave us the ode to Love (525 sq.), and the chorus beginning ἠλιβάτοις ὑπὸ κευθμῶσι γενοίμαν (732—775). Euripides may fairly claim credit for originality in the treatment of his subjects, while that very originality, by the novelty of its methods, is responsible for flaws in the poet's work, which a less original artist might have avoided.

THE HIPPOLYTUS.

We learn from the author of the Greek introduction, that the Hippolytus in the form in which we have it is a revised edition of an earlier play, the Ἱππόλυτος καλυπτόμενος, to which exception had been taken apparently on moral grounds. His words are ἐμφαίνεται δὲ ὕστερος γεγραμμένος· τὸ γὰρ ἀπρεπὲς καὶ κατηγορίας ἄξιον ἐν τούτῳ διώρθωται τῷ δράματι. There seems little doubt that reference is here made to the treatment of the character of Phaedra, and that it was the resetting of that character which involved the re-writing of the play. Much perhaps of the old play was incorporated in the new, but the evidence goes to prove that the second edition

was not a mere adaptation of the earlier one, but practically
an independent composition. It appears that Seneca bor-
rowed from the Ἱππόλυτος καλυπτόμενος the materials for his
Phaedra, and a brief examination of the latter play will
enable us to note the radical differences between Euripides'
first and second editions. As remarked above, it is in the
conception of Phaedra's character that the two plays differ.
After a laboured monologue from Hippolytus on sporting
matters, Phaedra appears accompanied by the nurse. Having
first complained of her enforced marriage to a hated and
unfaithful husband, who leaves her to pursue his amorous
intrigues elsewhere, she proceeds to bewail her own passion
for her step-son, tracing therein the fatal legacy of her
mother. The nurse endeavours to dissuade her from at-
tempting to gratify her desires, pointing out how perilous to
herself and her reputation such a course would be. Phaedra
admits the truth of her arguments, "*sed furor cogit sequi
pejora*". To the further reproaches of the nurse, who main-
tains that she is under the influence not of *amor* but of *libido*,
and warns her that Theseus may yet return from the nether
regions (where one of his adventures has led him), while
Hippolytus himself will assuredly reject her advances,
Phaedra still remains deaf. When however her aged attendant implores her by the memory of her long and devoted
services to pause in her mad course, her mistress suddenly
cries, "*paremus altrix; qui regi non vult amor vincatur*"
and announces her intention to die. The nurse, shocked at
her words, with an equally sudden change of front, now
urges the indulgence of her passion, offering to herself essay
the winning for her of Hippolytus' cold heart.

This brief analysis of the first act brings out with sufficient clearness the contrast between what we may assume
to be the Phaedra of the first, and the Phaedra of the second
play: a weak passionate woman, slave of her senses, scarcely
even struggling against her unholy desires on the one hand:
on the other we have a virtuous and modest woman, hardly
daring to commit to words the story of the fatal passion,

which an angry goddess has put into her heart, but anxious
to carry her sad secret with her to the grave : resolved on
death to save her honour, her own and her children's good
name, and although for an instant wavering when tempted
by the sophistry of her attendant, persevering in her purpose,
sparing neither herself nor the unhappy object of her love.
That there is nothing ἀπρεπές, nothing κατηγορίας ἄξιον in
the Phaedra of the Ἱππόλυτος στεφανίας cannot be urged:
but the greatness of her sin is palliated by the greatness of
her trial, and her very vengeance would to a Greek have in
it a semblance of virtue.

It is interesting to compare the same theme dealt with
at different times and in different countries, to compare the
treatment of Euripides, Seneca and Racine ; the simplicity
of the first, the merely literary character of the second, the
courtly rhetoric of the third.   Euripides wrote for the people,
Seneca for a circle of frigid poetasters and lovers of smart
lines, Racine for the educated and refined audiences of
polished aristocrats at the Hôtel de Bourgogne, trained in
the unities, and above all things correct; and the work of
the three poets was suited to their audiences.   Euripides
received the first prize at the hands of those great critics,
his fellow-citizens: no doubt the telling phrases of Seneca's
iambics and the graceful charm of some of his choruses
(notably that beginning *diva non miti generata ponto*) found
many to admire and quote them in that age of closet-dramas
and glittering polish: Racine's masterpiece from his day to
our own serves to mark the highest point attainable by an
artist, brilliant though he be, who imprisons his genius by
confining it within the limits proper to an age and a people
not his own, thereby reproducing types merely, without
infusing into them the life of the men and women among
whom he lived: a restriction to which we owe it that the
Phaedra of 428 B.C. speaks more truly to our hearts across
a score of centuries than the Phèdre of 1677.

It is a minor point, but one of interest, to notice how
impossible it was for the Frenchmen of that day, Racine

especially, to construct a drama, wherein should be no love-making. It would seem that the representation of that pas-time, which attracts and has attracted the attention of all ages, was necessary to give a human interest to the pro-ceedings of characters, who else would have been too far removed in time and manners from the audience, although that audience had sat at Boileau's feet and learnt the rules for tragedy. So even Hippolytus must have his Aricie; for whose presence Racine quotes Vergil in excuse, and is at ease.

In spite of all however Phèdre remains a brilliant drama, and the rhetorical effect of passages here and there through-out the play, is worthy of Corneille himself. To recognise by a contrast its merit, we need only peruse the Phaedra of the "ingenious Mr Edmund Smith", for which Addison thought it not beneath him to write a prologue, while in the epilogue Prior asks the favour of the audience for

> "An Oxford man, extremely read in Greek,
> Who from Euripides makes Phaedra speak".

THE TEXT.

The MSS of Euripides may be divided into two families. Of the first the most important members are:—

A.   Cod. Marcianus of the twelfth century, which contains the Hec. Or. Phœn. Andr. and Hipp. (lines 1—1223) with scholia. This is by far the most reliable MS.

B.   Cod. Vaticanus of the twelfth century, containing the Hippolytus, and eight other plays, with scholia.

C.   Cod. Hauniensis, a later MS, which seems to be derived from a corrupt version of B.

E.   Cod. Parisinus of the thirteenth century, which con-tains the Hippolytus and seven other plays, with short scholia.

A Byzantine grammarian of the thirteenth century seems to have used a MS of this family, which had become cor-

rupted by copyists' errors, and which he corrected according to the lights of his generation. Of this recension there
were three copies (one of which is now lost) at Florence,
and one at Paris.

The second family of MSS was derived from an archetype,
which had already suffered at the hands of grammarians and
interpolators: very few MSS of this group are extant, as the
recension seems to have early fallen out of use. There are
however two important MSS of this family :—

Cod. Palatinus, of the fourteenth century, at Rome, containing the Hippolytus and twelve other plays.

Cod. Florentinus, also of the fourteenth century, at Florence, in which are preserved all the eighteen plays of Euripides. No scholia are found in either.

These MSS are important in two ways: firstly, from the
fact that they are our only authority for several of Euripides'
plays; and secondly, that though the text has been tampered
with by correction to a very large extent, yet as representing
a different recension, they are very valuable for purposes of
comparison, while from the corrections may often be deduced the reading of an archetype probably earlier than any
of the first family of MSS. For a discussion of these two MSS
cf. Wilamowitz, *Anal. Eur.* 1—9. The author of the cento
made up largely of fragments of Euripides, and known as
the *Christus Patiens*, seems to have used a MS of this class.

The value of the early printed books is small, as the text
was mostly taken from worthless MSS. In 1496 Lascaris
printed at Florence four plays (Med. Hipp. Alc. Andr.), and
in 1503 appeared the Aldine edition at Venice, containing
the eighteen plays edited and corrected by Musurus.

ΙΠΠΟΛΥΤΟΣ.

ΑΦ. Πολλὴ μὲν ἐν βροτοῖσι κοὐκ ἀνώνυμος
θεὰ κέκλημαι Κύπρις οὐρανοῦ τ᾽ ἔσω,
ὅσοι τε πόντου τερμόνων τ᾽ Ἀτλαντικῶν
ναίουσιν εἴσω φῶς ὁρῶντες ἡλίου,
τοὺς μὲν σέβοντας τἀμὰ πρεσβεύω κράτη,   5
σφάλλω δ᾽ ὅσοι φρονοῦσιν εἰς ἡμᾶς μέγα.
ἔνεστι γὰρ δὴ κἀν θεῶν γένει τόδε,
τιμώμενοι χαίρουσιν ἀνθρώπων ὕπο.
δείξω δὲ μύθων τῶνδ᾽ ἀλήθειαν τάχα·
ὁ γάρ με Θησέως παῖς, Ἀμαζόνος τόκος   10
Ἱππόλυτος, ἁγνοῦ Πιτθέως παιδεύματα,
μόνος πολιτῶν τῆσδε γῆς Τροιζηνίας
λέγει κακίστην δαιμόνων πεφυκέναι,
ἀναίνεται δὲ λέκτρα κοὐ ψαύει γάμων·
Φοίβου δ᾽ ἀδελφὴν Ἄρτεμιν Διὸς κόρην   15
τιμᾷ μεγίστην δαιμόνων ἡγούμενος·
χλωρὰν δ᾽ ἀν᾽ ὕλην παρθένῳ ξυνὼν ἀεὶ
κυσὶν ταχείαις θῆρας ἐξαιρεῖ χθονός,
μείζω βροτείας προσπεσὼν ὁμιλίας.
τούτοισι μέν νυν οὐ φθονῶ· τί γάρ με δεῖ;   20
ἃ δ᾽ εἰς ἔμ᾽ ἡμάρτηκε, τιμωρήσομαι
Ἱππόλυτον ἐν τῇδ᾽ ἡμέρᾳ· τὰ πολλὰ δὲ

πάλαι προκόψασ᾽, οὐ πόνου πολλοῦ με δεῖ.
ἐλθόντα γάρ νιν Πιτθέως ποτ᾽ ἐκ δόμων
σεμνῶν ἐς ὄψιν καὶ τέλη μυστηρίων   25
Πανδίονος γῆν πατρὸς εὐγενὴς δάμαρ
ἰδοῦσα Φαίδρα καρδίαν κατείχετο
ἔρωτι δεινῷ τοῖς ἐμοῖς βουλεύμασι.
καὶ πρὶν μὲν ἐλθεῖν τήνδε γῆν Τροιζηνίαν,
πέτραν παρ᾽ αὐτὴν Παλλάδος κατόψιον   30
γῆς τῆσδε ναὸν Κύπριδος ἐγκαθείσατο.
[ἐρῶσ᾽ ἔρωτ᾽ ἔκδημον· Ἱππολύτῳ δ᾽ ἔπι
τὸ λοιπὸν ὠνόμαζεν ἱδρῦσθαι θεάν.]
ἐπεὶ δὲ Θησεὺς Κεκροπίαν λείπει χθόνα,
μίασμα φεύγων αἵματος Παλλαντιδῶν,   35
καὶ τήνδε σὺν δάμαρτι ναυστολεῖ χθόνα,
ἐνιαυσίαν ἔκδημον αἰνέσας φυγήν,
ἐνταῦθα δὴ στένουσα κἀκπεπληγμένη
κέντροις ἔρωτος ἡ τάλαιν᾽ ἀπόλλυται
σιγῇ· σύνοιδε δ᾽ οὔτις οἰκετῶν νόσον.   40
ἀλλ᾽ οὔτι ταύτῃ τόνδ᾽ ἔρωτα δεῖ πεσεῖν·
δείξω δὲ Θησεῖ πρᾶγμα, κἀκφανήσεται.
καὶ τὸν μὲν ἡμῖν πολέμιον νεανίαν
κτενεῖ πατὴρ ἀραῖσιν, ἃς ὁ πόντιος
ἄναξ Ποσειδῶν ὤπασεν Θησεῖ γέρας,   45
μηδὲν μάταιον εἰς τρὶς εὔξασθαι θεῷ.
ἡ δ᾽ εὐκλεὴς μέν, ἀλλ᾽ ὅμως ἀπόλλυται,
Φαίδρα· τὸ γὰρ τῆσδ᾽ οὐ προτιμήσω κακὸν
τὸ μὴ οὐ παρασχεῖν τοὺς ἐμοὺς ἐχθροὺς ἐμοὶ
δίκην τοσαύτην ὥστ᾽ ἐμοὶ καλῶς ἔχειν.   50
ἀλλ᾽ εἰσορῶ γὰρ τόνδε παῖδα Θησέως
στείχοντα θήρας μόχθον ἐκλελοιπότα,
Ἱππόλυτον, ἔξω τῶνδε βήσομαι τόπων.

πολὺς δ' ἄμ' αὐτῷ προσπόλων ὀπισθόπους
κῶμος λέλακεν Ἄρτεμιν τιμῶν θεὰν   55
ὕμνοισιν· οὐ γὰρ οἶδ' ἀνεῳγμένας πύλας
Ἅιδου, φάος δὲ λοίσθιον βλέπων τόδε.

ΙΠ. ἔπεσθ' ᾄδοντες ἔπεσθε
τὰν Διὸς οὐρανίαν
Ἄρτεμιν, ᾇ μελόμεσθα.   60

ΘΕ. πότνια πότνια σεμνοτάτα,
Ζανὸς γένεθλον,
χαῖρε χαῖρέ μοι, ὦ κόρα
Λατοῦς Ἄρτεμι καὶ Διός,   65
καλλίστα πολὺ παρθένων,
ἃ μέγαν κατ' οὐρανὸν
ναίεις εὐπατέρειαν αὐλάν,
Ζηνὸς πολύχρυσον οἶκον.
χαῖρέ μοι, ὦ καλλίστα   70
καλλίστα τῶν κατ' Ὄλυμπον
παρθένων, Ἄρτεμι.

ΙΠ. σοὶ τόνδε πλεκτὸν στέφανον ἐξ ἀκηράτου
λειμῶνος, ὦ δέσποινα, κοσμήσας φέρω,
ἔνθ' οὔτε ποιμὴν ἀξιοῖ φέρβειν βοτὰ   75
οὔτ' ἦλθέ πω σίδηρος, ἀλλ' ἀκήρατον
μέλισσα λειμῶν' ἠρινὸν διέρχεται·
Αἰδὼς δὲ ποταμίαισι κηπεύει δρόσοις,
ὅσοις διδακτὸν μηδέν, ἀλλ' ἐν τῇ φύσει
τὸ σωφρονεῖν εἴληχεν εἰς τὰ πάνθ' ὁμῶς,   80
τούτοις δρέπεσθαι· τοῖς κακοῖσι δ' οὐ θέμις.
ἀλλ' ὦ φίλη δέσποινα, χρυσέας κόμης
ἀνάδημα δέξαι χειρὸς εὐσεβοῦς ἄπο.
μόνῳ γάρ ἐστι τοῦτ' ἐμοὶ γέρας βροτῶν·
σοὶ καὶ ξύνειμι καὶ λόγοις σ' ἀμείβομαι,   85

κλύων μὲν αὐδήν, ὄμμα δ' οὐχ ὁρῶν τὸ σόν.
τέλος δὲ κάμψαιμ' ὥσπερ ἠρξάμην βίου.
ΘΕ. ἄναξ, θεοὺς γὰρ δεσπότας καλεῖν χρεών,
ἆρ' ἄν τί μου δέξαιο βουλεύσαντος εὖ;
ΙΠ. καὶ κάρτα γ'· ἦ γὰρ οὐ σοφοὶ φαινοίμεθ' ἄν.   90
ΘΕ. οἶσθ' οὖν βροτοῖσιν ὃς καθέστηκεν νόμος,
ΙΠ. οὐκ οἶδα· τοῦ δὲ καί μ' ἀνιστορεῖς πέρι;
ΘΕ. μισεῖν τὸ σεμνὸν καὶ τὸ μὴ πᾶσιν φίλον;
ΙΠ. ὀρθῶς γε· τίς δ' οὐ σεμνὸς ἀχθεινὸς βροτῶν;
ΘΕ. ἐν δ' εὐπροσηγόροισιν ἔστι τις χάρις;   95
ΙΠ. πλείστη γε, καὶ κέρδος γε σὺν μόχθῳ βραχεῖ.
ΘΕ. ἦ κἀν θεοῖσι ταὐτὸν ἐλπίζεις τόδε;
ΙΠ. εἴπερ γε θνητοὶ θεῶν νόμοισι χρώμεθα.
ΘΕ. πῶς οὖν σὺ σεμνὴν δαίμον' οὐ προσεννέπεις;
ΙΠ. τίν'; εὐλαβοῦ δὲ μή τι σοῦ σφαλῇ στόμα.   100
ΘΕ. τήνδ' ἣ πύλαισι σαῖς ἐφέστηκεν Κύπρις.
ΙΠ. πρόσωθεν αὐτὴν ἁγνὸς ὢν ἀσπάζομαι.
ΘΕ. σεμνή γε μέντοι κἀπίσημος ἐν βροτοῖς.
ΙΠ. οὐδείς μ' ἀρέσκει νυκτὶ θαυμαστὸς θεῶν.   106
ΘΕ. τιμαῖσιν, ὦ παῖ, δαιμόνων χρῆσθαι χρεών.   107
ΙΠ. ἄλλοισιν ἄλλος θεῶν τε κἀνθρώπων μέλει.   104
ΘΕ. εὐδαιμονοίης νοῦν ἔχων ὅσον σε δεῖ.   105
ΙΠ. χωρεῖτ', ὀπαδοί, καὶ παρελθόντες δόμους
σίτων μέλεσθε· τερπνὸν ἐκ κυναγίας
τράπεζα πλήρης· καὶ καταψήχειν χρεὼν   110
ἵππους, ὅπως ἂν ἅρμασι ζεύξας ὕπο
βορᾶς κορεσθεὶς γυμνάσω τὰ πρόσφορα·
τὴν σὴν δὲ Κύπριν πόλλ' ἐγὼ χαίρειν λέγω.
ΘΕ. ἡμεῖς δέ, τοὺς νέους γὰρ οὐ μιμητέον,
φρονοῦντες οὕτως ὡς πρέπει δούλοις λέγειν,   115
προσευξόμεσθα τοῖσι σοῖς ἀγάλμασι,

δέσποινα Κύπρι. χρὴ δὲ συγγνώμην ἔχειν,
εἴ τίς σ' ὑφ' ἥβης σπλάγχνον ἔντονον φέρων
μάταια βάζει· μὴ δόκει τούτου κλύειν·
σοφωτέρους γὰρ χρὴ βροτῶν εἶναι θεούς.   120

ΧΟ. Ὠκεανοῦ τις ὕδωρ   στρ.
στάζουσα πέτρα λέγεται
βαπτὰν κάλπισι ῥυτὰν
παγὰν προϊεῖσα κρημνῶν,
ὅθι μοί τις ἦν φίλα,   125
πορφύρεα φάρεα
ποταμίᾳ δρόσῳ
τέγγουσα, θερμᾶς δ' ἐπὶ νῶτα πέτρας
εὐαλίου κατέβαλλ'· ὅθεν μοι
πρῶτα φάτις ἦλθε δεσποίνας,   130
τειρομέναν νοσερᾷ   ἀντ.
κοίτᾳ δέμας ἐντὸς ἔχειν
οἴκων, λεπτὰ δὲ φάρη
ξανθὰν κεφαλὰν σκιάζειν.
*τριτάταν δέ νιν κλύω   135
τάνδε κατ' ἀμβροσίου
στόματος ἀμέραν
Δάματρος ἀκτᾶς δέμας ἁγνὸν ἴσχειν,*
κρυπτῷ πάθει θανάτου θέλουσαν
κέλσαι ποτὶ τέρμα δύστανον.   140
οὐ γὰρ ἔνθεος, ὦ κούρα,   στρ.
εἴτ' ἐκ Πανὸς εἴθ' Ἑκάτας
ἢ σεμνῶν Κορυβάντων
φοιτᾷς ἢ ματρὸς ὀρείας.
ἢ οὐκ ἀμφὶ τὰν πολύθηρον   145
Δίκτυνναν ἀμπλακίαις
ἀνίερος ἀθύτων πελάνων τρύχει;

φοιτᾷ γὰρ καὶ διὰ λίμνας
χέρσον θ' ὑπὲρ πελάγους
δίναις ἐν νοτίαις ἅλμας.   150
ἢ πόσιν τὸν Ἐρεχθειδᾶν   ἀντ.
ἀρχαγὸν τὸν εὐπατρίδαν
ποιμαίνει τις ἐν οἴκοις
κρυπτὰ κοίτα λεχέων σῶν;
ἢ ναυβάτας τις ἔπλευσεν   155
Κρήτας ἔξορμος ἀνὴρ
λιμένα τὸν εὐξεινότατον ναύταις,
φάμαν πέμπων βασιλείᾳ,
λύπᾳ δ' ὑπὲρ παθέων
εὐναία δέδεται ψυχάν;   160
φιλεῖ δὲ τᾷ δυστρόπῳ γυναικῶν
ἁρμονίᾳ κακὰ δύστανος
ἀμηχανία συνοικεῖν
ὠδίνων τε καὶ ἀφροσύνας.
δι' ἐμᾶς ᾖξέν ποτε νηδύος ἅδ' αὔρα·   165
τὰν δ' εὔλοχον οὐρανίαν
τόξων μεδέουσαν ἀύτευν
Ἄρτεμιν, καί μοι πολυζήλωτος ἀεὶ
σὺν θεοῖς ἐφοίτα.
ἀλλ' ἥδε τροφὸς γεραιὰ πρὸ θυρῶν   170
τήνδε κομίζουσ' ἔξω μελάθρων·
στυγνὸν δ' ὀφρύων νέφος αὐξάνεται.
τί ποτ' ἔστι μαθεῖν ἔραται ψυχά,
τί δεδήληται
δέμας ἀλλόχροον βασιλείας.   175
ΤΡ. ὦ κακὰ θνητῶν στυγεραί τε νόσοι.
τί σ' ἐγὼ δράσω; τί δὲ μὴ δράσω;
τόδε σοι φέγγος, λαμπρὸς ὅδ' αἰθήρ·

ἔξω δὲ δόμων ἤδη νοσερᾶς
δέμνια κοίτης.   180
δεῦρο γὰρ ἐλθεῖν πᾶν ἔπος ἦν σοι·
τάχα δ᾽ εἰς θαλάμους σπεύσεις τὸ πάλιν.
ταχὺ γὰρ σφάλλει κοὐδενὶ χαίρεις,
οὐδέ σ᾽ ἀρέσκει τὸ παρόν, τὸ δ᾽ ἀπὸν
φίλτερον ἡγεῖ.   185
κρεῖσσον δὲ νοσεῖν ἢ θεραπεύειν·
τὸ μέν ἐστιν ἁπλοῦν, τῷ δὲ συνάπτει
λύπη τε φρενῶν χερσίν τε πόνος.
πᾶς δ᾽ ὀδυνηρὸς βίος ἀνθρώπων,
κοὐκ ἔστι πόνων ἀνάπαυσις·   190
ἀλλ᾽ ὅ τι τοῦ ζῆν φίλτερον ἄλλο
σκότος ἀμπίσχων κρύπτει νεφέλαις.
δυσέρωτες δὴ φαινόμεθ᾽ ὄντες
τοῦδ᾽ ὅ τι τοῦτο στίλβει κατὰ γῆν,
δι᾽ ἀπειροσύνην ἄλλου βιότου   195
κοὐκ ἀπόδειξιν τῶν ὑπὸ γαίας·
μύθοις δ᾽ ἄλλως φερόμεσθα.
ΦΑ. αἴρετέ μου δέμας, ὀρθοῦτε κάρα·
λέλυμαι μελέων σύνδεσμα, φίλαι.
λάβετ᾽ εὐπήχεις χεῖρας, πρόπολοι.   200
βαρύ μοι κεφαλᾶς ἐπίκρανον ἔχειν·
ἄφελ᾽, ἀμπέτασον βόστρυχον ὤμοις.
ΤΡ. θάρσει, τέκνον, καὶ μὴ χαλεπῶς
μετάβαλλε δέμας.
ῥᾷον δὲ νόσον μετά θ᾽ ἡσυχίας   205
καὶ γενναίου λήματος οἴσεις·
μοχθεῖν δὲ βροτοῖσιν ἀνάγκη.
ΦΑ. αἰαῖ·
πῶς ἂν δροσερᾶς ἀπὸ κρηνῖδος

καθαρῶν ὑδάτων πῶμ᾽ ἀρυσαίμαν;
ὑπό τ᾽ αἰγείροις ἔν τε κομήτῃ   210
λειμῶνι κλιθεῖσ᾽ ἀναπαυσαίμαν.

ΤΡ. ὦ παῖ, τί θροεῖς;
οὐ μὴ παρ᾽ ὄχλῳ τάδε γηρύσει
μανίας ἔποχον ῥίπτουσα λόγον;

ΦΑ. πέμπετέ μ᾽ εἰς ὄρος· εἶμι πρὸς ὕλαν   215
καὶ παρὰ πεύκας, ἵνα θηροφόνοι
στείβουσι κύνες
βαλιαῖς ἐλάφοις ἐγχριμπτόμεναι·
πρὸς θεῶν, ἔραμαι κυσὶ θωΰξαι
καὶ παρὰ χαίταν ξανθὰν ῥῖψαι   220
Θεσσαλὸν ὅρπακ᾽, ἐπίλογχον ἔχουσ᾽
ἐν χειρὶ βέλος.

ΤΡ. τί ποτ᾽, ὦ τέκνον, τάδε κηραίνεις;
τί κυνηγεσίων καὶ σοὶ μελέτη;
τί δὲ κρηναίων νασμῶν ἔρασαι;   225
πάρα γὰρ δροσερὰ πύργοις συνεχὴς
κλιτύς, ὅθεν σοι πῶμα γένοιτ᾽ ἄν.

ΦΑ. δέσποιν᾽ ἁλίας Ἄρτεμι Λίμνας
καὶ γυμνασίων τῶν ἱπποκρότων,
εἴθε γενοίμαν ἐν σοῖς δαπέδοις,   230
πώλους Ἐνέτας δαμαλιζομένα.

ΤΡ. τί τόδ᾽ αὖ παράφρων ἔρριψας ἔπος;
νῦν δὴ μὲν ὄρος βᾶσ᾽ ἐπὶ θήρας
πόθον ἐστέλλου, νῦν δ᾽ αὖ ψαμάθοις
ἐπ᾽ ἀκυμάντοις πώλων ἔρασαι.   235
τάδε μαντείας ἄξια πολλῆς,
ὅστις σε θεῶν ἀνασειράζει
καὶ παρακόπτει φρένας, ὦ παῖ.

ΦΑ. δύστανος ἐγώ, τί ποτ᾽ εἰργασάμαν;

ποῖ παρεπλάγχθην γνώμας ἀγαθᾶς ;   240
ἐμάνην, ἔπεσον δαίμονος ἄτᾳ.
φεῦ φεῦ, τλάμων.
μαῖα, πάλιν μου κρύψον κεφαλάν·
αἰδούμεθα γὰρ τὰ λελεγμένα μοι.
κρύπτε· κατ' ὄσσων δάκρυ μοι βαίνει,   245
καὶ ἐπ' αἰσχύνην ὄμμα τέτραπται.
τὸ γὰρ ὀρθοῦσθαι γνώμην ὀδυνᾷ,
τὸ δὲ μαινόμενον κακόν· ἀλλὰ κρατεῖ
μὴ γιγνώσκοντ' ἀπολέσθαι.

ΤΡ. κρύπτω· τὸ δ' ἐμὸν πότε δὴ θάνατος   250
σῶμα καλύψει ;
πολλὰ διδάσκει μ' ὁ πολὺς βίοτος.
χρῆν γὰρ μετρίας εἰς ἀλλήλους
φιλίας θνητοὺς ἀνακίρνασθαι
καὶ μὴ πρὸς ἄκρον μυελὸν ψυχῆς,   255
εὔλυτα δ' εἶναι στέργηθρα φρενῶν
ἀπό τ' ὤσασθαι καὶ ξυντεῖναι.
τὸ δ' ὑπὲρ δισσῶν μίαν ὠδίνειν
ψυχὴν χαλεπὸν βάρος, ὡς κἀγὼ
τῆσδ' ὑπεραλγῶ.   260
βιότου δ' ἀτρεκεῖς ἐπιτηδεύσεις
φασὶ σφάλλειν πλέον ἢ τέρπειν
τῇ θ' ὑγιείᾳ μᾶλλον πολεμεῖν.
οὕτω τὸ λίαν ἧσσον ἐπαινῶ
τοῦ μηδὲν ἄγαν·   265
καὶ ξυμφήσουσι σοφοί μοι.

ΧΟ. γύναι γεραιά, βασιλίδος πιστὴ τροφὲ
Φαίδρας, ὁρῶ μὲν τάσδε δυστήνους τύχας,
ἄσημα δ' ἡμῖν ἥτις ἐστὶν ἡ νόσος·
σοῦ δ' ἂν πυθέσθαι καὶ κλύειν βουλοίμεθ' ἄν. 270

ΤΡ. οὐκ οἶδ᾽ ἐλέγχουσ᾽· οὐ γὰρ ἐννέπειν θέλει.
ΧΟ. οὐδ᾽ ἥτις ἀρχὴ τῶνδε πημάτων ἔφυ;
ΤΡ. εἰς ταὐτὸν ἥκεις· πάντα γὰρ σιγᾷ τάδε.
ΧΟ. ὡς ἀσθενεῖ τε καὶ κατέξανται δέμας.
ΤΡ. πῶς δ᾽ οὔ, τριταίαν οὖσ᾽ ἄσιτος ἡμέραν;   275
ΧΟ. πότερον ὑπ᾽ ἄτης ἢ θανεῖν πειρωμένη;
ΤΡ. θανεῖν· ἀσιτεῖ δ᾽ εἰς ἀπόστασιν βίου.
ΧΟ. θαυμαστὸν εἶπας, εἰ τάδ᾽ ἐξαρκεῖ πόσει.
ΤΡ. κρύπτει γὰρ ἥδε πῆμα κοὔ φησιν νοσεῖν.
ΧΟ. ὁ δ᾽ εἰς πρόσωπον οὐ τεκμαίρεται βλέπων;   280
ΤΡ. ἔκδημος ὢν γὰρ τῆσδε τυγχάνει χθονός.
ΧΟ. σὺ δ᾽ οὐκ ἀνάγκην προσφέρεις, πειρωμένη
    νόσον πυθέσθαι τῆσδε καὶ πλάνον φρενῶν;
ΤΡ. εἰς πᾶν ἀφῖγμαι κοὐδὲν εἴργασμαι πλέον·
    οὐ μὴν ἀνήσω γ᾽ οὐδὲ νῦν προθυμίας,   285
    ὡς ἂν παροῦσα καὶ σύ μοι ξυμμαρτυρῇς
    οἷα πέφυκα δυστυχοῦσι δεσπόταις.
    ἄγ᾽, ὦ φίλη παῖ, τῶν πάροιθε μὲν λόγων
    λαθώμεθ᾽ ἄμφω, καὶ σύ θ᾽ ἡδίων γενοῦ
    στυγνὴν ὀφρὺν λύσασα καὶ γνώμης ὁδόν,   290
    ἐγώ θ᾽ ὅπῃ σοι μὴ καλῶς τόθ᾽ εἱπόμην
    μεθεῖσ᾽ ἐπ᾽ ἄλλον εἶμι βελτίω λόγον.
    κεἰ μὲν νοσεῖς τι τῶν ἀπορρήτων κακῶν,
    γυναῖκες αἵδε συγκαθιστάναι νόσον·
    εἰ δ᾽ ἔκφορός σοι συμφορὰ πρὸς ἄρσενας,   295
    λέγ᾽, ὡς ἰατροῖς πρᾶγμα μηνυθῇ τόδε.
    εἶεν· τί σιγᾷς; οὐκ ἐχρῆν σιγᾶν, τέκνον,
    ἀλλ᾽ ἤ μ᾽ ἐλέγχειν, εἴ τι μὴ καλῶς λέγω,
    ἢ τοῖσιν εὖ λεχθεῖσι συγχωρεῖν λόγοις.
    φθέγξαι τι, δεῦρ᾽ ἄθρησον· ὦ τάλαιν᾽ ἐγώ.   300
    γυναῖκες, ἄλλως τούσδε μοχθοῦμεν πόνους,

ἴσον δ᾽ ἄπεσμεν τῷ πρίν· οὔτε γὰρ τότε
λόγοις ἐτέγγεθ᾽ ἥδε νῦν τ᾽ οὐ πείθεται.
ἀλλ᾽ ἴσθι μέντοι, πρὸς τάδ᾽ αὐθαδεστέρα
γίγνου θαλάσσης, εἰ θανεῖ, προδοῦσα σοὺς 305
παῖδας πατρῴων μὴ μεθέξοντας δόμων,
μὰ τὴν ἄνασσαν ἱππίαν Ἀμαζόνα,
ἢ σοῖς τέκνοισι δεσπότην ἐγείνατο
νόθον φρονοῦντα γνήσι᾽, οἶσθά νιν καλῶς.
Ἱππόλυτον. ΦΑ. οἴμοι. ΤΡ. θιγγάνει σέθεν
    τόδε;   310
ΦΑ. ἀπώλεσάς με, μαῖα, καί σε πρὸς θεῶν
    τοῦδ᾽ ἀνδρὸς αὖθις λίσσομαι σιγᾶν πέρι.
ΤΡ. ὁρᾷς; φρονεῖς μὲν εὖ, φρονοῦσα δ᾽ οὐ θέλεις
    παῖδάς τ᾽ ὀνῆσαι καὶ σὸν ἐκσῶσαι βίον.
ΦΑ. φιλῶ τέκν᾽· ἄλλῃ δ᾽ ἐν τύχῃ χειμάζομαι. 315
ΤΡ. ἁγνὰς μέν, ὦ παῖ, χεῖρας αἵματος φέρεις;
ΦΑ. χεῖρες μὲν ἁγναί, φρὴν δ᾽ ἔχει μίασμά τι.
ΤΡ. μῶν ἐξ ἐπακτοῦ πημονῆς ἐχθρῶν τινος;
ΦΑ. φίλος μ᾽ ἀπόλλυσ᾽ οὐχ ἑκοῦσαν οὐχ ἑκών.
ΤΡ. Θησεύς τιν᾽ ἡμάρτηκεν εἰς σ᾽ ἁμαρτίαν; 320
ΦΑ. μὴ δρῶσ᾽ ἔγωγ᾽ ἐκεῖνον ὀφθείην κακῶς.
ΤΡ. τί γὰρ τὸ δεινὸν τοῦθ᾽ ὅ σ᾽ ἐξαίρει θανεῖν;
ΦΑ. ἔα μ᾽ ἁμαρτεῖν· οὐ γὰρ εἰς σ᾽ ἁμαρτάνω.
ΤΡ. οὐ δῆθ᾽ ἑκοῦσά γ᾽, ἐν δὲ σοὶ λελείψομαι.
ΦΑ. τί δρᾷς; βιάζει χειρὸς ἐξαρτωμένη; 325
ΤΡ. καὶ σῶν γε γονάτων, κοὐ μεθήσομαί ποτε.
ΦΑ. κάκ᾽, ὦ τάλαινα, σοὶ τάδ᾽, εἰ πεύσει, κακά.
ΤΡ. μεῖζον γὰρ ἢ σοῦ μὴ τυχεῖν τί μοι κακόν;
ΦΑ. ὀλεῖ· τὸ μέντοι πρᾶγμ᾽ ἐμοὶ τιμὴν φέρει. 329
ΤΡ. οὔκουν λέγουσα τιμιωτέρα φανεῖ; 332
ΦΑ. ἐκ τῶν γὰρ αἰσχρῶν ἐσθλὰ μηχανώμεθα· 331

ΤΡ. κἄπειτα κρύπτεις χρῆσθ' ἱκνουμένης ἐμοῦ;   330
ΦΑ. ἄπελθε πρὸς θεῶν δεξιάν τ' ἐμὴν μέθες.   333
ΤΡ. οὐ δῆτ', ἐπεί μοι δῶρον οὐ δίδως ὃ χρῆν.
ΦΑ. δώσω· σέβας γὰρ χειρὸς αἰδοῦμαι τὸ σόν.   335
ΤΡ. σιγῷμ' ἂν ἤδη· σὸς γὰρ οὑντεῦθεν λόγος.
ΦΑ. ὦ τλῆμον, οἷον, μῆτερ, ἠράσθης ἔρον,
ΤΡ. ὃν ἔσχε ταύρου, τέκνον, ἢ τί φῂς τόδε;
ΦΑ. σύ τ', ὦ τάλαιν' ὅμαιμε, Διονύσου δάμαρ,
ΤΡ. τέκνον, τί πάσχεις; συγγόνους κακορροθεῖς;   340
ΦΑ. τρίτη τ' ἐγὼ δύστηνος ὡς ἀπόλλυμαι.
ΤΡ. ἔκ τοι πέπληγμαι· ποῖ προβήσεται λόγος;
ΦΑ. ἐκεῖθεν ἡμεῖς, οὐ νεωστὶ δυστυχεῖς.
ΤΡ. οὐδέν τι μᾶλλον οἶδ' ἃ βούλομαι κλύειν.
ΦΑ. φεῦ·
    πῶς ἂν σύ μοι λέξειας ἁμὲ χρῇς λέγειν;   345
ΤΡ. οὐ μάντις εἰμὶ τἀφανῆ γνῶναι σαφῶς.
ΦΑ. τί τοῦθ' ὃ δὴ λέγουσιν ἀνθρώπους ἐρᾶν;
ΤΡ. ἥδιστον, ὦ παῖ, ταὐτὸν ἀλγεινόν θ' ἅμα.
ΦΑ. ἡμεῖς ἂν εἶμεν θατέρῳ κεχρημένοι.
ΤΡ. τί φῄς; ἐρᾷς, ὦ τέκνον, ἀνθρώπων τίνος;   350
ΦΑ. ὅστις ποθ' οὗτός ἐσθ' ὁ τῆς Ἀμαζόνος—
ΤΡ. Ἱππόλυτον αὐδᾷς; ΦΑ. σοῦ τάδ', οὐκ ἐμοῦ
    κλύεις.
ΤΡ. οἴμοι, τί λέξεις, τέκνον; ὥς μ' ἀπώλεσας.
    γυναῖκες, οὐκ ἀνασχέτ', οὐκ ἀνέξομαι
    ζῶσ'· ἐχθρὸν ἦμαρ, ἐχθρὸν εἰσορῶ φάος.   355
    ῥίψω μεθήσω σῶμ', ἀπαλλαχθήσομαι
    βίου θανοῦσα· χαίρετ'· οὐκέτ' εἴμ' ἐγώ.
    οἱ σώφρονες γὰρ οὐχ ἑκόντες, ἀλλ' ὅμως
    κακῶν ἐρῶσι. Κύπρις οὐκ ἄρ' ἦν θεός,
    ἀλλ' εἴ τι μεῖζον ἄλλο γίγνεται θεοῦ,   360

ἢ τήνδε κἀμὲ καὶ δόμους ἀπώλεσεν.

ΧΟ. ἄιες ὤ, ἔκλυες ὤ   στρ.
ἀνήκουστα τᾶς
τυράννου πάθεα μέλεα θρεομένας;
ὀλοίμαν ἔγωγε, πρὶν σᾶν, φίλα,
κατανύσαι φρενῶν. ἰώ μοι, φεῦ φεῦ.   365
ὦ τάλαινα τῶνδ' ἀλγέων·
ὦ πόνοι τρέφοντες βροτούς.
ὄλωλας, ἐξέφηνας εἰς φάος κακά.
τίς σε παναμέριος ὅδε χρόνος μένει;
τελευτάσεταί τι καινὸν δόμοις.   370
ἄσημα δ' οὐκέτ' ἐστὶν οἷ φθίνει τύχα
Κύπριδος, ὦ τάλαινα παῖ Κρησία.

ΦΛ. Τροιζήνιαι γυναῖκες, αἱ τόδ' ἔσχατον
οἰκεῖτε χώρας Πελοπίας προνώπιον,
ἤδη ποτ' ἄλλων νυκτὸς ἐν μακρῷ χρόνῳ   375
θνητῶν ἐφρόντισ' ᾗ διέφθαρται βίος.
καί μοι δοκοῦσιν οὐ κατὰ γνώμης φύσιν
πράσσειν κάκιον, ἔστι γὰρ τό γ' εὖ φρονεῖν
πολλοῖσιν, ἀλλὰ τῇδ' ἀθρητέον τόδε·
τὰ χρήστ' ἐπιστάμεσθα καὶ γιγνώσκομεν,   380
οὐκ ἐκπονοῦμεν δ', οἱ μὲν ἀργίας ὕπο,
οἱ δ' ἡδονὴν προθέντες ἀντὶ τοῦ καλοῦ
ἄλλην τιν'. εἰσὶ δ' ἡδοναὶ πολλαὶ βίου,
[μακραί τε λέσχαι καὶ σχολή, τερπνὸν κακόν,
αἰδώς τε. δισσαὶ δ' εἰσίν, ἢ μὲν οὐ κακή,   385
ἢ δ' ἄχθος οἴκων. εἰ δ' ὁ καιρὸς ἦν σαφής,
οὐκ ἂν δύ' ἤστην ταῦτ' ἔχοντε γράμματα.]   387
λέξω δὲ καὶ σοὶ τῆς ἐμῆς γνώμης ὁδόν·   391
ἐπεί μ' ἔρως ἔτρωσεν, ἐσκόπουν ὅπως
κάλλιστ' ἐνέγκαιμ' αὐτόν. ἠρξάμην μὲν οὖν

ἐκ τοῦδε, σιγᾶν τήνδε καὶ κρύπτειν νόσον.
γλώσσῃ γὰρ οὐδὲν πιστόν, ἢ θυραῖα μὲν　395
φρονήματ᾽ ἀνδρῶν νουθετεῖν ἐπίσταται,
αὐτὴ δ᾽ ὑφ᾽ αὑτῆς πλεῖστα κέκτηται κακά.
τὸ δεύτερον δὲ τὴν ἄνοιαν εὖ φέρειν
τῷ σωφρονεῖν νικῶσα προυνοησάμην.
τρίτον δ᾽, ἐπειδὴ τοισίδ᾽ οὐκ ἐξήνυτον　400
Κύπριν κρατῆσαι, κατθανεῖν ἔδοξέ μοι
κράτιστον, οὐδεὶς ἀντερεῖ, βουλευμάτων.
ταῦτ᾽ οὖν ἐπειδὴ τυγχάνω φρονοῦσ᾽ ἐγώ,　388
οὐκ ἔσθ᾽ ὁποίῳ φαρμάκῳ διαφθερεῖν　389
ἔμελλον, ὥστε τοὔμπαλιν πεσεῖν φρενῶν.　390
ἐμοὶ γὰρ εἴη μήτε λανθάνειν καλὰ
μήτ᾽ αἰσχρὰ δρώσῃ μάρτυρας πολλοὺς ἔχειν.
τὸ δ᾽ ἔργον ἤδη τὴν νόσον τε δυσκλεᾶ,　405
γυνή τε πρὸς τοῖσδ᾽ οὖσ᾽ ἐγίγνωσκον καλῶς,
μίσημα πᾶσιν. ὡς ὄλοιτο παγκάκως
ἥτις πρὸς ἄνδρας ἤρξατ᾽ αἰσχύνειν λέχη
πρώτη θυραίους. ἐκ δὲ γενναίων δόμων
τόδ᾽ ἦρξε θηλείαισι γίγνεσθαι κακόν.　410
ὅταν γὰρ αἰσχρὰ τοῖσιν ἐσθλοῖσιν δοκῇ,
ἢ κάρτα δόξει τοῖς κακοῖς γ᾽ εἶναι καλά.
μισῶ δὲ καὶ τὰς σώφρονας μὲν ἐν λόγοις,
λάθρα δὲ τόλμας οὐ καλὰς κεκτημένας.
αἳ πῶς ποτ᾽, ὦ δέσποινα ποντία Κύπρι,　415
βλέπουσιν εἰς πρόσωπα τῶν ξυνευνετῶν
οὐδὲ σκότον φρίσσουσι τὸν ξυνεργάτην
τέρεμνά τ᾽ οἴκων μή ποτε φθογγὴν ἀφῇ;
ἡμᾶς γὰρ αὐτὸ τοῦτ᾽ ἀποκτείνει, φίλαι,
ὡς μήποτ᾽ ἄνδρα τὸν ἐμὸν αἰσχύνασ᾽ ἁλῶ,　420
μὴ παῖδας οὓς ἔτικτον· ἀλλ᾽ ἐλεύθεροι

παρρησίᾳ θάλλοντες οἰκοῖεν πόλιν
κλεινῶν 'Αθηνῶν, μητρὸς οὕνεκ' εὐκλεεῖς.
δουλοῖ γὰρ ἄνδρα, κἂν θρασύσπλαγχνός τις ᾖ,
ὅταν ξυνειδῇ μητρὸς ἢ πατρὸς κακά.   425
μόνον δὲ τοῦτό φασ' ἀμιλλᾶσθαι βίῳ,
γνώμην δικαίαν κἀγαθήν, ὅτῳ παρῇ.
κακοὺς δὲ θνητῶν ἐξέφην', ὅταν τύχῃ,
προθεὶς κάτοπτρον ὥστε παρθένῳ νέᾳ
χρόνος· παρ' οἷσι μήποτ' ὀφθείην ἐγώ.   430
ΧΟ. φεῦ φεῦ· τὸ σῶφρον ὡς ἀπανταχοῦ καλὸν
καὶ δόξαν ἐσθλὴν ἐν βροτοῖς καρπίζεται.
ΤΡ. δέσποιν', ἐμοί τοι συμφορὰ μὲν ἀρτίως
ἡ σὴ παρέσχε δεινὸν ἐξαίφνης φόβον·
νῦν δ' ἐννοοῦμαι φαῦλος οὖσα· κἀν βροτοῖς   435
αἱ δεύτεραί πως φροντίδες σοφώτεραι.
οὐ γὰρ περισσὸν οὐδὲν οὐδ' ἔξω λόγου
πέπονθας· ὀργαὶ δ' εἴς σ' ἐπέσκηψαν θεᾶς.
ἐρᾷς· τί τοῦτο θαῦμα; σὺν πολλοῖς βροτῶν.
κἄπειτ' ἔρωτος οὕνεκα ψυχὴν ὀλεῖς;   440
οὐκ ἄρ' ἀγὼν δὴ τοῖς ἐρῶσι νῦν μέγας
ὅσοι τε μέλλουσ', εἰ θανεῖν αὐτοὺς χρεών;
Κύπρις γὰρ οὐ φορητός, ἢν πολλὴ ῥυῇ·
ἢ τὸν μὲν εἴκονθ' ἡσυχῇ μετέρχεται,
ὃν δ' ἂν περισσὸν καὶ φρονοῦνθ' εὕρῃ μέγα,   445
τοῦτον λαβοῦσα, πῶς δοκεῖς; καθύβρισεν.
φοιτᾷ δ' ἀν' αἰθέρ', ἔστι δ' ἐν θαλασσίῳ
κλύδωνι Κύπρις, πάντα δ' ἐκ ταύτης ἔφυ·
ἥδ' ἐστὶν ἡ σπείρουσα καὶ διδοῦσ' ἔρον,
οὗ πάντες ἐσμὲν οἱ κατὰ χθόν' ἔκγονοι.   450
ὅσοι μὲν οὖν γραφάς τε τῶν παλαιτέρων
ἔχουσιν αὐτοί τ' εἰσὶν ἐν μούσαις ἀεί,

ἴσασι μὲν Ζεὺς ὥς ποτ᾽ ἠράσθη γάμων
Σεμέλης, ἴσασι δ᾽ ὡς ἀνήρπασέν ποτε
ἡ καλλιφεγγὴς Κέφαλον εἰς θεοὺς Ἕως   455
ἔρωτος οὕνεκ᾽· ἀλλ᾽ ὅμως ἐν οὐρανῷ
ναίουσι κοὐ φεύγουσιν ἐκποδὼν θεούς,
στέργουσι δ᾽, οἶμαι, συμφορᾷ νικώμενοι.
σὺ δ᾽ οὐκ ἀνέξει; χρῆν σ᾽ ἐπὶ ῥητοῖς ἄρα
πατέρα φυτεύειν ἢ ᾽πὶ δεσπόταις θεοῖς   460
ἄλλοισιν, εἰ μὴ τούσδε γε στέρξεις νόμους.
πόσους δοκεῖς δὴ κάρτ᾽ ἔχοντας εὖ φρενῶν
νοσοῦνθ᾽ ὁρῶντας λέκτρα μὴ δοκεῖν ὁρᾶν;
πόσους δὲ παισὶ πατέρας ἡμαρτηκόσι
συνεκκομίζειν Κύπριν; ἐν σοφοῖσι γὰρ   465
τάδ᾽ ἐστὶ θνητῶν, λανθάνειν τὰ μὴ καλά.
οὐδ᾽ ἐκπονεῖν τοι χρῆν βίον λίαν βροτούς·
οὐδὲ στέγην γὰρ ἧς κατηρεφεῖς δόμοι
καλῶς ἀκριβώσειαν· εἰς δὲ τὴν τύχην
πεσοῦσ᾽ ὅσην σὺ πῶς ἂν ἐκνεῦσαι δοκεῖς;   470
ἀλλ᾽ εἰ τὰ πλείω χρηστὰ τῶν κακῶν ἔχεις,
ἄνθρωπος οὖσα κάρτα γ᾽ εὖ πράξειας ἄν.
ἀλλ᾽ ὦ φίλη παῖ, λῆγε μὲν κακῶν φρενῶν,
λῆξον δ᾽ ὑβρίζους᾽· οὐ γὰρ ἄλλο πλὴν ὕβρις
τάδ᾽ ἐστί, κρείσσω δαιμόνων εἶναι θέλειν·   475
τόλμα δ᾽ ἐρῶσα· θεὸς ἐβουλήθη τάδε.
νοσοῦσα δ᾽ εὖ πως τὴν νόσον καταστρέφου.
εἰσὶν δ᾽ ἐπῳδαὶ καὶ λόγοι θελκτήριοι·
φανήσεταί τι τῆσδε φάρμακον νόσου.
ἦ τἄρ᾽ ἂν ὀψέ γ᾽ ἄνδρες ἐξεύροιεν ἄν,   480
εἰ μὴ γυναῖκες μηχανὰς εὑρήσομεν.
ΧΟ. Φαίδρα, λέγει μὲν ἥδε χρησιμώτερα
πρὸς τὴν παροῦσαν συμφοράν, αἰνῶ δὲ σέ.

ὁ δ᾽ αἶνος οὗτος δυσχερέστερος ψόγων
τῶν τῆσδε καὶ σοὶ μᾶλλον ἀλγίων κλύειν.   485

ΦΑ. τοῦτ᾽ ἔσθ᾽ ὃ θνητῶν εὖ πόλεις οἰκουμένας
δόμους τ᾽ ἀπόλλυσ᾽, οἱ καλοὶ λίαν λόγοι.
οὐ γάρ τι τοῖσιν ὠσὶ τερπνὰ χρὴ λέγειν,
ἀλλ᾽ ἐξ ὅτου τις εὐκλεὴς γενήσεται.

ΤΡ. τί σεμνομυθεῖς; οὐ λόγων εὐσχημόνων   490
δεῖ σ᾽, ἀλλὰ τἀνδρός· ὡς τάχος δὲ πειστέον,
τὸν εὐθὺν ἐξειπόντας ἀμφὶ σοῦ λόγον.
εἰ μὲν γὰρ ἦν σοι μὴ ᾽πὶ συμφοραῖς βίος
τοιαῖσδε, σώφρων δ᾽ οὖσ᾽ ἐτύγχανες γυνή,
οὐκ ἄν ποτ᾽ εὐνῆς οὕνεχ᾽ ἡδονῆς τε σῆς   495
προῆγον ἄν σε δεῦρο· νῦν δ᾽ ἀγὼν μέγας
σῶσαι βίον σόν, κοὐκ ἐπίφθονον τόδε.

ΦΑ. ὦ δεινὰ λέξασ᾽, οὐχὶ συγκλῄσεις στόμα
καὶ μὴ μεθήσεις αὖθις αἰσχίστους λόγους;

ΤΡ. αἴσχρ᾽, ἀλλ᾽ ἀμείνω τῶν καλῶν τάδ᾽ ἐστί σοι.   500
κρεῖσσον δὲ τοὔργον, εἴπερ ἐκσώσει γέ σε,
ἢ τοὔνομ᾽ ᾧ σὺ κατθανεῖ γαυρουμένη.

ΦΑ. καὶ μή σε πρὸς θεῶν, εὖ λέγεις γάρ, αἰσχρὰ δέ,
πέρα προβῇς τῶνδ᾽· ὡς ὑπείργασμαι μὲν εὖ
ψυχὴν ἔρωτι, τἀσχρὰ δ᾽ ἢν λέγῃς καλῶς,   505
εἰς τοῦθ᾽ ὃ φεύγω νῦν ἀναλωθήσομαι.

ΤΡ. εἴ τοι δοκεῖ σοι, χρῆν μὲν οὔ σ᾽ ἁμαρτάνειν·
εἰ δ᾽ οὖν, πιθοῦ μοι· δευτέρα γὰρ ἡ χάρις.
ἔστιν κατ᾽ οἴκους φίλτρα μοι θελκτήρια
ἔρωτος, ἦλθε δ᾽ ἄρτι μοι γνώμης ἔσω,   510
ἅ σ᾽ οὔτ᾽ ἐπ᾽ αἰσχροῖς οὔτ᾽ ἐπὶ βλάβῃ φρενῶν
παύσει νόσου τῆσδ᾽, ἢν σὺ μὴ γένῃ κακή.
[δεῖ δ᾽ ἐξ ἐκείνου δή τι τοῦ ποθουμένου
σημεῖον, ἢ λόγον τιν᾽ ἢ πέπλων ἄπο

λαβεῖν, συνάψαι τ᾽ ἐκ δυοῖν μίαν χάριν.]   515
ΦΑ. πότερα δὲ χριστὸν ἢ ποτὸν τὸ φάρμακον;
ΤΡ. οὐκ οἶδ᾽· ὄνασθαι, μὴ μαθεῖν βούλου, τέκνον.
ΦΑ. δέδοιχ᾽ ὅπως μοι μὴ λίαν φανῇς σοφή.
ΤΡ. πάντ᾽ ἂν φοβηθεῖσ᾽ ἴσθι· δειμαίνεις δὲ τί;
ΦΑ. μή μοί τι Θησέως τῶνδε μηνύσῃς τόκῳ.   520
ΤΡ. ἔασον, ὦ παῖ· ταῦτ᾽ ἐγὼ θήσω καλῶς.
μόνον σύ μοι, δέσποινα ποντία Κύπρι,
συνεργὸς εἴης. τἄλλα δ᾽ οἷ᾽ ἐγὼ φρονῶ
τοῖς ἔνδον ἡμῖν ἀρκέσει λέξαι φίλοις.
ΧΟ. Ἔρως Ἔρως, ὁ κατ᾽ ὀμμάτων   στρ. 525
στάζων πόθον, εἰσάγων γλυκεῖαν
ψυχαῖς χάριν οὓς ἐπιστρατεύσῃ,
μή μοί ποτε σὺν κακῷ φανείης
μηδ᾽ ἄρρυθμος ἔλθοις.
οὔτε γὰρ πυρὸς οὔτ᾽   530
ἄστρων ὑπέρτερον βέλος,
οἷον τὸ τᾶς Ἀφροδίτας
ἵησιν ἐκ χερῶν
Ἔρως ὁ Διὸς παῖς.
ἄλλως ἄλλως παρά τ᾽ Ἀλφεῷ   ἀντ. 535
Φοίβου τ᾽ ἐπὶ Πυθίοις τεράμνοις
βούταν φόνον Ἑλλὰς αἲ᾽ ἀέξει·
Ἔρωτα δὲ τὸν τύραννον ἀνδρῶν,
τὸν τᾶς Ἀφροδίτας
φιλτάτων θαλάμων   540
κλῃδοῦχον, οὐ σεβίζομεν,
πέρθοντα καὶ διὰ πάσας
ἰόντα συμφορᾶς
θνατοῖς, ὅταν ἔλθῃ.
τὰν μὲν Οἰχαλίᾳ   στρ. 545

πῶλον ἄζυγα λέκτρων
ἄνανδρον τὸ πρὶν καὶ ἄνυμφον, οἴκων
ζεύξασ᾽ ἀπ᾽ εἰρεσίᾳ, δρομάδα
ναϊάδ᾽ ὅπως τε Βάκχαν,   550
σὺν αἵματι, σὺν καπνῷ
φονίοις ἐφ᾽ ὕμνοισιν
Ἀλκμήνας τόκῳ Κύπρις ἐξέδωκεν·
ὦ τλάμων ὑμεναίων.
ὦ Θήβας ἱερὸν   ἀντ. 555
τεῖχος, ὦ στόμα Δίρκας,
συνείπαιτ᾽ ἂν ἁ Κύπρις οἷον ἔρπει.
βροντᾷ γὰρ ἀμφιπύρῳ τοκάδα
τὰν Διογόνοιο Βάκχου   560
νυμφευσαμένα πότμῳ
φονίῳ κατεύνασεν.
δεινὰ γὰρ τὰ πάντ᾽ ἐπιπνεῖ, μέλισσα δ᾽
οἷά τις πεπόταται.

ΦΑ. σιγήσατ᾽, ὦ γυναῖκες· ἐξειργάσμεθα.   565
ΧΟ. σιγῶ· τὸ μέντοι φροίμιον κακὸν τόδε.   568
ΦΑ. ἐπίσχετ᾽, αὐδὴν τῶν ἔσωθεν ἐκμάθω.   567
ΧΟ. τί δ᾽ ἔστι, Φαίδρα, δεινὸν ἐν δόμοισι σοῖς; 566
ΦΑ. ἰώ μοι, αἰαῖ αἰαῖ·
ὦ δυστάλαινα τῶν ἐμῶν παθημάτων.   570
ΧΟ. τίνα θροεῖς αὐδάν; τίνα βοᾷς λόγον;
ἔνεπε τίς φοβεῖ σε φάμα, γύναι,
φρένας ἐπίσσυτος.
ΦΑ. ἀπωλόμεσθα. ταῖσδ᾽ ἐπιστᾶσαι πύλαις   575
ἀκούσαθ᾽ οἷος κέλαδος ἐν δόμοις πίτνει.
ΧΟ. σὺ παρὰ κλῇθρα· σοὶ μέλει πομπίμα
φάτις δωμάτων.
ἔνεπε δ᾽ ἔνεπέ μοι, τί ποτ᾽ ἔβα κακόν;   580

ΦΑ. ὁ τῆς φιλίππου παῖς Ἀμαζόνος βοᾷ
Ἱππόλυτος, αὐδῶν δεινὰ πρόσπολον κακά.

ΧΟ. ἀχὰν μὲν κλύω, σαφὲς δ' οὐκ ἔχω   585
γεγωνεῖν ὅπᾳ
διὰ πύλας ἔμολεν ἔμολε σοὶ βοά.

ΦΑ. καὶ μὴν σαφῶς γε τὴν κακῶν προμνήστριαν,
τὴν δεσπότου προδοῦσαν ἐξαυδᾷ λέχος.   590

ΧΟ. ὤμοι ἐγὼ κακῶν· προδέδοσαι, φίλα.
τί σοι μήσομαι;
τὰ κρύπτ' ἄρα πέφηνε, διὰ δ' ὄλλυσαι

ΦΑ. αἰαῖ, ἒ ἔ.

ΧΟ. πρόδοτος ἐκ φίλων.   595

ΦΑ. ἀπώλεσέν μ' εἰποῦσα συμφορὰς ἐμάς,
φίλως, καλῶς δ' οὐ τήνδ' ἰωμένη νόσον.

ΧΟ. πῶς οὖν; τί δράσεις, ὦ παθοῦσ' ἀμήχανα;

ΦΑ. οὐκ οἶδα πλὴν ἕν, κατθανεῖν ὅσον τάχος
τῶν νῦν παρόντων πημάτων ἄκος μόνον.   600

ΙΠ. ὦ γαῖα μῆτερ ἡλίου τ' ἀναπτυχαί,
οἵων λόγων ἄρρητον εἰσήκουσ' ὄπα.

ΤΡ. σίγησον, ὦ παῖ, πρίν τιν' αἰσθέσθαι βοῆς.

ΙΠ. οὐκ ἔστ' ἀκούσας δείν' ὅπως σιγήσομαι.

ΤΡ. ναὶ πρός σε τῆσδε δεξιᾶς εὐωλένου.   605

ΙΠ. οὐ μὴ προσοίσεις χεῖρα μηδ' ἅψει πέπλων;

ΤΡ. ὦ πρός σε γονάτων, μηδαμῶς μ' ἐξεργάσῃ.

ΙΠ. τί δ', εἴπερ ὡς φὴς μηδὲν εἴρηκας κακόν;

ΤΡ. ὁ μῦθος, ὦ παῖ, κοινὸς οὐδαμῶς ὅδε.

ΙΠ. τά τοι κάλ' ἐν πολλοῖσι κάλλιον λέγειν.   610

ΤΡ. ὦ τέκνον, ὅρκους μηδαμῶς ἀτιμάσῃς.

ΙΠ. ἡ γλῶσσ' ὀμώμοχ', ἡ δὲ φρὴν ἀνώμοτος.

ΤΡ. ὦ παῖ, τί δράσεις; σοὺς φίλους διεργάσει;

ΙΠ. ἀπέπτυσ'· οὐδεὶς ἄδικός ἐστί μοι φίλος.   614

ΤΡ. σύγγνωθ'· ἁμαρτεῖν εἰκὸς ἀνθρώπους, τέκνον.

ΙΙΙ. ὦ Ζεῦ, τί δὴ κίβδηλον ἀνθρώποις κακὸν
γυναῖκας εἰς φῶς ἡλίου κατῴκισας;
εἰ γὰρ βρότειον ἤθελες σπεῖραι γένος,
οὐκ ἐκ γυναικῶν χρῆν παρασχέσθαι τόδε,
ἀλλ' ἀντιθέντας σοῖσιν ἐν ναοῖς βροτοὺς   620
ἢ χρυσὸν ἢ σίδηρον ἢ χαλκοῦ βάρος
παίδων πρίασθαι σπέρμα, τοῦ τιμήματος
τῆς ἀξίας ἕκαστον· ἐν δὲ δώμασι
ναίειν ἐλευθέροισι θηλειῶν ἄτερ.
[νῦν δ' εἰς δόμους μὲν πρῶτον ἄξεσθαι κακὸν 625
μέλλοντες ὄλβον δωμάτων ἐκτίνομεν.]
τούτῳ δὲ δῆλον ὡς γυνὴ κακὸν μέγα·
προσθεὶς γὰρ ὁ σπείρας τε καὶ θρέψας πατὴρ
φερνὰς ἀπῴκισ', ὡς ἀπαλλαχθῇ κακοῦ·
ὁ δ' αὖ λαβὼν ἀτηρὸν εἰς δόμους φυτὸν   630
γέγηθε κόσμον προστιθεὶς ἀγάλματι
καλὸν κακίστῳ καὶ πέπλοισιν ἐκπονεῖ
δύστηνος, ὄλβον δωμάτων ὑπεξελών.
ἔχει δ' ἀνάγκην, ὥστε κηδεύσας καλοῖς
γαμβροῖσι χαίρων σώζεται πικρὸν λέχος,   635
ἢ χρηστὰ λέκτρα, πενθεροὺς δ' ἀνωφελεῖς
λαβὼν πιέζει τἀγαθῷ τὸ δυστυχές.
ῥᾷστον δ' ὅτῳ τὸ μηδέν, ἀλλ' ἀνωφελὴς
εὐηθίᾳ κατ' οἶκον ἵδρυται γυνή.
σοφὴν δὲ μισῶ· μὴ γὰρ ἔν γ' ἐμοῖς δόμοις   640
εἴη φρονοῦσα πλεῖον ἢ γυναῖκα χρή.
τὸ γὰρ κακοῦργον μᾶλλον ἐντίκτει Κύπρις
ἐν ταῖς σοφαῖσιν· ἡ δ' ἀμήχανος γυνὴ
γνώμῃ βραχείᾳ μωρίαν ἀφῃρέθη.
χρῆν δ' εἰς γυναῖκα πρόσπολον μὲν οὐ περᾶν, 645

ἄφθογγα δ᾽ αὐταῖς συγκατοικίζειν δάκη
θηρῶν, ἵν᾽ εἶχον μήτε προσφωνεῖν τινα
μήτ᾽ ἐξ ἐκείνων φθέγμα δέξασθαι πάλιν.
νῦν δ᾽ αἱ μὲν ἐννοοῦσιν αἱ κακαὶ κακὰ
βουλεύματ᾽, ἔξω δ᾽ ἐκφέρουσι πρόσπολοι.   650
ὡς καὶ σύ γ᾽ ἡμῖν πατρός, ὦ κακὸν κάρα,
λέκτρων ἀθίκτων ἦλθες εἰς συναλλαγάς·
ἀγὼ ῥυτοῖς νασμοῖσιν ἐξομόρξομαι,
εἰς ὦτα κλύζων. πῶς ἂν οὖν εἴην κακός,
ὃς οὐδ᾽ ἀκούσας τοιάδ᾽ ἁγνεύειν δοκῶ;   655
εὖ δ᾽ ἴσθι, τοὐμόν σ᾽ εὐσεβὲς σώζει, γύναι·
εἰ μὴ γὰρ ὅρκοις θεῶν ἄφρακτος ᾑρέθην,
οὐκ ἄν ποτ᾽ ἔσχον μὴ οὐ τάδ᾽ ἐξειπεῖν πατρί.
νῦν δ᾽ ἐκ δόμων μέν, ἔστ᾽ ἂν ἔκδημος χθονὸς
Θησεύς, ἄπειμι· σῖγα δ᾽ ἕξομεν στόμα.   660
θεάσομαι δὲ σὺν πατρὸς μολὼν ποδὶ
πῶς νιν προσόψει καὶ σὺ καὶ δέσποινα σή·
τῆς σῆς δὲ τόλμης εἴσομαι γεγευμένος.
ὄλοισθε. μισῶν δ᾽ οὔποτ᾽ ἐμπλησθήσομαι
γυναῖκας, οὐδ᾽ εἴ φησί τίς μ᾽ ἀεὶ λέγειν·   665
ἀεὶ γὰρ οὖν πώς εἰσι κἀκεῖναι κακαί.
ἢ νύν τις αὐτὰς σωφρονεῖν διδαξάτω,
ἢ κἄμ᾽ ἐάτω ταῖσδ᾽ ἐπεμβαίνειν ἀεί.

ΦΑ. τάλανες ὦ κακοτυχεῖς   ἀντ.
γυναικῶν πότμοι.
τίν᾽ αὖ νῦν τέχναν ἔχομεν ἢ λόγους   670
σφαλεῖσαι κάθαμμα λύειν ψόγου;
ἐτύχομεν δίκας· ἰὼ γᾶ καὶ φῶς.
πᾷ ποτ᾽ ἐξαλύξω τύχας;
πῶς δὲ πῆμα κρύψω, φίλαι;
τίς ἂν θεῶν ἀρωγὸς ἢ τίς ἂν βροτῶν   675

πάρεδρος ἢ ξυνεργὸς ἀδίκων ἔργων
φανείη; τὸ γὰρ παρ' ἡμῖν πάθος
παρὸν δυσεκπέρατον ἔρχεται βίῳ.
κακοτυχεστάτα γυναικῶν ἐγώ.

ΧΟ. φεῦ φεῦ· πέπρακται, κοὐ κατώρθωνται τέχναι, 680
δέσποινα, τῆς σῆς προσπόλου, κακῶς δ' ἔχει.

ΦΑ. ὦ παγκακίστη καὶ φίλων διαφθορεῦ,
οἷ' εἰργάσω με. Ζεύς σ' ὁ γεννήτωρ ἐμὸς
πρόρριζον ἐκτρίψειεν οὐτάσας πυρί.
οὐκ εἶπον, οὐ σῆς προυνοησάμην φρενός,   685
σιγᾶν ἐφ' οἷσι νῦν ἐγὼ κακύνομαι;
σὺ δ' οὐκ ἀνέσχου· τοιγὰρ οὐκέτ' εὐκλεεῖς
θανούμεθ'. ἀλλὰ δεῖ με δὴ καινῶν λόγων.
οὗτος γὰρ ὀργῇ συντεθηγμένος φρένας
ἐρεῖ καθ' ἡμῶν πατρὶ σὰς ἁμαρτίας,   690
[ἐρεῖ δὲ Πιτθεῖ τῷ γέροντι συμφορὰς]
πλήσει δὲ πᾶσαν γαῖαν αἰσχίστων λόγων.
ὄλοιο καὶ σὺ χὤστις ἄκοντας φίλους
πρόθυμός ἐστι μὴ καλῶς εὐεργετεῖν.

ΤΡ. δέσποιν', ἔχεις μὲν τἀμὰ μέμψασθαι κακά· 695
τὸ γὰρ δάκνον σου τὴν διάγνωσιν κρατεῖ·
ἔχω δὲ κἀγὼ πρὸς τάδ', εἰ δέξει, λέγειν.
ἔθρεψά σ' εὔνους τ' εἰμί· τῆς νόσου δέ σοι
ζητοῦσα φάρμαχ' εὗρον οὐχ ἀβουλόμην.
εἰ δ' ἐξέπραξα, κάρτ' ἂν ἐν σοφοῖσιν ἦν·   700
πρὸς τὰς τύχας γὰρ τὰς φρένας κεκτήμεθα.

ΦΑ. ἦ καὶ δίκαια ταῦτα κἀξαρκοῦντά μοι,
τρώσασαν ἡμᾶς εἶτα συγχωρεῖν λόγοις;

ΤΡ. μακρηγοροῦμεν· οὐκ ἐσωφρόνουν ἐγώ,
ἀλλ' ἔστι κἀκ τῶνδ' ὥστε σωθῆναι, τέκνον. 705

ΦΑ. παῦσαι λέγουσα· καὶ τὰ πρὶν γὰρ οὐ καλῶς

παρῄνεσάς μοι κἀπεχείρησας κακά.
ἀλλ' ἐκποδὼν ἄπελθε καὶ σαυτῆς πέρι
φρόντιζ'· ἐγὼ δὲ τἀμὰ θήσομαι καλῶς.
ὑμεῖς δέ, παῖδες εὐγενεῖς Τροιζήνιαι,   710
τοσόνδε μοι παράσχετ' ἐξαιτουμένῃ,
σιγῇ καλύπτειν ἀνθάδ' εἰσηκούσατε.
ΧΟ. ὄμνυμι σεμνὴν Ἄρτεμιν Διὸς κόρην,
μηδὲν κακῶν σῶν εἰς φάος δείξειν ποτέ.
ΦΑ. καλῶς ἔλεξας. ἐν δὲ πρόσθ' εἰποῦσ' ἐρῶ·   715
εὕρημα δή τι τῆσδε συμφορᾶς ἔχω,
ὥστ' εὐκλεᾶ μὲν παισὶ προσθεῖναι βίον,
αὐτή τ' ὄνασθαι πρὸς τὰ νῦν πεπτωκότα.
οὐ γάρ ποτ' αἰσχυνῶ γε Κρησίους δόμους,
οὐδ' εἰς πρόσωπον Θησέως ἀφίξομαι   720
αἰσχροῖς ἐπ' ἔργοις οὕνεκα ψυχῆς μιᾶς.
ΧΟ. μέλλεις δὲ δὴ τί δρᾶν ἀνήκεστον κακόν;
ΦΑ. θανεῖν· ὅπως δέ, τοῦτ' ἐγὼ βουλεύσομαι.
ΧΟ. εὔφημος ἴσθι.
ΦΑ.   καὶ σύ γ' εὖ με νουθέτει.
ἐγὼ δὲ Κύπριν, ἥπερ ἐξόλλυσί με,   725
ψυχῆς ἀπαλλαχθεῖσα τῇδ' ἐν ἡμέρᾳ
τέρψω· πικροῦ δ' ἔρωτος ἡσσηθήσομαι.
ἀτὰρ κακόν γε χἀτέρῳ γενήσομαι
θανοῦσ', ἵν' εἰδῇ μὴ 'πὶ τοῖς ἐμοῖς κακοῖς
ὑψηλὸς εἶναι· τῆς νόσου δὲ τῆσδέ μοι   730
κοινῇ μετασχὼν σωφρονεῖν μαθήσεται.
ΧΟ. ἠλιβάτοις ὑπὸ κευθμῶσι γενοίμαν,   στρ.
ἵνα με πτεροῦσσαν ὄρνιν
θεὸς ἔν τε ποταναῖς ἀγέλαις θείη.
ἀρθείην δ' ἐπὶ πόντιον   735
κῦμα τᾶς Ἀδριηνᾶς

ἀκτᾶς Ἠριδανοῦ θ᾽ ὕδωρ·
ἔνθα πορφύρεον σταλάσσουσ᾽
εἰς οἶδμα πατρὸς τάλαιναι
κόραι Φαέθοντος οἴκτῳ δακρύων   740
τὰς ἠλεκτροφαεῖς αὐγάς.
Ἑσπερίδων δ᾽ ἐπὶ μηλόσπορον ἀκτὰν   ἀντ.
ἀνύσαιμι τᾶν ἀοιδῶν,
ἵν᾽ ὁ ποντομέδων πορφυρέας λίμνας
ναύταις οὐκέθ᾽ ὁδὸν νέμει,   745
σεμνὸν τέρμονα ναίων
οὐρανοῦ, τὸν Ἄτλας ἔχει,
κρῆναί τ᾽ ἀμβρόσιαι χέονται
Ζηνὸς μελάθρων παρὰ κοίταις,
ἵν᾽ ἁ βιόδωρος αὔξει ζαθέα   750
χθὼν εὐδαιμονίαν θεοῖς.
ὦ λευκόπτερε Κρησία   στρ.
πορθμίς, ἁ διὰ πόντιον
κῦμ᾽ ἁλίκτυπον ἅλμας
ἐπόρευσας ἐμὰν ἄνασσαν   755
ὀλβίων ἀπ᾽ οἴκων,
κακονυμφοτάταν ὄνασιν.
ἦ γὰρ ἀπ᾽ ἀμφοτέρων ἢ
Κρησίας ἐκ γᾶς δύσορνις
ἔπτατ᾽ ἐπὶ κλεινὰς Ἀθήνας,   760
Μουνύχου δ᾽ ἀκταῖσιν ἐκδήσαντο πλεκτὰς πεισμάτων ἀρ-
χὰς ἐπ᾽ ἀπείρου τε γᾶς ἔβασαν.
ἀνθ᾽ ὧν οὐχ ὁσίων ἐρώ-   ἀντ.
των δεινᾷ φρένας Ἀφροδί-   765
τας νόσῳ κατεκλάσθη·
χαλεπᾷ δ᾽ ὑπέραντλος οὖσα

συμφορᾷ, τεράμνων
ἀπὸ νυμφιδίων κρεμαστὸν
ἅψεται ἀμφὶ βρόχον λευ-   770
κᾷ καθαρμόζουσα δείρᾳ,
δαίμονα στυγνὰν καταιδε-
σθεῖσα τάν τ᾽ εὔδοξον ἀνθαιρουμένα φάμαν ἀπαλλάσ-
σουσά τ᾽ ἀλγεινὸν φρενῶν ἔρωτα.   775

ΕΞ. ἰοὺ ἰού·
βοηδρομεῖτε πάντες οἱ πέλας δόμων·
ἐν ἀγχόναις δέσποινα, Θησέως δάμαρ.

ΧΟ. φεῦ φεῦ, πέπρακται· βασιλὶς οὐκέτ᾽ ἔστι δὴ
γυνή, κρεμαστοῖς ἐν βρόχοις ἠρτημένη.

ΕΞ. οὐ σπεύσετ᾽; οὐκ οἴσει τις ἀμφιδέξιον   780
σίδηρον, ᾧ τόδ᾽ ἄμμα λύσομεν δέρης;

ΧΟ. φίλαι, τί δρῶμεν; ἦ δοκεῖ περᾶν δόμους
λῦσαί τ᾽ ἄνασσαν ἐξ ἐπισπαστῶν βρόχων;

ΗΜ. τί δ᾽; οὐ πάρεισι πρόσπολοι νεανίαι;
τὸ πολλὰ πράσσειν οὐκ ἐν ἀσφαλεῖ βίου.   785

ΕΞ. ὀρθώσατ᾽ ἐκτείναντες ἄθλιον νέκυν·
πικρὸν τόδ᾽ οἰκούρημα δεσπόταις ἐμοῖς.

ΗΜ. ὄλωλεν ἡ δύστηνος, ὡς κλύω, γυνή·
ἤδη γὰρ ὡς νεκρόν νιν ἐκτείνουσι δή.

ΘΗ. γυναῖκες, ἴστε τίς ποτ᾽ ἐν δόμοις βοή;   790
ἠχὼ βαρεῖα προσπόλων μ᾽ ἀφίκετο.
οὐ γάρ τί μ᾽ ὡς θεωρὸν ἀξιοῖ δόμος
πύλας ἀνοίξας εὐφρόνως προσεννέπειν.
μῶν Πιτθέως τι γῆρας εἴργασται νέον;
πρόσω μὲν ἤδη βίοτος, ἀλλ᾽ ὅμως ἔτ᾽ ἂν   795
λυπηρὸς ἡμῖν τοῦδ᾽ ἂν ἐκλίποι δόμους.

ΧΟ. οὐκ εἰς γέροντας ἥδε σοι τείνει τύχη,

Θησεῦ· νέοι θανόντες ἀλγυνοῦσί σε.

ΘΗ. οἴμοι· τέκνων μοι μή τι συλᾶται βίος;

ΧΟ. ζῶσιν, θανούσης μητρὸς ὡς ἄλγιστά σοι.   800

ΘΗ. τί φής; ὄλωλεν ἄλοχος; ἐκ τίνος τύχης;

ΧΟ. βρόχον κρεμαστὸν ἀγχόνης ἀνήψατο.

ΘΗ. λύπῃ παχνωθεῖσ᾽ ἢ ἀπὸ συμφορᾶς τίνος;

ΧΟ. τοσοῦτον ἴσμεν· ἄρτι γὰρ κἀγὼ δόμοις,
Θησεῦ, πάρειμι σῶν κακῶν πενθήτρια.   805

ΘΗ. αἰαῖ· τί δῆτα τοῖσδ᾽ ἀνέστεμμαι κάρα
πλεκτοῖσι φύλλοις, δυστυχὴς θεωρὸς ὤν;
χαλᾶτε κλῇθρα, πρόσπολοι, πυλωμάτων,
*ἐκλύεθ᾽ ἁρμούς, ὡς ἴδω δυσδαίμονα
γυναικός, ἥ με κατθανοῦσ᾽ ἀπώλεσεν.*   810

ΧΟ. ἰὼ ἰὼ τάλαινα μελέων κακῶν·
ἔπαθες, εἰργάσω
τοσοῦτον ὥστε τούσδε συγχέαι δόμους.
αἰαῖ τόλμας, ὦ βιαίως θανοῦσ᾽
ἀνοσίῳ τε συμφορᾷ, σᾶς χερὸς
πάλαισμα μελέας.   815
τίς ἄρα σάν, τάλαιν᾽, ἀμαυροῖ ζόαν;

ΘΗ. ὤμοι ἐγὼ πόνων· ἔπαθον, ὦ πόλις,   στρ.
τὰ μάκιστ᾽ ἐμῶν κακῶν. ὦ τύχα,
ὥς μοι βαρεῖα καὶ δόμοις ἐπεστάθης,
κηλὶς ἄφραστος ἐξ ἀλαστόρων τινός.   820
κατακονὰ μὲν οὖν ἀβίοτος βίου·
κακῶν δ᾽ ὦ τάλας πέλαγος εἰσορῶ
τοσοῦτον ὥστε μήποτ᾽ ἐκνεῦσαι πάλιν
μηδ᾽ ἐκπερᾶσαι κῦμα τῆσδε συμφορᾶς.
[ἐκλύεθ᾽ ἁρμούς, ὡς ἴδω πικρὰν θέαν]
τίνα λόγον τάλας, τίνα τύχαν σέθεν   826
βαρύποτμον, γύναι, προσαυδῶν τύχω;

ὄρνις γὰρ ὥς τις ἐκ χερῶν ἄφαντος εἶ,
πήδημ᾽ ἐς Ἅιδου κραιπνὸν ὁρμήσασά μοι.
αἰαῖ αἰαῖ, μέλεα μέλεα τάδε πάθη.   830
πρόσωθεν δέ ποθεν ἀνακομίζομαι
τύχαν δαιμόνων
ἀμπλακίαισι τῶν πάροιθέν τινος.

ΧΟ. οὐ σοὶ τάδ᾽, ὦναξ, ἦλθε δὴ μόνῳ κακά·
πολλῶν μετ᾽ ἄλλων δ᾽ ὤλεσας κεδνὸν λέχος. 835

ΘΗ. τὸ κατὰ γᾶς θέλω, τὸ κατὰ γᾶς κνέφας   ἀντ.
μετοικεῖν σκότῳ θανὼν ὁ τλάμων,
τῆς σῆς στερηθεὶς φιλτάτης ὁμιλίας·
ἀπώλεσας γὰρ μᾶλλον ἢ κατέφθισο.
τίνα κλύω; πόθεν θανάσιμος τύχα   840
γύναι, σάν, τάλαιν᾽, ἔβα καρδίαν;
εἴποι τις ἂν τὸ πραχθέν, ἢ μάτην ὄχλον
στέγει τύραννον δῶμα προσπόλων ἐμῶν;
ὤμοι μοι σέθεν ******
μέλεος, οἷον εἶδον ἄλγος δόμων,   845
οὐ τλητὸν οὐδὲ ῥητόν· ἀλλ᾽ ἀπωλόμην·
ἔρημος οἶκος, καὶ τέκν᾽ ὀρφανεύεται.
ἔλιπες ἔλιπες, ὦ φίλα
γυναικῶν ἀρίστα θ᾽ ὁπόσας ἐφορᾷ
φέγγος ἀελίου τε καὶ   850
νυκτὸς ἀστερωπὸς σελάνα.

ΧΟ. τάλας, ὦ τάλας· ὅσον κακὸν ἔχει δόμος.
δάκρυσί μου βλέφαρα
καταχυθέντα τέγγεται σᾷ τύχᾳ·
τὸ δ᾽ ἐπὶ τῷδε πῆμα φρίσσω πάλαι.   855

ΘΗ. ἔα ἔα·
τί δή ποθ᾽ ἥδε δέλτος ἐκ φίλης χερὸς
ἠρτημένη; θέλει τι σημῆναι νέον;

ἀλλ' ἢ λέχους μοι καὶ τέκνων ἐπιστολὰς
ἔγραψεν ἡ δύστηνος ἐξαιτουμένη;
θάρσει, τάλαινα· λέκτρα γὰρ τὰ Θησέως   860
οὐκ ἔστι δῶμά θ' ἥτις εἴσεισιν γυνή.
καὶ μὴν τύποι γε σφενδόνης χρυσηλάτου
τῆς οὐκέτ' οὔσης τῆσδε προσσαίνουσί με.
φέρ', ἐξελίξας περιβολὰς σφραγισμάτων
ἴδω τί λέξαι δέλτος ἥδε μοι θέλει.   865

ΧΟ. φεῦ φεῦ· * τόδ' αὖ νεοχμὸν ἐκδοχαῖς
ἐπιφέρει θεὸς κακόν. ἐμοὶ μὲν οὖν
ἀβίοτος βίου τύχα πρὸς τὸ κρανθὲν εἴη τυχεῖν.
ὀλομένους γάρ, οὐκέτ' ὄντας λέγω,
φεῦ φεῦ, τῶν ἐμῶν τυράννων δόμους.   870
[ὦ δαῖμον, εἴ πως ἔστι, μὴ σφήλῃς δόμους,
αἰτουμένης δὲ κλῦθί μου· πρὸς γάρ τινος
οἰωνὸν ὥστε μάντις εἰσορῶ κακόν.]

ΘΗ. οἴμοι· τόδ' οἷον ἄλλο πρὸς κακῷ κακόν,
οὐ τλητὸν οὐδὲ λεκτόν. ὦ τάλας ἐγώ.   875

ΧΟ. τί χρῆμα; λέξον, εἴ τί μοι λόγου μέτα.

ΘΗ. βοᾷ βοᾷ δέλτος ἄλαστα. πᾷ φύγω
βάρος κακῶν; ἀπὸ γὰρ ὀλόμενος οἴχομαι,
οἷον οἷον εἶδον ἐν γραφαῖς μέλος
φθεγγόμενον τλάμων.   880

ΧΟ. αἰαῖ, κακῶν ἀρχηγὸν ἐκφαίνεις λόγον.

ΘΗ. τόδε μὲν οὐκέτι στόματος ἐν πύλαις
καθέξω δυσεκπέρατον, ὀλοὸν
κακόν· ἰὼ πόλις.
Ἱππόλυτος εὐνῆς τῆς ἐμῆς ἔτλη θιγεῖν   885
βίᾳ, τὸ σεμνὸν Ζηνὸς ὄμμ' ἀτιμάσας.
ἀλλ' ὦ πάτερ Πόσειδον, ἃς ἐμοί ποτε
ἀρὰς ὑπέσχου τρεῖς, μιᾷ κατέργασαι

τούτων ἐμὸν παῖδ', ἡμέραν δὲ μὴ φύγοι
τήνδ', εἴπερ ἡμῖν ὤπασας σαφεῖς ἀράς.   890

ΧΟ. ἄναξ, ἀπεύχου ταῦτα πρὸς θεῶν πάλιν·
γνώσει γὰρ αὖθις ἀμπλακών. ἐμοὶ πιθοῦ.

ΘΗ. οὐκ ἔστι· καὶ πρός γ' ἐξελῶ σφε τῆσδε γῆς,
δυοῖν δὲ μοίραιν θατέρᾳ πεπλήξεται·
ἢ γὰρ Ποσειδῶν αὐτὸν εἰς Ἅιδου δόμους   895
θανόντα πέμψει τὰς ἐμὰς ἀρὰς σέβων,
ἢ τῆσδε χώρας ἐκπεσὼν ἀλώμενος
ξένην ἐπ' αἶαν λυπρὸν ἀντλήσει βίον.

ΧΟ. καὶ μὴν ὅδ' αὐτὸς παῖς σὸς εἰς καιρὸν πάρα,
Ἱππόλυτος· ὀργῆς δ' ἐξανεὶς κακῆς, ἄναξ   900
Θησεῦ, τὸ λῷστον σοῖσι βούλευσαι δόμοις.

ΙΠ. κραυγῆς ἀκούσας σῆς ἀφικόμην, πάτερ,
σπουδῇ· τὸ μέντοι πρᾶγμ' ἐφ' ᾧτινι στένεις
οὐκ οἶδα, βουλοίμην δ' ἂν ἐκ σέθεν κλύειν.
ἔα, τί χρῆμα; σὴν δάμαρθ' ὁρῶ, πάτερ,   905
νεκρόν· μεγίστου θαύματος τόδ' ἄξιον·
ἣν ἀρτίως ἔλειπον, ἣ φάος τόδε
οὔπω χρόνον παλαιὸν εἰσεδέρκετο.
τί χρῆμα πάσχει; τῷ τρόπῳ διόλλυται;
πάτερ, πυθέσθαι βούλομαι σέθεν πάρα.   910
σιγᾷς; σιωπῆς δ' οὐδὲν ἔργον ἐν κακοῖς·
ἡ γὰρ ποθοῦσα πάντα καρδία κλύειν
κἂν τοῖς κακοῖσι λίχνος οὖσ' ἁλίσκεται.
οὐ μὴν φίλους γε κἄτι μᾶλλον ἢ φίλους
κρύπτειν δίκαιον σὰς πάτερ δυσπραξίας.   915

ΘΗ. ὦ πόλλ' ἁμαρτάνοντες ἄνθρωποι μάτην,
τί δὴ τέχνας μὲν μυρίας διδάσκετε
καὶ πάντα μηχανᾶσθε κἀξευρίσκετε,
ἓν δ' οὐκ ἐπίστασθ' οὐδ' ἐθηράσασθέ πω,

φρονεῖν διδάσκειν οἷσιν οὐκ ἔνεστι νοῦς;   920
ΙΠ. δεινὸν σοφιστὴν εἶπας, ὅστις εὖ φρονεῖν
τοὺς μὴ φρονοῦντας δυνατός ἐστ᾽ ἀναγκάσαι.
ἀλλ᾽ οὐ γὰρ ἐν δέοντι λεπτουργεῖς, πάτερ,
δέδοικα μή σου γλῶσσ᾽ ὑπερβάλῃ κακοῖς.
ΘΗ. φεῦ, χρῆν βροτοῖσι τῶν φίλων τεκμήριον   925
σαφές τι κεῖσθαι καὶ διάγνωσιν φρενῶν,
ὅστις τ᾽ ἀληθής ἐστιν ὅς τε μὴ φίλος·
δισσάς τε φωνὰς πάντας ἀνθρώπους ἔχειν,
τὴν μὲν δικαίαν, τὴν δ᾽ ὅπως ἐτύγχανεν,
ὡς ἡ φρονοῦσα τἄδικ᾽ ἐξηλέγχετο   930
πρὸς τῆς δικαίας, κοὐκ ἂν ἠπατώμεθα.
ΙΠ. ἀλλ᾽ ἦ τις εἰς σὸν οὖς με διαβαλὼν ἔχει
φίλων, νοσοῦμεν δ᾽ οὐδὲν ὄντες αἴτιοι;
ἔκ τοι πέπληγμαι· σοὶ γὰρ ἐκπλήσσουσί με
λόγοι παραλλάσσοντες ἔξεδροι φρενῶν.   935
ΘΗ. φεῦ τῆς βροτείας (ποῖ προβήσεται;) φρενός·
τί τέρμα τόλμης καὶ θράσους γενήσεται;
εἰ γὰρ κατ᾽ ἀνδρὸς βίοτον ἐξογκώσεται,
ὁ δ᾽ ὕστερος τοῦ πρόσθεν εἰς ὑπερβολὴν
πανοῦργος ἔσται, θεοῖσι προσβαλεῖν χθονὶ   940
ἄλλην δεήσει γαῖαν, ἢ χωρήσεται
τοὺς μὴ δικαίους καὶ κακοὺς πεφυκότας.
σκέψασθε δ᾽ εἰς τόνδ᾽, ὅστις ἐξ ἐμοῦ γεγὼς
ᾔσχυνε τἀμὰ λέκτρα κἀξελέγχεται
πρὸς τῆς θανούσης ἐμφανῶς κάκιστος ὤν.   945
δεῖξον δ᾽, ἐπειδή γ᾽ εἰς μίασμ᾽ ἐλήλυθας,
τὸ σὸν πρόσωπον δεῦρ᾽ ἐναντίον πατρί.
σὺ δὴ θεοῖσιν ὡς περισσὸς ὢν ἀνὴρ
ξύνει; σὺ σώφρων καὶ κακῶν ἀκήρατος;
οὐκ ἂν πιθοίμην τοῖσι σοῖς κόμποις ἐγὼ   950

θεοῖσι προσθεὶς ἀμαθίαν φρονεῖν κακῶς.
ἤδη νῦν αὔχει καὶ δι᾽ ἀψύχου βορᾶς
σίτοις καπήλευ᾽, Ὀρφέα τ᾽ ἄνακτ᾽ ἔχων
βάκχευε πολλῶν γραμμάτων τιμῶν καπνούς·
ἐπεί γ᾽ ἐλήφθης. τοὺς δὲ τοιούτους ἐγὼ   955
φεύγειν προφωνῶ πᾶσι· θηρεύουσι γὰρ
σεμνοῖς λόγοισιν, αἰσχρὰ μηχανώμενοι.
τέθνηκεν ἥδε· τοῦτό σ᾽ ἐκσώσειν δοκεῖς;
ἐν τῷδ᾽ ἁλίσκει πλεῖστον, ὦ κάκιστε σύ·
ποῖοι γὰρ ὅρκοι κρείσσονες, τίνες λόγοι   960
τῆσδ᾽ ἂν γένοιντ᾽ ἄν, ὥστε σ᾽ αἰτίαν φυγεῖν;
μισεῖν σε φήσεις τήνδε καὶ τὸ δὴ νόθον
τοῖς γνησίοισι πολέμιον πεφυκέναι·
κακὴν ἄρ᾽ αὐτὴν ἔμπορον βίου λέγεις,
εἰ δυσμενείᾳ σῇ τὰ φίλτατ᾽ ὤλεσεν.   965
ἀλλ᾽ ὡς τὸ μῶρον ἀνδράσιν μὲν οὐκ ἔνι,
γυναιξὶ δ᾽ ἐμπέφυκεν; οἶδ᾽ ἐγὼ νέους
οὐδὲν γυναικῶν ὄντας ἀσφαλεστέρους,
ὅταν ταράξῃ Κύπρις ἡβῶσαν φρένα·
τὸ δ᾽ ἄρσεν αὐτοὺς ὠφελεῖ προσκείμενον.   970
νῦν οὖν τί ταῦτα σοῖς ἁμιλλῶμαι λόγοις
νεκροῦ παρόντος μάρτυρος σαφεστάτου;
ἔξερρε γαίας τῆσδ᾽ ὅσον τάχος φυγάς,
καὶ μήτ᾽ Ἀθήνας τὰς θεοδμήτους μόλῃς,
μήτ᾽ εἰς ὅρους γῆς ἧς ἐμὸν κρατεῖ δόρυ.   975
εἰ γὰρ παθών γε σοῦ τάδ᾽ ἡσσηθήσομαι,
οὐ μαρτυρήσει μ᾽ Ἴσθμιος Σίνις ποτὲ
κτανεῖν ἑαυτόν, ἀλλὰ κομπάζειν μάτην,
οὐδ᾽ αἱ θαλάσσῃ σύννομοι Σκειρωνίδες
φήσουσι πέτραι τοῖς κακοῖς μ᾽ εἶναι βαρύν.   980
ΧΟ. οὐκ οἶδ᾽ ὅπως εἴποιμ᾽ ἂν εὐτυχεῖν τινα

θνητῶν· τὰ γὰρ δὴ πρῶτ᾿ ἀνέστραπται πάλιν.

III. πάτερ, μένος μὲν ξύντασίς τε σῶν φρενῶν
δεινή· τὸ μέντοι πρᾶγμ᾿ ἔχον καλοὺς λόγους,
εἴ τις διαπτύξειεν, οὐ καλὸν τόδε.   985
ἐγὼ δ᾿ ἄκομψος εἰς ὄχλον δοῦναι λόγον,
εἰς ἥλικας δὲ κὠλίγους σοφώτερος.
ἔχει δὲ μοῖραν καὶ τόδ᾿· οἱ γὰρ ἐν σοφοῖς
φαῦλοι παρ᾿ ὄχλῳ μουσικώτεροι λέγειν.
ὅμως δ᾿ ἀνάγκη, συμφορᾶς ἀφιγμένης,   990
γλῶσσάν μ᾿ ἀφεῖναι. πρῶτα δ᾿ ἄρξομαι λέγειν
ὅθεν μ᾿ ὑπῆλθες πρῶτον ὡς διαφθερῶν
οὐκ ἀντιλέξοντ᾿· εἰσορᾷς φάος τόδε
καὶ γαῖαν· ἐν τοῖσδ᾿ οὐκ ἔνεστ᾿ ἀνὴρ ἐμοῦ,
οὐδ᾿ ἦν σὺ μὴ φῇς, σωφρονέστερος γεγώς.   995
ἐπίσταμαι γὰρ πρῶτα μὲν θεοὺς σέβειν,
φίλοις τε χρῆσθαι μὴ ἀδικεῖν πειρωμένοις,
ἀλλ᾿ οἷσιν αἰδὼς μήτ᾿ ἐπαγγέλλειν κακὰ
μήτ᾿ ἀνθυπουργεῖν αἰσχρὰ τοῖσι χρωμένοις·
οὐκ ἐγγελαστὴς τῶν ὁμιλούντων, πάτερ,   1000
ἀλλ᾿ αὑτὸς οὐ παροῦσι κἀγγὺς ὢν φίλος.
ἑνὸς δ᾿ ἄθικτος, ᾧ με νῦν ἑλεῖν δοκεῖς·
λέχους γὰρ εἰς τόδ᾿ ἡμέρας ἁγνὸν δέμας.
οὐκ οἶδα πρᾶξιν τήνδε πλὴν λόγῳ κλύων
γραφῇ τε λεύσσων· οὐδὲ ταῦτα γὰρ σκοπεῖν   1005
πρόθυμός εἰμι, παρθένον ψυχὴν ἔχων.
καὶ δὴ τὸ σῶφρον τοὐμὸν οὐ πείθει σ᾿ ἴσως·
δεῖ δή σε δεῖξαι τῷ τρόπῳ διεφθάρην.
πότερα τὸ τῆσδε σῶμ᾿ ἐκαλλιστεύετο
πασῶν γυναικῶν; ἢ σὸν οἰκήσειν δόμον   1010
ἔγκληρον εὐνὴν προσλαβὼν ἐπήλπισα;
μάταιος ἄρ᾿ ἦν, οὐδαμοῦ μὲν οὖν φρενῶν.

ἀλλ' ὡς τυραννεῖν ἡδύ; τοῖσι σώφροσιν
ἥκιστά γ', εἰ δὴ τὰς φρένας διέφθορε
θνητῶν ὅσοισιν ἁνδάνει μοναρχία.   1015
ἐγὼ δ' ἀγῶνας μὲν κρατεῖν Ἑλληνικοὺς
πρῶτος θέλοιμ' ἄν, ἐν πόλει δὲ δεύτερος
σὺν τοῖς ἀρίστοις εὐτυχεῖν ἀεὶ φίλοις.
πράσσειν τε γὰρ πάρεστι, κίνδυνός τ' ἀπὼν
κρείσσω δίδωσι τῆς τυραννίδος χάριν.   1020
ἓν οὐ λέλεκται τῶν ἐμῶν, τὰ δ' ἄλλ' ἔχεις·
εἰ μὲν γὰρ ἦν μοι μάρτυς οἷός εἰμ' ἐγώ,
καὶ τῆσδ' ὁρώσης φέγγος ἠγωνιζόμην,
ἔργοις ἂν εἶδες τοὺς κακοὺς διεξιών.
νῦν δ' ὅρκιόν σοι Ζῆνα καὶ πέδον χθονὸς   1025
ὄμνυμι τῶν σῶν μήποθ' ἅψασθαι γάμων
μηδ' ἂν θελῆσαι μηδ' ἂν ἔννοιαν λαβεῖν.
ἦ τἄρ' ὀλοίμην ἀκλεὴς ἀνώνυμος,
ἄπολις ἄοικος, φυγὰς ἀλητεύων χθόνα,
καὶ μήτε πόντος μήτε γῆ δέξαιτό μου   1030
σάρκας θανόντος, εἰ κακὸς πέφυκ' ἀνήρ.
εἰ δ' ἥδε δειμαίνουσ' ἀπώλεσεν βίον
οὐκ οἶδ'· ἐμοὶ γὰρ οὐ θέμις πέρα λέγειν.
ἐσωφρόνησε δ' οὐκ ἔχουσα σωφρονεῖν,
ἡμεῖς δ' ἔχοντες οὐ καλῶς ἐχρώμεθα.   1035
ΧΟ. ἀρκοῦσαν εἶπας αἰτίας ἀποστροφήν,
ὅρκους παρασχών, πίστιν οὐ σμικράν, θεῶν.
ΘΗ. ἆρ' οὐκ ἐπῳδὸς καὶ γόης πέφυχ' ὅδε,
ὃς τὴν ἐμὴν πέποιθεν εὐοργησίᾳ
ψυχὴν κρατήσειν τὸν τεκόντ' ἀτιμάσας;   1040
ΙΠ. καὶ σοῦ γε κάρτα ταῦτα θαυμάζω, πάτερ·
εἰ γὰρ σὺ μὲν παῖς ἦσθ', ἐγὼ δὲ σὸς πατήρ,
ἔκτεινά τοί σ' ἂν κοὐ φυγαῖς ἐζημίουν,

εἴπερ γυναικὸς ἠξίους ἐμῆς θιγεῖν.

ΘΗ. ὡς ἄξιον τόδ᾽ εἶπας· οὐχ οὕτω θανεῖ·   1045
ταχὺς γὰρ Ἅιδης ῥᾷστος ἀνδρὶ δυσσεβεῖ·   1047
ἀλλ᾽ ἐκ πατρῴας φυγὰς ἀλητεύων χθονὸς   1048
ὥσπερ σὺ σαυτῷ τόνδε προύθηκας νόμον·   1046
[ξένην ἐπ᾽ αἶαν λυπρὸν ἀντλήσεις βίον·
μισθὸς γὰρ οὗτός ἐστιν ἀνδρὶ δυσσεβεῖ.]   1050

ΙΠ. οἴμοι, τί δράσεις; οὐδὲ μηνυτὴν χρόνον
δέξει καθ᾽ ἡμῶν, ἀλλά μ᾽ ἐξελᾷς χθονός;

ΘΗ. πέραν γε πόντου καὶ τόπων Ἀτλαντικῶν,
εἴ πως δυναίμην, ὡς σὸν ἐχθαίρω κάρα.

ΙΠ. οὐδ᾽ ὅρκον οὐδὲ πίστιν οὐδὲ μάντεων   1055
φήμας ἐλέγξας ἄκριτον ἐκβαλεῖς με γῆς;

ΘΗ. ἡ δέλτος ἥδε κλῆρον οὐ δεδεγμένη
κατηγορεῖ σου πιστά· τοὺς δ᾽ ὑπὲρ κάρα
φοιτῶντας ὄρνεις πόλλ᾽ ἐγὼ χαίρειν λέγω.

ΙΠ. ὦ θεοί, τί δῆτα τοὐμὸν οὐ λύω στόμα,   1060
ὅστις γ᾽ ὑφ᾽ ὑμῶν, οὓς σέβω, διόλλυμαι;
οὐ δῆτα· πάντως οὐ πίθοιμ᾽ ἂν οὕς με δεῖ,
μάτην δ᾽ ἂν ὅρκους συγχέαιμ᾽ οὓς ὤμοσα.

ΘΗ. οἴμοι· τὸ σεμνὸν ὥς μ᾽ ἀποκτείνει τὸ σόν.
οὐκ εἶ πατρῴας ἐκτὸς ὡς τάχιστα γῆς;   1065

ΙΠ. ποῖ δῆθ᾽ ὁ τλήμων τρέψομαι; τίνος ξένων
δόμους ἔσειμι τῇδ᾽ ἐπ᾽ αἰτίᾳ φυγών;

ΘΗ. ὅστις γυναικῶν λυμεῶνας ἥδεται
ξένους κομίζων καὶ συνοικουροὺς κακῶν.

ΙΠ. αἰαῖ· πρὸς ἧπαρ δακρύων τ᾽ ἐγγὺς τόδε,   1070
εἰ δὴ κακός γε φαίνομαι δοκῶ τέ σοι.

ΘΗ. τότε στενάζειν καὶ προγιγνώσκειν σ᾽ ἐχρῆν,
ὅτ᾽ εἰς πατρῴαν ἄλοχον ὑβρίζειν ἔτλης.

ΙΠ. ὦ δώματ᾽, εἴθε φθέγμα γηρύσαισθέ μοι

καὶ μαρτυρήσαιτ᾽ εἰ κακὸς πέφυκ᾽ ἀνήρ.   1075

ΘΗ. εἰς τοὺς ἀφώνους μάρτυρας φεύγεις σοφῶς·
τὸ δ᾽ ἔργον οὐ λέγον σε μηνύει κακόν.

ΙΠ. φεῦ·
εἴθ᾽ ἦν ἐμαυτὸν προσβλέπειν ἐναντίον
στάνθ᾽, ὡς ἐδάκρυσ᾽ οἷα πάσχομεν κακά.

ΘΗ. πολλῷ γε μᾶλλον σαυτὸν ἤσκησας σέβειν   1080
ἢ τοὺς τεκόντας ὅσια δρᾶν, δίκαιος ὤν.

ΙΠ. ὦ δυστάλαινα μῆτερ, ὦ πικραὶ γοναί·
μηδείς ποτ᾽ εἴη τῶν ἐμῶν φίλων νόθος.

ΘΗ. οὐχ ἕλξετ᾽ αὐτόν, δμῶες; οὐκ ἀκούετε
πάλαι ξενοῦσθαι τόνδε προυννέποντά με;   1085

ΙΠ. κλαίων τις αὐτῶν ἄρ᾽ ἐμοῦ γε θίξεται·
σὺ δ᾽ αὐτός, εἴ σοι θυμός, ἐξώθει χθονός.

ΘΗ. δράσω τάδ᾽, εἰ μὴ τοῖς ἐμοῖς πείσει λόγοις·
οὐ γάρ τις οἶκτος σῆς μ᾽ ὑπέρχεται φυγῆς.

ΙΠ. ἄραρεν, ὡς ἔοικεν· ὦ τάλας ἐγώ·   1090
ὡς οἶδα μὲν ταῦτ᾽, οἶδα δ᾽ οὐχ ὅπως φράσω.
ὦ φιλτάτη μοι δαιμόνων Λητοῦς κόρη
σύνθακε συγκύναγε, φευξούμεσθα δὴ
κλεινὰς Ἀθήνας. ἀλλὰ χαίρετ᾽, ὦ πόλις
καὶ γαῖ᾽ Ἐρεχθέως· ὦ πέδον Τροιζήνιον,   1095
ὡς ἐγκαθηβᾶν πόλλ᾽ ἔχεις εὐδαίμονα,
χαῖρ᾽· ὕστατον γάρ σ᾽ εἰσορῶν προσφθέγγομαι.
ἴτ᾽, ὦ νέοι μοι τῆσδε γῆς ὁμήλικες,
προσείπαθ᾽ ἡμᾶς καὶ προπέμψατε χθονός·
ὡς οὔποτ᾽ ἄλλον ἄνδρα σωφρονέστερον   1100
ὄψεσθε, κεἰ μὴ ταῦτ᾽ ἐμῷ δοκεῖ πατρί.

ΧΟ. ἦ μέγα μοι τὰ θεῶν μελεδήμαθ᾽, ὅταν φρένας
        ἔλθῃ,   στρ.
λύπας παραιρεῖ·

ξύνεσιν δέ τιν᾽ ἐλπίδι κεύθων   1105
λείπομαι ἔν τε τύχαις θνατῶν καὶ ἐν ἔργμασι
    λεύσσων·
ἄλλα γὰρ ἄλλοθεν ἀμείβεται,
μετὰ δ᾽ ἵσταται ἀνδράσιν αἰὼν
πολυπλάνητος αἰεί.   1110
εἴθε μοι εὐξαμένᾳ θεόθεν τάδε μοῖρα παρά-
    σχοι,   ἀντ.
τύχαν μετ᾽ ὄλβου
καὶ ἀκήρατον ἄλγεσι θυμόν·
δόξα δὲ μήτ᾽ ἀτρεκὴς μήτ᾽ αὖ παράσημος ἐνείη·
ῥᾴδια δ᾽ ἤθεα τὸν αὔριον   1116
μεταβαλλομένα χρόνον αἰεὶ
βίον συνευτυχοίην.
οὐκέτι γὰρ καθαρὰν φρέν᾽ ἔχω τὰ παρ᾽ ἐλπίδα
    λεύσσων,   στρ. 1120
ἐπεὶ τὸν Ἑλλανίας
φανερώτατον ἀστέρ᾽ Ἀθάνας
εἴδομεν εἴδομεν ἐκ πατρὸς ὀργᾶς
ἄλλαν ἐπ᾽ αἶαν ἱέμενον.   1125
ὦ ψάμαθοι πολιήτιδος ἀκτᾶς
δρυμός τ᾽ ὄρειος, ὅθι κυνῶν
ὠκυπόδων μέτα θῆρας ἔναιρεν
Δίκτυνναν ἀμφὶ σεμνάν.   1130
οὐκέτι συζυγίαν πώλων Ἐνετᾶν ἐπιβάσει ἀντ.
τὸν ἀμφὶ Λίμνας τρόχον
κατέχων ποδὶ γυμνάδος ἵππου.
μοῦσα δ᾽ ἄυπνος ὑπ᾽ ἄντυγι χορδᾶν   1135
λήξει πατρῷον ἀνὰ δόμον·
ἀστέφανοι δὲ κόρας ἀνάπαυλαι
Λατοῦς βαθεῖαν ἀνὰ χλόαν·

νυμφιδία δ' ἀπόλωλε φυγᾷ σᾷ   1140
λέκτρων ἅμιλλα κούραις.
ἐγὼ δὲ σᾷ δυστυχίᾳ δάκρυσι διοίσω
πότμον ἄποτμον· ὦ τάλαινα
μᾶτερ, ἔτεκες ἀνόνατα· φεῦ,   1145
μανίω θεοῖσιν·
ἰὼ ἰὼ συζύγιαι Χάριτες,
τί τὸν ταλαν' ἐκ πατρίας γᾶς
τὸν οὐδὲν ἄτας αἴτιον
πέμπετε τῶνδ' ἀπ' οἴκων;   1150
καὶ μὴν ὀπαδὸν Ἱππολύτου τόνδ' εἰσορῶ
σπουδῇ σκυθρωπὸν πρὸς δόμους ὁρμώμενον.

ΑΓ. ποῖ γῆς ἄνακτα τῆσδε Θησέα μολὼν
εὕροιμ' ἄν, ὦ γυναῖκες; εἴπερ ἴστ', ἐμοὶ
σημήνατ'· ἆρα τῶνδε δωμάτων ἔσω;   1155
ΧΟ. ὅδ' αὐτὸς ἔξω δωμάτων πορεύεται.
ΑΓ. Θησεῦ, μερίμνης ἄξιον φέρω λόγον
σοὶ καὶ πολίταις οἵ τ' Ἀθηναίων πόλιν
ναίουσι καὶ γῆς τέρμονας Τροιζηνίας.
ΘΗ. τί δ' ἔστι; μῶν τις συμφορὰ νεωτέρα   1160
δισσὰς κατείληφ' ἀστυγείτονας πόλεις;
ΑΓ. Ἱππόλυτος οὐκέτ' ἔστιν, ὡς εἰπεῖν ἔπος·
δέδορκε μέντοι φῶς ἐπὶ σμικρᾶς ῥοπῆς.
ΘΗ. πρὸς τοῦ; δι' ἔχθρας μῶν τις ἦν ἀφιγμένος,
ὅτου κατῄσχυν' ἄλοχον ὡς πατρὸς βίᾳ;   1165
ΑΓ. οἰκεῖος αὐτὸν ὤλεσ' ἁρμάτων ὄχος
ἀραί τε τοῦ σοῦ στόματος, ἃς σὺ σῷ πατρὶ
πόντου κρέοντι παιδὸς ἠράσω πέρι.
ΘΗ. ὦ θεοὶ Πόσειδόν θ', ὡς ἄρ' ἦσθ' ἐμὸς πατὴρ
ὀρθῶς, ἀκούσας τῶν ἐμῶν κατευγμάτων.   1170
πῶς καὶ διώλετ'; εἰπέ· τῷ τρόπῳ Δίκης

ἔπαισεν αὐτὸν ῥόπτρον αἰσχύναντ' ἐμέ;

ΑΓ. ἡμεῖς μὲν ἀκτῆς κυμοδέγμονος πέλας
ψήκτραισιν ἵππων ἐκτενίζομεν τρίχας
κλαίοντες· ἦλθε γάρ τις ἄγγελος λέγων   1175
ὡς οὐκέτ' ἐν γῇ τῇδ' ἀναστρέψοι πόδα
Ἱππόλυτος, ἐκ σοῦ τλήμονας φυγὰς ἔχων.
ὁ δ' ἦλθε ταὐτὸ δακρύων ἔχων μέλος
ἡμῖν ἐπ' ἀκτάς· μυρία δ' ὀπισθόπους
φίλων ἅμ' ἔστειχ' ἡλίκων ὁμήγυρις.   1180
χρόνῳ δὲ δή ποτ' εἶπ' ἀπαλλαχθεὶς γόων·
τί ταῦτ' ἀλύω; πειστέον πατρὸς λόγοις.
ἐντύναθ' ἵππους ἅρμασι ζυγηφόρους,
δμῶες· πόλις γὰρ οὐκέτ' ἔστιν ἥδε μοι.
τοὐνθένδε μέντοι πᾶς ἀνὴρ ἠπείγετο,   1185
καὶ θᾶσσον ἢ λέγοι τις ἐξηρτυμένας
πώλους παρ' αὐτὸν δεσπότην ἐστήσαμεν.
μάρπτει δὲ χερσὶν ἡνίας ἀπ' ἄντυγος,
αὐταῖσιν ἀρβύλαισιν ἁρμόσας πόδας.
καὶ πρῶτα μὲν θεοῖς εἶπ' ἀναπτύξας χέρας· 1190
Ζεῦ, μηκέτ' εἴην, εἰ κακὸς πέφυκ' ἀνήρ·
αἴσθοιτο δ' ἡμᾶς ὡς ἀτιμάζει πατὴρ
ἤτοι θανόντας ἢ φάος δεδορκότας.
κἂν τῷδ' ἐπῆγε κέντρον εἰς χεῖρας λαβὼν
πώλοις· ὁμαρτῇ πρόσπολοι δ' ἐφ' ἅρματος* 1195
πέλας χαλινῶν εἱπόμεσθα δεσπότῃ
τὴν εὐθὺς Ἄργους κἀπιδαυρίας ὁδόν.
ἐπεὶ δ' ἔρημον χῶρον εἰσεβάλλομεν,
ἀκτή τις ἔστι τοὐπέκεινα τῆσδε γῆς
πρὸς πόντον ἤδη κειμένη Σαρωνικόν.   1200
ἔνθεν τις ἠχὼ χθόνιος ὡς βροντὴ Διὸς
βαρὺν βρόμον μεθῆκε φρικώδη κλύειν·

ὀρθὸν δὲ κρᾶτ' ἔστησαν οὕς τ' ἐς οὐρανὸν
ἵπποι· παρ' ἡμῖν δ' ἦν φόβος νεανικὸς
πόθεν ποτ' εἴη φθόγγος. εἰς δ' ἁλιρρόθους   1205
ἀκτὰς ἀποβλέψαντες ἱερὸν εἴδομεν
κῦμ' οὐρανῷ στηρίζον, ὥστ' ἀφῃρέθη
Σκιρωνίδ' ἄκραν ὄμμα τοὐμὸν εἰσορᾶν·
ἔκρυπτε δ' Ἰσθμὸν καὶ πέτραν Ἀσκληπιοῦ.
κἄπειτ' ἀνοιδῆσάν τε καὶ πέριξ ἀφρὸν   1210
πολὺν καχλάζον ποντίῳ φυσήματι
χωρεῖ πρὸς ἀκτάς, οὗ τέθριππος ἦν ὄχος.
αὐτῷ δὲ σὺν κλύδωνι καὶ τρικυμίᾳ
κῦμ' ἐξέθηκε ταῦρον ἄγριον τέρας,
οὗ πᾶσα μὲν χθὼν φθέγματος πληρουμένη   1215
φρικῶδες ἀντεφθέγγετ', εἰσορῶσι δὲ
κρεῖσσον θέαμα δεργμάτων ἐφαίνετο.
εὐθὺς δὲ πώλοις δεινὸς ἐμπίπτει φόβος
καὶ δεσπότης μὲν ἱππικοῖσιν ἤθεσι
πολὺς ξυνοικῶν ἥρπασ' ἡνίας χεροῖν,   1220
ἕλκει δὲ κώπην ὥστε ναυβάτης ἀνὴρ
ἱμᾶσιν εἰς τοὔπισθεν ἀρτήσας δέμας·
αἱ δ' ἐνδακοῦσαι στόμια πυριγενῆ γναθμοῖς
βίᾳ φέρουσιν, οὔτε ναυκλήρου χερὸς
οὔθ' ἱπποδέσμων οὔτε κολλητῶν ὄχων   1225
μεταστρέφουσαι. κεἰ μὲν εἰς τὰ μαλθακὰ
γαίας ἔχων οἴακας ἰθύνοι δρόμον,
προυφαίνετ' ἐκ τοῦ πρόσθεν, ὥστ' ἀναστρέφειν,
ταῦρος φόβῳ τέτρωρον ἐκμαίνων ὄχον·
εἰ δ' εἰς πέτρας φέροιντο μαργῶσαι φρένας,   1230
σιγῇ πελάζων ἄντυγι ξυνείπετο
εἰς τοῦθ' ἕως ἔσφηλε κἀνεχαίτισεν,
ἁψῖδα πέτρῳ προσβαλὼν ὀχήματος.

σύμφυρτα δ' ἦν ἅπαντα· σύριγγές τ' ἄνω
τροχῶν ἐπήδων ἀξόνων τ' ἐνήλατα.   1235
αὐτὸς δ' ὁ τλήμων ἡνίαισιν ἐμπλακεὶς
δεσμὸν δυσεξήνυστον ἕλκεται δεθείς,
σποδούμενος μὲν πρὸς πέτραις φίλον κάρα,
θραύων δὲ σάρκας, δεινὰ δ' ἐξαυδῶν κλύειν·
στῆτ', ὦ φάτναισι ταῖς ἐμαῖς τεθραμμέναι,   1240
μή μ' ἐξαλείψητ'· ὦ πατρὸς τάλαιν' ἀρά.
τίς ἄνδρ' ἄριστον βούλεται σῶσαι παρών;
πολλοὶ δὲ βουληθέντες ὑστέρῳ ποδὶ
ἐλειπόμεσθα. χὡ μὲν ἐκ δεσμῶν λυθεὶς
τμητῶν ἱμάντων οὐ κάτοιδ' ὅτῳ τρόπῳ   1245
πίπτει, βραχὺν δὴ βίοτον ἐμπνέων ἔτι·
ἵπποι δ' ἔκρυφθεν καὶ τὸ δύστηνον τέρας
ταύρου λεπαίας οὐ κάτοιδ' ὅπου χθονός.
δοῦλος μὲν οὖν ἔγωγε σῶν δόμων, ἄναξ,
ἀτὰρ τοσοῦτόν γ' οὐ δυνήσομαί ποτε   1250
τὸν σὸν πιθέσθαι παῖδ' ὅπως ἐστὶν κακός,
οὐδ' εἰ γυναικῶν πᾶν κρεμασθείη γένος
καὶ τὴν ἐν Ἴδῃ γραμμάτων πλήσειέ τις
πεύκην, ἐπεί νιν ἐσθλὸν ὄντ' ἐπίσταμαι.

ΧΟ. αἰαῖ· κέκρανται συμφορὰ νέων κακῶν,   1255
οὐδ' ἔστι μοίρας τοῦ χρεών τ' ἀπαλλαγή.

ΘΗ. μίσει μὲν ἀνδρὸς τοῦ πεπονθότος τάδε
λόγοισιν ἥσθην τοῖσδε· νῦν δ' αἰδούμενος
θεούς τ' ἐκεῖνόν θ', οὕνεκ' ἐστὶν ἐξ ἐμοῦ,
οὔθ' ἥδομαι τοῖσδ' οὔτ' ἐπάχθομαι κακοῖς.   1260

ΑΓ. πῶς οὖν; κομίζειν ἢ τί χρὴ τὸν ἄθλιον
δράσαντας ἡμᾶς σῇ χαρίζεσθαι φρενί;
φρόντιζ'· ἐμοῖς δὲ χρώμενος βουλεύμασιν
οὐκ ὠμὸς εἰς σὸν παῖδα δυστυχοῦντ' ἔσει.

ΘΗ. κομίζετ᾽ αὐτόν, ὡς ἰδὼν ἐν ὄμμασι   1265
τὸν τἄμ᾽ ἀπαρνηθέντα μὴ χρᾶναι λέχη
λόγοις τ᾽ ἐλέγξω δαιμόνων τε συμφοραῖς.

ΧΟ. σὺ τὰν θεῶν ἄκαμπτον φρένα καὶ βροτῶν
ἄγεις, Κύπρι· σὺν δ᾽
ὁ ποικιλόπτερος ἀμφιβαλὼν   1270
ὠκυτάτῳ πτερῷ.
ποτᾶται δ᾽ ἐπὶ γαῖαν εὐάχητόν θ᾽
ἁλμυρὸν ἐπὶ πόντον.
θέλγει δ᾽ Ἔρως, ᾧ μαινομένᾳ κραδίᾳ
πτανὸς ἐφορμάσῃ   1275
χρυσοφαής,
φύσιν ὀρεσκόων
σκυλάκων πελαγίων θ᾽ ὅσα τε γᾶ τρέφει,
τὰν Ἅλιος αἰθομέναν δέρκεται,
ἄνδρας τε· συμπάντων δὲ   1280
βασιληίδα τιμάν, Κύπρι,
τῶνδε μόνα κρατύνεις.

ΑΡ. σὲ τὸν εὐπατρίδαν Αἰγέως κέλομαι
παῖδ᾽ ἐπακοῦσαι·
Λητοῦς δὲ κόρη σ᾽ Ἄρτεμις αὐδῶ.   1285
Θησεῦ, τί τάλας τοῖσδε συνήδει,
παῖδ᾽ οὐχ ὁσίως σὸν ἀποκτείνας,
ψευδέσι μύθοις δ᾽ ἀλόχου πεισθεὶς
ἀφανῆ, φανερὰν ἔσχεθες ἄταν;
πῶς οὐχ ὑπὸ γῆς τάρταρα κρύπτεις   1290
δέμας αἰσχυνθείς,
ἢ πτηνὸς ἄνω μεταβὰς βίοτον
πήματος ἔξω πόδα τοῦδ᾽ ἀπέχεις;
ὡς ἔν γ᾽ ἀγαθοῖς ἀνδράσιν οὔ σοι
κτητὸν βιότου μέρος ἐστίν.   1295

ἄκουε, Θησεῦ, σῶν κακῶν κατάστασιν·
καίτοι προκόψω γ' οὐδέν, ἀλγυνῶ δὲ σέ.
ἀλλ' εἰς τόδ' ἦλθον, παιδὸς ἐκδεῖξαι φρένα
τοῦ σοῦ δικαίαν, ὡς ὑπ' εὐκλείας θάνῃ,
καὶ σῆς γυναικὸς οἶστρον ἢ τρόπον τινὰ   1300
γενναιότητα· τῆς γὰρ ἐχθίστης θεῶν
ἡμῖν, ὅσαισι παρθένειος ἡδονή,
δηχθεῖσα κέντροις παιδὸς ἠράσθη σέθεν.
γνώμῃ δὲ νικᾶν τὴν Κύπριν πειρωμένη
τροφοῦ διώλετ' οὐχ ἑκοῦσα μηχαναῖς,   1305
ἣ σῷ δι' ὅρκων παιδὶ σημαίνει νόσον.
ὁ δ', ὥσπερ οὖν δίκαιον, οὐκ ἐφέσπετο
λόγοισιν, οὐδ' αὖ πρὸς σέθεν κακούμενος
ὅρκων ἀφεῖλε πίστιν, εὐσεβὴς γεγώς.
ἡ δ' εἰς ἔλεγχον μὴ πέσῃ φοβουμένη   1310
ψευδεῖς γραφὰς ἔγραψε καὶ διώλεσε
δόλοισι σὸν παῖδ', ἀλλ' ὅμως ἔπεισέ σε.
ΘΗ. οἴμοι.
ΑΡ. δάκνει σε, Θησεῦ, μῦθος; ἀλλ' ἔχ' ἥσυχος,
τοὐνθένδ' ἀκούσας ὡς ἂν οἰμώξῃς πλέον.
ἆρ' οἶσθα πατρὸς τρεῖς ἀρὰς σαφεῖς ἔχων;   1315
ὧν τὴν μίαν παρεῖλες, ὦ κάκιστε σύ,
εἰς παῖδα τὸν σόν, ἐξὸν εἰς ἐχθρόν τινα.
πατὴρ μὲν οὖν σοι πόντιος φρονῶν καλῶς
ἔδωχ' ὅσονπερ χρῆν, ἐπείπερ ᾔνεσεν·
σὺ δ' ἔν τ' ἐκείνῳ κἀν ἐμοὶ φαίνει κακός,   1320
ὃς οὔτε πίστιν οὔτε μάντεων ὄπα
ἔμεινας, οὐκ ἤλεγξας, οὐ χρόνῳ μακρῷ
σκέψιν παρέσχες, ἀλλὰ θᾶσσον ἤ σ' ἐχρῆν
ἀρὰς ἐφῆκας παιδὶ καὶ κατέκτανες.
ΘΗ. δέσποιν', ὀλοίμην.

ΑΡ.   δείν᾽ ἔπραξας, ἀλλ᾽ ὅμως   1325
ἔτ᾽ ἔστι καὶ σοὶ τῶνδε συγγνώμης τυχεῖν·
Κύπρις γὰρ ἤθελ᾽ ὥστε γίγνεσθαι τάδε,
πληροῦσα θυμόν. θεοῖσι δ᾽ ὧδ᾽ ἔχει νόμος·
οὐδεὶς ἀπαντᾶν βούλεται προθυμίᾳ
τῇ τοῦ θέλοντος, ἀλλ᾽ ἀφιστάμεσθ᾽ ἀεί.   1330
ἐπεὶ σάφ᾽ ἴσθι, Ζῆνα μὴ φοβουμένη
οὐκ ἄν ποτ᾽ ἦλθον εἰς τόδ᾽ αἰσχύνης ἐγὼ
ὥστ᾽ ἄνδρα πάντων φίλτατον βροτῶν ἐμοὶ
θανεῖν ἐᾶσαι. τὴν δὲ σὴν ἁμαρτίαν
τὸ μὴ εἰδέναι μὲν πρῶτον ἐκλύει κάκης·   1335
ἔπειτα δ᾽ ἡ θανοῦσ᾽ ἀνάλωσεν γυνὴ
λόγων ἐλέγχους ὥστε σὴν πεῖσαι φρένα.
μάλιστα μέν νυν σοὶ τάδ᾽ ἔρρωγεν κακά,
λύπη δὲ κἀμοί· τοὺς γὰρ εὐσεβεῖς θεοὶ
θνήσκοντας οὐ χαίρουσι· τούς γε μὴν κακοὺς   1340
αὐτοῖς τέκνοισι καὶ δόμοις ἐξόλλυμεν.

ΧΟ. καὶ μὴν ὁ τάλας ὅδε δὴ στείχει,
σάρκας νεαρὰς ξανθόν τε κάρα
διαλυμανθείς. ὢ πόνος οἴκων,
οἷον ἐκράνθη δίδυμον μελάθροις   1345
πένθος θεόθεν καταληπτόν.

ΙΠ. αἰαῖ αἰαῖ·
δύστανος ἐγώ, πατρὸς ἐξ ἀδίκου
χρησμοῖς ἀδίκοις διελυμάνθην.
ἀπόλωλα τάλας, οἴμοι μοι.   1350
διά μου κεφαλᾶς ἄσσουσ᾽ ὀδύναι,
κατὰ δ᾽ ἐγκέφαλον πηδᾷ σφάκελος.
σχές, ἀπειρηκὸς σῶμ᾽ ἀναπαύσω.
[ἒ ἔ·]
ὢ στυγνὸν ὄχημ᾽ ἵππειον, ἐμῆς   1355

βόσκημα χερός,
διά μ᾽ ἔφθειρας, κατὰ δ᾽ ἔκτεινας.
φεῦ φεῦ· πρὸς θεῶν, ἀτρέμας, δμῶες,
χροὸς ἑλκώδους ἅπτεσθε χεροῖν.
τίς ἐφέστηκεν δεξιὰ πλευροῖς; 1360
πρόσφορά μ᾽ αἴρετε, σύντονα δ᾽ ἕλκετε
τὸν κακοδαίμονα καὶ κατάρατον
πατρὸς ἀμπλακίαις. Ζεῦ Ζεῦ, τάδ᾽ ὁρᾷς;
ὅδ᾽ ὁ σεμνὸς ἐγὼ καὶ θεοσέπτωρ,
ὅδ᾽ ὁ σωφροσύνῃ πάντας ὑπερσχὼν 1365
προὖπτον ἐς Ἅιδαν στείχω κατὰ γᾶς,
ὀλέσας βίοτον· μόχθους δ᾽ ἄλλως
τῆς εὐσεβίας
εἰς ἀνθρώπους ἐπόνησα.
αἰαῖ αἰαῖ· 1370
καὶ νῦν ὀδύνα μ᾽ ὀδύνα βαίνει.
μέθετέ με τάλανα·
καί μοι Θάνατος Παιὰν ἔλθοι.
προσαπόλλυτέ μ᾽ ὄλλυτε τὸν δυσδαίμον᾽·
* ἀμφιτόμου λόγχας ἔραμαι 1375
διαμοιρᾶσαι,
διά τ᾽ εὐνᾶσαι τὸν ἐμὸν βίοτον.
ὦ πατρὸς ἐμοῦ δύστανος ἀρά,
μιαιφόνων τι συγγόνων,
παλαιῶν προγεννητόρων, 1380
ἐξορίζεται κακὸν οὐδὲ μέλλει,
ἔμολέ τ᾽ ἐπ᾽ ἐμὲ
τί ποτε τὸν οὐδὲν ὄντ᾽ ἐπαίτιον κακῶν;
ἰώ μοι, τί φῶ;
πῶς ἀπαλλάξω βιοτὰν 1385
ἐμὰν τοῦδ᾽ ἀναλγήτου πάθους;

εἴθε με κοιμίσειε τὸν δυσδαίμον᾿
 Ἅιδου μέλαινα νύκτερός τ᾿ ἀνάγκα.

ΑΡ. ὦ τλῆμον, οἵαις συμφοραῖς συνεζύγης·
 τὸ δ᾿ εὐγενές σε τῶν φρενῶν ἀπώλεσεν.   1390

ΙΠ. ἔα·
 ὦ θεῖον ὀδμῆς πνεῦμα· καὶ γὰρ ἐν κακοῖς
 ὢν ᾐσθόμην σου κἀνεκουφίσθην δέμας·
 ἔστ᾿ ἐν τόποισι τοισίδ᾿ Ἄρτεμις θεά;

ΑΡ. ὦ τλῆμον, ἔστι, σοί γε φιλτάτη θεῶν.

ΙΠ. ὁρᾷς με, δέσποιν᾿, ὡς ἔχω, τὸν ἄθλιον;   1395

ΑΡ. ὁρῶ· κατ᾿ ὄσσων δ᾿ οὐ θέμις βαλεῖν δάκρυ.

ΙΠ. οὐκ ἔστι σοι κυναγὸς οὐδ᾿ ὑπηρέτης,

ΑΡ. οὐ δῆτ᾿· ἀτάρ μοι προσφιλής γ᾿ ἀπόλλυσαι.

ΙΠ. οὐδ᾿ ἱππονώμας οὐδ᾿ ἀγαλμάτων φύλαξ.

ΑΡ. Κύπρις γὰρ ἡ πανοῦργος ὧδ᾿ ἐμήσατο.   1400

ΙΠ. ὤμοι· φρονῶ δὴ δαίμον᾿ ἥ μ᾿ ἀπώλεσε.

ΑΡ. τιμῆς ἐμέμφθη, σωφρονοῦντι δ᾿ ἤχθετο.

ΙΠ. τρεῖς ὄντας ἡμᾶς ὤλεσ᾿, ᾔσθημαι, μία.

ΑΡ. πατέρα τε καὶ σὲ καὶ τρίτην ξυνάορον.

ΙΠ. ᾤμωξα τοίνυν καὶ πατρὸς δυσπραξίας.   1405

ΑΡ. ἐξηπατήθη δαίμονος βουλεύμασιν.

ΙΠ. ὦ δυστάλας σὺ τῆσδε συμφορᾶς, πάτερ.

ΘΗ. ὄλωλα, τέκνον, οὐδέ μοι χάρις βίου.

ΙΠ. στένω σὲ μᾶλλον ἢ 'μὲ τῆς ἁμαρτίας.

ΘΗ. εἰ γὰρ γενοίμην, τέκνον, ἀντὶ σοῦ νεκρός.   1410

ΙΠ. ὦ δῶρα πατρὸς σοῦ Ποσειδῶνος πικρά.

ΘΗ. ὡς μήποτ᾿ ἐλθεῖν ὤφελ᾿ εἰς τοὐμὸν στόμα.

ΙΠ. τί δ᾿; ἔκτανές τἂν μ᾿, ὡς τότ᾿ ἦσθ᾿ ὠργισμένος.

ΘΗ. δόξης γὰρ ἦμεν πρὸς θεῶν ἐσφαλμένοι.

ΙΠ. φεῦ·
 εἴθ᾿ ἦν ἀραῖον δαίμοσιν βροτῶν γένος.   1415

ΑΡ. ἔασον· οὐ γὰρ οὐδὲ γῆς ὑπὸ ζόφον
θεᾶς ἄτιμοι Κύπριδος ἐκ προθυμίας
ὀργαὶ κατασκήψουσιν εἰς τὸ σὸν δέμας
[σῆς εὐσεβείας κἀγαθῆς φρενὸς χάριν].
ἐγὼ γὰρ αὐτῆς ἄλλον ἐξ ἐμῆς χερὸς   1420
ὃς ἂν μάλιστα φίλτατος κυρῇ βροτῶν
τόξοις ἀφύκτοις τοῖσδε τιμωρήσομαι.
σοὶ δ', ὦ ταλαίπωρ', ἀντὶ τῶνδε τῶν κακῶν
τιμὰς μεγίστας ἐν πόλει Τροιζηνίᾳ
δώσω· κόραι γὰρ ἄζυγες γάμων πάρος   1425
κόμας κεροῦνταί σοι, δι' αἰῶνος μακροῦ
πένθη μέγιστα δακρύων καρπουμένῳ.
ἀεὶ δὲ μουσοποιὸς εἰς σὲ παρθένων
ἔσται μέριμνα, κοὐκ ἀνώνυμος πεσὼν
ἔρως ὁ Φαίδρας εἰς σὲ σιγηθήσεται.   1430
σὺ δ', ὦ γεραιοῦ τέκνον Αἰγέως, λαβὲ
σὸν παῖδ' ἐν ἀγκάλαισι καὶ προσέλκυσαι·
ἄκων γὰρ ὤλεσάς νιν· ἀνθρώποισι δὲ
θεῶν διδόντων εἰκὸς ἐξαμαρτάνειν.
καὶ σοὶ παραινῶ πατέρα μὴ στυγεῖν σέθεν,   1435
Ἱππόλυτ'· ἔχεις γὰρ μοῖραν ᾗ διεφθάρης.
καὶ χαῖρ'· ἐμοὶ γὰρ οὐ θέμις φθιτοὺς ὁρᾶν
οὐδ' ὄμμα χραίνειν θανασίμοισιν ἐκπνοαῖς·
ὁρῶ δέ σ' ἤδη τοῦδε πλησίον κακοῦ.

ΙΠ. χαίρουσα καὶ σὺ στεῖχε, παρθέν' ὀλβία·   1440
μακρὰν δὲ λείπεις ῥᾳδίως ὁμιλίαν.
λύω δὲ νεῖκος πατρὶ χρῃζούσης σέθεν·
καὶ γὰρ πάροιθε σοῖς ἐπειθόμην λόγοις.
αἰαῖ, κατ' ὄσσων κιγχάνει μ' ἤδη ·σκότος·
λαβοῦ, πάτερ, μου καὶ κατόρθωσον δέμας.   1445

ΘΗ. ὤμοι, τέκνον, τί δρᾷς με τὸν δυσδαίμονα;

ΙΠ. ὄλωλα καὶ δὴ νερτέρων ὁρῶ πύλας.
ΘΗ. ἦ τὴν ἐμὴν ἄναγνον ἐκλιπὼν φρένα;
ΙΠ. οὐ δῆτ', ἐπεί σε τοῦδ' ἐλευθερῶ φόνου.
ΘΗ. τί φής; ἀφήσεις αἵματός μ' ἐλεύθερον;   1450
ΙΠ. τὴν τοξόδαμνον Ἄρτεμιν μαρτύρομαι.
ΘΗ. ὦ φίλταθ', ὡς γενναῖος ἐκφαίνει πατρί.
ΙΠ. ὦ χαῖρε καὶ σύ, χαῖρε πολλά μοι, πάτερ.
ΘΗ. ὤμοι φρενὸς σῆς εὐσεβοῦς τε κἀγαθῆς.
ΙΠ. τοιῶνδε παίδων γνησίων εὔχου τυχεῖν.   1455
ΘΗ. μή νυν προδῷς με, τέκνον, ἀλλὰ καρτέρει.
ΙΠ. κεκαρτέρηται τἄμ'· ὄλωλα γάρ, πάτερ·
    κρύψον δέ μου πρόσωπον ὡς τάχος πέπλοις.
ΘΗ. ὦ κλείν' Ἀθηνῶν Παλλάδος θ' ὁρίσματα,
    οἵου στερήσεσθ' ἀνδρός. ὦ τλήμων ἐγώ·   1460
    ὡς πολλά, Κύπρι, σῶν κακῶν μεμνήσομαι.
ΧΟ. κοινὸν τόδ' ἄχος πᾶσι πολίταις
    ἦλθεν ἀέλπτως.
    πολλῶν δακρύων ἔσται πίτυλος·
    τῶν γὰρ μεγάλων ἀξιοπενθεῖς   1465
    φῆμαι μᾶλλον κατέχουσιν.

NOTES.

1. **πολλή...κοὐκ ἀνώνυμος.** Since ἀνώνυμος means 'inglorious' (cf. Ion 1372 ἀνώνυμος εἰ θεοῦ μελάθροις εἶχον οἰκέτην βίον: so too I. T. 502, Hel. 16), on the analogy of phrases like γνωτὰ κοὐκ ἄγνωτα etc. πολλὴ should mean 'powerful'. Schol. δυνατή. κέκλημαι, as Monk points out, has then merely the force of εἰμί. Cf. Hec. 484. If however Aphrodite is regarded as arguing her power from the number of names under which she is worshipped, then πολλὴ κοὐκ ἀνώνυμος must = πολυώνυμος κοὐκ ἀν., the force of -ωνυμος being thrown back on πολλὴ from ἀνώνυμος: κέκλημαι must then of course receive its natural meaning. Cf. Soph. Ant. 1115 and Jebb's note. Theocr. 15, 109 addresses Aphrodite as πολυώνυμε.

3. **ὅσοι τε.** Split up into τοὺς μὲν σέβοντας l. 5, and ὅσοι φρονοῦσιν l. 6. Herodotus in four places (II. 21, 23; IV. 8, 36) ridicules the theory of a river Oceanos, as described by older writers, encircling the earth: but the modified idea of a vast sea, stretching westward from the pillars of Heracles, in which the earth is as it were an island, frequently occurs in the 5th and 4th centuries. Eur. generally calls in its aid to express vaguely a limit of the world, e.g. infr. 746, 1053 (where the suggestion, that πόντος in all these passages is the Euxine, is, as Wecklein remarks, rendered improbable, as it is unlikely that Theseus would be fixing a definite limit both east and west, beyond which his son should be banished). Cf. too Or. 1377; Arist. (?) de mundo 3, where the earth is called νῆσος ὑπὸ τῆς Ἀτλαντικῆς καλουμένης θαλάσσης περιρρεομένη.

5. **πρεσβεύω** = προτιμῶ. Cf. Soph. Tr. 1067. The transition from the original meaning is well marked in Aesch. Eum. 1 where the priestess says: 'I assign the first place to her whose age demands it, Earth': πρῶτον μὲν...πρεσβεύω θεῶν τὴν πρωτόμαντιν Γαῖαν.

7. In Suppl. 232 it was the 'young men' with whom Adrastus

'consulted' who were said τιμώμενοι χαίρειν. Here and Bacch. 319, Alc. 54 the same quality is attributed to the gods.

10. Cf. I. T. 238 'Αγαμέμνονος παῖ καὶ Κλυταιμνήστρας τέκνον. Eur. follows the tradition, which made Hippolyte the Amazon wife of Theseus. Pausanias (I. 41) adheres to the more usual story that Antiope was carried off by Theseus, and that her sister Hippolyte, failing in an attempt to rescue her, retired to Megara, where she died and was buried.

11. **παιδεύματα,** 'pupil'. For the plural of an abstract noun similarly used of the result of repeated actions cf. Soph. Phil. 36 τεχνήματα (of a goblet). Cf. also Soph. Ant. 568 νυμφεῖα, of Antigone. Eur. Hec. 265 προσφάγματα, of Helen. Pittheus was king of Troezen, and father of Aethra the mother of Theseus. When the latter on the death of Hippolyte married Phaedra, Hippolytus was taken to Troezen, and educated by his grandfather, who was renowned for his uprightness and learning. Pausanias says that his judgment-seat was still to be seen in Troezen, and that he was *said* (δή) to have written a book on the art of speaking. Phaedra too had the advantage of a lawgiver's influence on her early years in Crete. Notice the emphatic proximity of ἁγνοῦ to 'Ιππόλυτος.

13. **πεφυκέναι,** more than εἶναι: to be necessarily, by very nature.

14. **ἀναίνεται,** 'spurns': a rare word except in Homer: Sophocles never uses it: here its meaning is as in Il. ix. 510 (of men refusing submission to deities) ὃς δέ κ' ἀνήνηται καί τε στερεῶς ἀποείπῃ. Sometimes, like Lat. *aspernari*, it means to refuse, without connoting scorn, Od. iv. 651. With the participle, as I. A. 1502 θανοῦσα δ' οὐκ ἀναίνομαι, Bacch. 251, it resembles Lat. *recuso*, 'do under protest'.

ψαύει γάμων. Cf. Pind. Ol. 6. 58 'Αφροδίτης ἔψαυσεν.

16. Notice the precise correspondence of rhythm with l. 13, which brings into contrast μεγίστην and κακίστην.

17. **χλωράν,** 'fresh green': heightens the effect of παρθένῳ: everything is unsullied and bright, even the scene of the hunt: cf. 73 ἀκηράτου: on the meaning of χλωρὸς cf. Verrall on Med. 906.

18. **ἐξαιρεῖ,** of ridding a land of wild beasts. Cf. H. F. 154 of the Nemean lion. So Xen. Hell. ii. 2. 19 μὴ σπένδεσθαι τοῖς 'Αθηναίοις, ἀλλ' ἐξαιρεῖν. Paus. says that Hippolytus dedicated a temple to "Αρτεμις Λυκεία, presumably to commemorate τὴν Τροιζ. λυμαινομένους λύκους ἐξελεῖν.

19. **μείζω,** sc. ὁμιλίαν. Schol. explains προσπεσὼν by ἐντυχών.

προσπίπτειν seems never elsewhere to be used with the accus., except in the sense 'to supplicate', where the meaning accounts for the construction.

20. **τούτοισι.** Hipp. and Artemis. 'It is not envy', says Aphrodite, 'which I feel. Why indeed should I? But the sins of Hipp. against me I will punish'.

23. **δεῖ με πόνου**, for the more usual δεῖ μοι: cf. infr. 490, 686, Cycl. 330, Aesch. Cho. 518. προκόψασ' 'having prepared the way': properly of pioneers preparing the way for an army. Cf. Alc. 1079. For προκόψασα we should expect προκόψασαν: the so called *nominativus pendens* is to be explained by the fact that οὐ πόνου πολλοῦ με δεῖ = ῥᾳδίως ἐκτελῶ.

25. The principal mysteries at Athens were those connected with the worship of Dionysus—the Anthesteria, and of Demeter— the Thesmophoria and Eleusinia, in February, October, and September respectively. The two former were celebrated by women only, so that Eur. here refers to the Eleusinia. At the time of their celebration we know Athens was crowded with visitors. Hipp. would present himself for final admission (as ἐπόπτης, cf. σεμνῶν ἐς ὄψιν) to full privileges five years after his initiation as a μύστης. Cf. Soph. fr. 719 ὡς τρισόλβιοι | κεῖνοι βροτῶν, οἳ ταῦτα δερχθέντες τέλη | μόλωσ' ἐς Ἅιδου. Plat. Phaedr. 250 B. For the intimate connection of Orphism with the Eleusinian mysteries cf. Girard, Sentiment Religieux, p. 113, 114; Rhes. 944. The selection of Pandion's name may be due to the belief that in his reign Dionysus and Demeter came to Athens.

27. **κατείχετο.** Monk's correction for MSS κατέσχετο. Cf. Elmsley on Her. 634. Thompson on Plat. Phaedr. 238 D defends the 2nd aor. mid. used as passive.

29—33. These lines have been condemned by many editors either wholly or in part, and it is hard to believe them genuine. I have bracketed 32, 33 following Blomfield. Whether we take the reading of most MSS ἔκδηλον, or that of Pal. and Flor. ἔκδημον, these lines are entirely inconsistent with the character of Phaedra assumed in this play: it is but necessary to read 390 sq. to see that Eur. could not have written 32, 33. ὠνόμαζεν too can hardly be tortured into meaning. Lines 29—31 are weak certainly, but not sufficiently so as to justify expulsion. The awkwardness of the goddess' reference to herself in the third person (Κύπριδος 31) may be explained partly by a desire to balance Παλλάδος in the corresponding position in the previous line : partly because it would be natural to refer to the temple under the name by which it was commonly known. (These considerations however do not excuse θεὰν in 33, to which a similar objection attaches.) I believe 32, 33 to have been originally an explanation of κατόψιον γῆς τῆσδε, and that ἔκδημον is the right reading ; the word may have been suggested by 37. The addition was intended to show why the temple was built overlooking Troezen, viz. because Phaedra's absent love (ἔρως ἔκδημος) was dwelling there. This point being overlooked ἔκδηλον was written by a stupid corrector, in the sense of *scilicet*—like the scholiastic δῆλον, δηλονότι. 'Phaedra built a temple to Cypris, because of her love, of course'. If this view be adopted there will be no need for the arbitrary alteration of ὠνόμαζεν to ὀνομάσουσιν, and we may imagine the meaning of the aforesaid corrector to have been : 'but posterity declared by the name it gave—Hippolyteum—that it was to gain Hippolytus that the goddess was settled in a home'. [The temple of Aphrodite (if that, and not the so-called tomb of Hippolytus, is what Eur. refers to, cf. n. on 30) was really built by Theseus, though Eur. for his own purposes here ascribes it to Phaedra ; it once occurred to me that πάνδημος (under which title Aphrodite was there worshipped) might have suggested here ἔνδημον, when the meaning would be that Phaedra, a Cretan, on coming to Athens, dedicated a temple to the Aphrodite of her adopted home, in seeming honour of her husband, though it was in truth to gain Hippolytus.]

30. **πέτραν.** The Acropolis rose 500 feet from the plain, steep on all sides except the West, where on the slope were the temple of Aphrodite Pandemos, dedicated by Theseus on his consolidation of Attica, and a tomb of Hippolytus. There was also a tomb of Hipp. at Troezen, where a different legend of his death and burial prevailed.

κατόψιον. The statue of Athene Promachos on the Acropolis, 70 feet in height, could, Paus. tells us (1. 28), be seen from ships rounding Sunium. It is not however necessary to press κατόψιον to imply actual sight in this passage. The word only occurs here and in Ap. Rh., though Aesch. uses κάτοπτος.

33. **ἱδρῦσθαι θεάν.** Cf. Ar. Pl. 1153 ἱδρῦσαι Ἑρμῆν.

35. Theseus came to Troezen to be purified of the murder of Pallas, son of Pandion, bringing Phaedra with him. Orestes too was purified at Troezen. Paus. ii. 31.

37. **αἰνέσας φυγήν,** 'having acquiesced in exile for a year' (ἀπενιαυτισμός). Cf. Alc. 2 ἔτλην θῆσσαν τράπεζαν αἰνέσαι.

38. **ἐκπεπλ.** A very strong word. Note the fine effect of the emphatic position of σιγῇ followed by an abrupt pause. 'Maddened by passion's goad, poor wretch, she wastes, nor yet a word'.

40. **νόσον,** 'weakness' of any sort: used especially of love. Cf. Med. 1364, Andr. 220, infr. 393, 477, 766.

41. 'But not on this wise' etc. Cf. Med. 365 ἀλλ᾽ οὔτι ταῦτα ταύτῃ, μὴ δοκεῖτέ πω.

ταύτῃ refers to what precedes, that Phaedra should die silent.

δεῖ, it is to my interest)(χρὴ of moral necessity and ἀνάγκη of fate.

43. **πολέμιον.** 'The youth who has taken up arms against me' : a declared and public foe)(ἐχθρός a private enemy.

46. 'That thrice fulfilment should attend his prayer'. Schol. μίαν μὲν ᾐτήσατο τὸ ἀνελθεῖν ἐξ ᾅδου, δευτέραν ἐκ λαβυρίνθου, καὶ τρίτην τοῦ Ἱππολύτου.

47. **ἀλλ᾽ ὅμως.** Cf. Hec. 843 παράσχες χεῖρα τῇ πρεσβύτιδι | τιμωρόν, εἰ καὶ μηδέν ἐστιν, ἀλλ᾽ ὅμως. Bacch. 1023 and Sandys' n. Aristophanes ridicules Eur.'s fondness for ἀλλ᾽ ὅμως at the end of a line (cf. inf. 358) Ach. 402 ΔΙ. ἐκκάλεσον αὐτόν. ΘΕ. ἀλλ᾽ ἀδύνατον. ΔΙ. ἀλλ᾽ ὅμως.

ἡ δ᾽...Φαίδρα, 'but she, Phaedra I mean'. This resembles the Homeric use of the article ; the noun is in apposition. Cf. Monro Hom. Gr. § 258, Goodwin § 140 n. 2 a.

ἀπόλλυται prophetic present. Cf. Pind. P. 4. 49.

48. On the syntax οὐ προτιμήσω...τὸ μὴ οὐ παρασχεῖν cf. Goodwin § 263, 2 and n. Phoen. 1175 εἰργαθεῖν...τὸ μὴ οὐχ ἑλεῖν. For προτιμᾶν cf. Aesch. Eum. 640.

50. **ὥστ᾽ ἐμοὶ καλῶς ἔχειν.** Cf. Hec. 854 βούλομαι...τήνδε σοι δοῦναι δίκην, | εἴ πως φανείη γ᾽ ὥστε σοί τ᾽ ἔχειν καλῶς κ.τ.λ.

55. **λέλακεν** of confused or rapid speech : entirely poet. word, and in this sense mainly trag. In Homer more generally of animals and things. ὀπισθόπους here and 1179 of his friends escorting him into exile. κῶμος 'joyful band' contrasts with πύλας Ἅιδου. ἀνεῳγμένας 'are standing wide' (perf.); on the partic. cf. Goodwin § 280.

57. **τόδε φάος,** 'today's sun'.

58. Hippolytus here enters from the chase with a band of huntsmen, who sing the lines 61—72, thus forming a secondary chorus. This is the only instance of such a secondary chorus in Eur.

60. **μελόμεσθα.** The use of the middle is poetic.

64. **μοι**, 'I bid you'. Below 66 πολλῷ would be more usual. Goodwin 188, 2.

67—69. Pal. has αἴ...ναίετ': also εὐπατέρεια (a Homeric word used only of women) properly applies to Artemis and not to αὐλή. The latter difficulty led Gaisford to conjecture εὐπατέρει' ἀν' αὐλάν, which makes a clumsy sentence, where either αὐλάν or οἶκον is otiose. The intrepid Nauck expels 67, and reads ναίεις, εὐπατέρει', ἀν' οἶκον Ζανὸς πολύχρυσον. But neither of these treatments takes notice of the reading of Pal. (from which, though a later MS, truer readings can often be deduced than those found in the older extant MSS). Cobet starting with αἴ, and regarding ναίετ' as due to its influence, reads αἰγλάεντα κατ' οὐρανὸν ναίουσ' εὐπατέρειαν αὐλὰν Ζανὸς πολύχρυσον, thus remedying metre and sense. That εὐπ. αὐλὴ can = 'hall of a noble sire' is proved by e.g. I. T. 1083 ἔσωσας ἐκ πατροκτόνου χέρος, 'from a murderous father's hand'.

71. The broad summit (μακρὸς) of Olympus, towering through the clouds 10,000 feet into the bright ether, is in the Iliad the site of Zeus' Hephaestus-built house, while on the precipitous spurs (πολυδειράς, Il. 1. 499) just beneath were the houses of the other gods. Olympus and οὐρανός, frequently used together, should be distinguished. The latter is the brazen (πολύχαλκος) star-set (Il. xviii. 485) vault, ever revolving, supported by Atlas (Od. 1. 54): the term is then extended to embrace the region above it, home of the gods and realm of Zeus (Il. xv. 192). Through the cloud-door kept by the ὧραι (Il. v. 750) lay the way to earth. Compare the myth of the procession of the gods in Plato's Phaedrus. It is doubtful whether Homer imagined that Olympus actually pierced the vault of Heaven.

73. From this strikingly beautiful opening scene is derived the title of the play—Ἱππόλυτος στεφανηφόρος.

74. **κοσμήσας**, in older sense = 'prepare', e.g. Hom. Od. vii. 13 κ. δόρπον.

77. **ἠρινόν.** The more strictly Attic form is found in Pal. and Flor. (which were taken from a corrected archetype). Valck. proposed ἐαρινή. It is perhaps worthy of notice that the priestesses of Artemis were called μέλισσαι. Cf. Schol. on Pind. Pyth. 4. 60. With 76 cf. Soph. Tr. 200 ὦ Ζεῦ τὸν Οἴτης ἄτομον ὃς λειμῶν' ἔχεις. 'Where neither shepherd deems to graze his flocks, nor yet has come the scythe, but the bee takes her way there-through, a virgin spring-clad lawn'.

78. The conceit of analogy between the virgin goddess and the untrodden meadow tempts Eur. into the bold figure of Αἰδὼς tending and keeping ever fresh its bright beauty, as a maiden's purity is ever reflected on her face. 'And Aidôs the gardener doth tend it with water from the rill, that it may furnish garlands for all those, in whom is no taught goodness, but at their birth a wise Sobriety in everything alike took them for her own'. I have retained the reading of the MSS throughout this disputed passage, and believe my version to be defensible. Porson proposed ὅστις for ὅσοις on the ground that εἴληχεν in the intransitive sense of 'it has fallen to the lot of' is very rare, and has been followed by all editors, who do not either excise the passage or on the analogy of Bacch. 316 read ὅσοις...ἔνεστι. The sense I have given to εἴληχεν is supported by Hom. Il. xxiii. 79 ἐμὲ μὲν κὴρ λάχε γεινόμενον: Theocr. 4. 40 τῷ σκληρῷ μάλα δαίμονος ὅς με λελόγχῃ: Poet. ap. Alciphr. 3. 49 ὦ δαῖμον ὅς με εἴληχας, while in the poet's allegorizing vein (which may, as Wecklein points out, be due to Orphic influence) it would not be unnatural tὸ personify τὸ σωφρονεῖν, taking it as the subject, instead of the object of the verb. For φύσις=birth, cf. Soph. Ant. 659, El. 325, 1125 etc. For δρέπεσθαι cf. Ar. Ran. 1300 δρέπειν λείμωνα. For the superiority of natural over acquired excellence cf. Pind. Ol. 2. 86 σοφὸς ὁ πολλὰ εἰδὼς φυᾷ· μαθόντες δὲ λάβροι κ.τ.λ. This is in direct opposition to Socrates' teaching that ἀρετή is διδακτή. τούτοις is antecedent to ὅσοις: coming so late in the sentence it acquires emphasis, 'by them and by no others'.

82. **χρυσέας**, used in the general sense of 'glorious', common in Pindar (cf. Gildersleeve's Index s.v.): or Eur. may be thinking of his friend Phidias' recent chryselephantine work, in which the hair would be of gold. Hipp. of course places his wreath upon a statue of Artemis before the palace. There was also a statue of Aphrodite, infr. 101, 116.

86. Cf. Soph. Aj. 15 ὦ φθέγμ' Ἀθάνας...ὡς εὐμαθές σου κἂν ἄποπτος ᾖς, ὅμως | φώνημ' ἀκούω. Prof. Jebb holds the view that when introduced as taking part in the action of a drama, a god or goddess was visibly represented on the stage, as inf. 1283 sq.

87. **κάμψαιμ'**. Cf. Eur. El. 956 πέρας κάμψῃ βίου: of turning the καμπτήρ in the δίαυλος, which was the goal in the short race, which was run down a single arm only of the course: 'may I round the goal of life, even as I began'.

88. **δεσπότας.** This strikes the key-note of the play: a man

may be ἄναξ: he may not be δεσπότης, but must yield to the gods. Hipp. supr. 74 had called Artemis δέσποινα.

89. ἆρα (like ἦ) merely expresses interrogation. ἆρ' οὐ = *nonne*, ἆρα μή = *num*.

δέξαιό μου. Cf. fr. 757 ἃ γοῦν παραινῶ, ταῦτά μου δέξαι, γύναι.

92. τοῦ δὲ καί, 'and furthermore'. Cf. Hec. 519 πῶς καὶ νιν ἐξεπράξατ'; Porson on Phoen. 1373 gives examples of καί '*inter-rogativis postpositum*'.

93. σεμνόν, 'exclusiveness', based on not being as other men are. Cf. Med. 216 (where possibly we might read τοὺς μὲν ὀμμάτων ὕπο—some under our eyes, here in Corinth)(τοὺς δ' ἐν θυραίοις, some abroad, Medea's experience being large). It is easy to imagine that contemporary political experience suggested or added point to this and the following lines. Pericles had been σεμνότης itself, and had suffered for it: popular feeling had run high against him in 430, one year before his death, and two before the production of this play: while Cleon the εὐπροσήγορος (*affabilis* as Valck. renders it) was gaining both χάρις and κέρδος σὺν μόχθῳ βραχεῖ.

96. καὶ κέρδος γε, 'aye, and profit too'.

97. ἐλπίζεις, 'expect', 'think', Aesch. Cho. 187 πῶς γὰρ ἐλπίσω | ἀστῶν τιν' ἄλλον τῆσδε δεσπόζειν κόμης;

98. εἴπερ, 'if as I think,' *siquidem*. Homer ascribes the θέμιστες to the gods; these were individual decisions prompted by heaven: on these precedents νόμος was formed.

99. σεμνήν. 'Think you'—the attendant had asked—'that the gods too regard τὸ σεμνὸν with disfavour?' 'Certainly' Hipp. had replied. It seems curious logic to conclude, 'why then do you not render observance to a goddess, who is σεμνή?' After emphasizing σεμνὸς in the bad sense from 90—98, without warning the poet emphasizes it in the good sense from 99—103. This has led Wecklein to adopt Tournier's σεπτὴν in this line and σεπτή in 103, a conjecture which is refuted by 100, where Hipp. warns the attendant that his 'lips should not offend' by mentioning by name the Ἐρινύες—αἱ σεμναὶ θεαί (cf. Or. 37 and 409 οἶδ' ἃς ἔλεξας, ὀνομάσαι δ' οὐ βούλομαι. | σεμναὶ γάρ). Two alternatives remain, either that Eur. wrote carelessly, or that he wished to imply that though τὸ σεμνὸν was objectionable in a mortal, it was a laudable attribute of deity: the former is unsatisfactory, though many some-what similar cases will be noticed in this play: the latter perhaps far-fetched. We are of course at liberty to summon the *deus ex* *machina* of critics and assert that explanatory lines have fallen out. See on 138.

102. **ἀγνὸς ὤν**, 'for I am pure'. πρόσωθεν ἀσπάζομαι, cf. Plat. Rep. vi. 499 A where it = to be civil at a distance, i.e. decline to have anything to do with.

104. I have followed Gomperz in transposing 104, 5 to follow 106, 7.

106. **με**, by the so-called Attic construction with ἀρέσκω, for μοι. Soph. Aj. 584, infr. 184, Or. 210.

θαυμαστὸς νυκτί, 'whose worship is by night'. For θαιμάζω =*colere* cf. Eur. El. 84 and 519 μολὼν δ' ἐθαύμασ' ἄθλιον τύμβον πατρός.

107. **χρῆσθαι**, 'recognise', by conforming to.

105. **ἔχων** = καὶ ἔχοις—the optative meaning being continued in the participle.

110. **καταψήχειν**, 'rub down'. Cf. Ar. fr. 134 ψήχει ἠρέμα τὸν βουκέφαλον.

112. **βορᾶς κορεσθείς**: a rather coarse expression for an Orphic.

113. **τὴν σήν**, contemptuous, cf. *iste*. Eur. Heracl. 284 τὸ σὸν γὰρ "Αργος οὐ δέδοικ' ἐγώ. χαίρειν λέγω, cf. Med. 1044 χαιρέτω βουλεύματα: infr. 1059: often in Plato, e.g. Phileb. 59 B. Cf. too fr. 342, 6, 7.

115. The inappositeness of λέγειν to φρονοῦντες has led to suggestions of φρονοῦντες...φρονεῖν and λέγοντες...λέγειν, and many more, culminating in φρονοῦντες οὕτως ὡς πρέπει δούλοις λεχέων of Bothe, who wisely explains the two last words by '*mariti, nihil amplius*'. If alteration be needed I would propose λέγοντες οὕτως ὡς πρέπει, δούλους (or δούλοις, cf. 940) τε δεῖ. δούλοις is antithetic to δέσποινα, 117.

117. Monk points out that συγγνώμην ἔχειν means either *veniam dare*, as here, Soph. El. 400 and commonly, or *veniam mereri*, Eur. Phoen. 995, Thuc. iii. 44, 1.

118. **εὔτονον**, the reading of A and other MSS, would, as Blomfield pointed out, mean *robustus*: **ἔντονον**, = *violens*, has been generally received.

σε...μάταια βάζει, for the double accus. cf. Hom. Il. xvi. 207 ταῦτά μ' ἀγειρόμενοι θάμ' ἐβάζετε. μάταια, 'random'. μὴ δόκει κλύειν 'make as though thou heardest not', cf. Med. 67 οὐ δοκῶν κλύειν: infr. 463: Hec. 874 εἶργε μὴ δοκῶν ἐμὴν χάριν, 'pretending not to be doing so for my sake', Thuc. iii. 47, 3 μὴ προσποιεῖσθαι. Latin *dissimulare.*

121—170. The parodos or entrance of the chorus, who speculate on the possible causes of Phaedra's illness, of which they have just heard.

121. The order is: πέτρα τις λέγεται στ. ὠκ. ὕδωρ, προϊεῖσα κρ. ῥυτὰν παγὰν κάλπισι βαπτάν. For πέτρα λέγεται στάζουσα, cf. Or. 331 ἵνα μεσόμφαλοι λέγονται μυχοί, Soph. O. T. 1451 ἔνθα κλῄζεται οὑμὸς Κιθαιρών. παγὰν ῥυτὰν κ. β. 'a welling spring, (full enough) to be drawn in pitchers'. These lines and infr. 653 seem to be parodied in Ar. Ran. 1339, 40 κάλπισί τ' ἐκ ποταμῶν δρόσον ἄρατε, θέρμετε δ' ὕδωρ, ὡς ἂν θεῖον ὄνειρον ἀποκλύσω. ὠκεανός was regarded as the source of all waters, cf. Hom. Il. xxi. 196 ἐξ οὗ περ πάντες ποταμοὶ καὶ πᾶσα θάλασσα | καὶ πᾶσαι κρῆναι καὶ φρείατα μακρὰ νάουσιν. βάπτω is 1. 'to dip', 'to dye', 2. 'to draw by means of dipping'. Hec. 610 λαβοῦσα τεῦχος βάψασ' ἔνεγκε δεῦρο ποντίας ἁλός, Theocr. 5. 127 ἀνθ' ὕδατος τῇ κάλπιδι κηρία βάψαι.

126. **φάρεα**, φᾶρ- in Homer: φὶρ- or φᾶρ- in trag.: πορφ. φ. Hom. Il. viii. 221. For the jingle, intentional or not, cf. Hec. 538—540: πρευμενὴς, πρύμνας, πρευμενοῦς.

129. **καταβάλλω** = *depono*, 'lay down': a rare meaning, cf. Il. ix. 206 κρεῖον κάββαλεν ἐν πυρὸς αὐγῇ, Ar. Ach. 165.

130. **φάτις δεσποίνας.** Wecklein compares φάτις ἀνδρῶν μνηστήρων, Hom. Od. xxiii. 362.

131. **τειρομ. νοσερᾷ κοίτᾳ**, 'wasting on a bed of sickness': κοίτη is rare in this sense. Eur. still had it in his mind infr. 180, an instance of the common tendency to repeat a rare word or phrase, which has taken a writer's fancy, cf. Hec. 85, 98 ἀλίαστος, ἐλιάσθην. Some MSS omit κοίτᾳ, others (inferior) have it after ἔχειν. This confusion has led to conjectures and transpositions, which seem needless. Weckl. reads τειρ. νοσερᾶς αὐτὰν δέμας ἐντὸς ἔχειν κοίτας, urging that it would be nothing noteworthy that Phaedra should keep to the house (ἐντὸς οἴκων), and that the sense required is that she kept in bed, which sense he produces. It is however at least doubtful whether κοίτη can be given so concrete a meaning, as to allow of the expression ἐντὸς κοίτας. (κοίτη means a 'lying down', or a 'way of lying down', cf. Verrall on Med. 434.) Compare besides infr. 179 ἔξω δὲ δόμων ἤδη κ.τ.λ., where the emphatic ἤδη seems to show that Phaedra has been indoors some time. It is a fairly pertinent remark that an invalid has been

confined to the house. I give the reading of B, C, Pal. and Flor. δέμας, 'living body')(σῶμα, 'corpse'. This rule holds in Homer, but is violated by Soph. e.g. Ant. 205 (see Jebb), Eur. e.g. Hec. 735, where it is exceptionally harsh, as in 723 he had used δέμας Ἀγαμέμνονος = Ἀγαμέμνων, cf. infr. 135.

135—8. The MSS give τριτάταν δέ νιν κλύω | τάνδε κατ' ἀμβρο- σίου | στόματος ἀμέραν | Δάματρος ἀκτᾶς δέμας ἁγνὸν ἴσχειν, which will be found in the text. Whether we translate, 'and this is the third day I hear that she keeps her body free from bread in (lit. down upon) her mouth', or 'keeps from her lips the pure form of bread', κατ' ἀμβροσίου στόματος is well-nigh impossible. Neither can we take κατ'...ἴσχειν by tmesis, as there is no instance of the use of κατέχειν with accus. and gen. with the meaning 'to keep from': κατέχειν is to check something already in motion. For τάνδε κατ' ἀμβ. I had conjectured τάνδ' ἑκὰς ἀμβρ. before finding that Reiske had made a similar suggestion. The poet's allegorizing vein (so noticeable in this play) seems to have led him to personify bread as a living element, a personification perhaps suggested by the mention of Δαμάτηρ and to which the attribute ἁγνὸν is suitable (though it is probably also antithetic to Phaedra's 'guilty' passion). Thus we have the picture of the sinful Phaedra, holding as it were at arm's length the pure element, which took its name from the dread mother who was a special object of reverence to the Orphic and other cults, whose aim was purity of life. With this view ἑκὰς agrees well. In Soph. fr. 239 the mystic vine is regarded as endowed with life; and δέμας is the word selected in its descrip- tion (οἰνάνθης δέμας). On ἀκτή, cf. Hes. Sc. 290, Eur. fr. 884. Dr Verrall (Med. 982) objects to ἀμβροσίου, denying its use as a mere epithet of beauty. It should however be borne in mind that Eust. (on Il. iv. p. 333, 13) actually ascribes this use of ἀμβρόσιος to Euripides: and 'lips divinely fair' harmonises with the picture of wasting loveliness, better than ἀβρώτου, which Dr Verrall proposes, and which is somewhat tautological. If ἀμβρο- σίου is to be rejected ἀβροτάτου would correspond metrically, and still preserve the contrast. Wecklein reads τρ. δέ νιν κλύω | τάνδ' ἀβρωσίᾳ | στόματος ἀμέραν | Δάμ. ἀκτᾶς δέμας ἁγνὸν ἴσχειν, reading in 126 πορφύρεα (trisyll.) φάρη, and translates 'keeps her body free from bread'. This puts a false shade of meaning on ἁγνὸν, which would imply that food was a pollution, and is unsuited to the passage.

138. The awkward repetition of so strange a phrase as δέμας ἔχειν (132, 138) in different senses may defend the similarly care-less use of σεμνὸς (93, 99): cf. φοιτᾷς, φοιτᾷ (144, 148), προνώπιος, Bacch. 639, 644.

140. 'Wishing to put into the last haven, the sad haven of death'. For κέλσαι cf. Aesch. Prom. 183, Eur. Hec. 1057 ὤμοι ἐγώ...πᾷ κέλσω; θανάτου poet. genit. of designation, cf. Hom. Il. iii. 309 θανάτοιο τέλος.

141 sq. The editors seem to have overlooked the contrast be-tween φοιτᾷς (144) and τρύχει (147), 'roaming madly afield' and 'pining at home'. All the chorus know thus far is that Phaedra has shut herself up in the house and refused all food. This, and the fact that the metre requires that the first syllable of 141 should be long, lead to the conjecture οὐ γὰρ ἔνθεος ὦ κούρα. Further, the first syl-lable of 145 should also be long. Now several MSS in the previous line for φοιτᾷς have φοιταλέου (in some both are found). May not the last two syllables of φοιταλέου represent the first two of the next line, viz. ἦ οὐ (as one syll.) =*nonne?* The history of the lines will be that first φοιτᾷς became displaced, and then confused with the first syllables of the next line. (I have *metr. gr.* adopted Bothe's transposition φοιτᾷς ἦ ματρὸς ὀρείας.) Thus we get the natural sense, 'Thou art not suffering from a mere frenzy fit: art thou not rather wasting by reason of some neglect of the rites of the goddess of thy native island? For (γάρ 148) Dictynna's power defies the limit of the seas, and can follow thee even here to Troezen'. Weckl. reads οὐ in 141 and οὐδ' in 145. This latter change seems to weaken the general sense, and to destroy the special force of γὰρ in 148. Other possibilities present themselves to the chorus and are in turn discussed.

142. For the belief that fits of madness—'panic fears'—were caused by divine agency cf. Med. 1172, Rhes. 36. The Corybantes were the priests of the Phrygian Rhea or Cybele: the latter was also identified with the Thracian Hecate, whose priests or attendants were the Cabiri: Bendis probably was the original Thracian name. What Eur. thought or whether he had any definite idea on the per-plexed relations of Demeter, Artemis, Hecate, Rhea etc. cannot be guessed: the point of interest for him was that all were worshipped with wild mysterious rites. Pan is addressed as the companion of the 'mighty mother' by Pindar fr. 63. For μητρὶ οὐρείᾳ of Cybele, cf. Eur. fr. 475. 10—20. The generation to which Eurip. belonged

had seen the introduction and spread of several eastern cults, mostly orgiastic. From Suidas, s.v. μητραγύρτης, we learn that a few years before the production of this play, a man who had come to Athens, and initiated women into the mysteries of the mother of the gods, had been put to death by the Athenians; but a plague ensuing, they had propitiated the great mother by building a shrine in her honour.

147. **ἀνίεροs ἀθύτων πελάνων**, 'unhallowed by reason of sacrificial offerings unmade'. Since leaving Crete Phaedra might have ceased to pay due respect to the Cretan goddess. The πέλανος of meal, oil and honey was generally burnt on the altar; cf. Ion 226 εἰ μὲν ἐθύσατε πέλανον κ.τ.λ., Aesch. Pers. 204. For the genit. cf. Soph. O. T. 191 ἄχαλκος ἀσπίδων, Eur. Phoen. 324 ἄπεπλος φαρέων, Goodw. Gr. Gr. 180, 1 n.

148. **φοιτᾷ**, sc. the goddess Dictynna. For φοιτᾷν (of a divinity) cf. Soph. Ant. 785 ἔρως, φοιτᾷς ὑπερπόντιος: infr. 169, 447. Also cf. n. on 138 supr.

λίμναs, 'the sea'. Homeric. Cf. Od. iii. 1 ἠέλιος δ' ἀνόρουσε λιπὼν περικαλλέα λίμνην. Eur. Hec. 446, Soph. fr. 341: 423, 2. The choice of the word here may be due to the popularity (especially in the Peloponnese) of the worship of Ἄρτεμις Λιμνᾶτις. 'For she roameth through the waters, and to the land beyond the sea, in the salt waves' plashing eddies'. χέρσον, 'the mainland' of Peloponnese: for the accus. without prep. cf. supr. 26, 29, infr. 157, Soph. O. C. 378.

152. **εὐπατρίδαν**, cf. infr. 1283 σὲ τὸν εὐπατρίδαν κέλομαι ἐπακοῦσαι, also of Theseus. The epithet is applied to him as a typical representative of the old Athenian nobility.

153. **ποιμαίνει**, 'beguiles'. Theocr. 11. 80 ἐποίμαινεν τὸν ἔρωτα: so βουκολεῖν Aesch. Ag. 669. Lucian speaks of sham philosophers, who τοὺς ἀμαθεῖς ποιμαίνουσι. Another reading is πημαίνει.

154. **λεχέων σῶν**, 'thee his wedded wife'. The genit. is governed by κρυπτά, as in Aesch. Supp. 301 κοὐ κρυπτά γ' Ἥρας ταῦτα τἀμπαλάγματα. Weckl. reads σοῦ taking κοῖτα λεχέων together, as in Alc. 926 λέκτρων κοῖτας. Cf. H. F. 798.

157. **λιμένα**. The bay of Pogon, where the Greek ships were ordered to assemble before the battle of Salamis. Her. viii. 42.

158. **πέμπων**. Schol. κομίζων: a straining of the use of πέμπω = 'escort'.

160. **εὐναία**, with δέδεται: 'she is confined to her bed', cf. Soph.

O. T. 1340 ἀπάγετ' ἐκτόπιον, and the passages quoted by Prof. Jebb in n. on 478, Appendix p. 226.

161. **δέ**, 'but after all it may be mere hysterical weakness. We too have suffered so'.

162. **ἁρμονίᾳ**, 'composition', a physiological word, used by Hippocrates. δυστρόπῳ κακᾷ, 'weak and wayward'.

163. **ἀμηχανία ὠδίνων τε καὶ ἀφροσύνας**, a feeling of helplessness against birth-pains and unhealthy cravings. ὠδ. ἀφρ. objective genitives, cf. Hadley Gr. Gr. 729 c, rem.

165. **αὔρα**, in figurative sense, connotes a veering or changing, cf. Eur. El. 1148 μετάτροποι αὖραι, Ar. Pax 945 μετάτροπος αὖρα: so here = 'capricious yearnings'.

166. **εὔλοχον...ἀύτευν**, a hexameter verse, perhaps from some old hymn to Artemis. ἀύτευν, Ion. form of the 1st sing. imperf. indic. of the Homeric verb ἀυτέω, cf. Med. 423 ὑμνεῦσαι, Aesch. Prom. 645. Artemis, as she could assist women in labour (εὔλοχον), cf. Hor. Od. iii. 22. 1, might too slay them with her ἀγανὰ βέλη (τόξων μεδέουσαν): a god could work not only blessing, but also the corresponding curse. Apollo the purifier also sent plagues upon the disobedient.

169. **σὺν θεοῖς ἐφοίτα**: so I have read for MSS σὺν θεοῖσι φοιτᾷ. 'And ever, by heaven's grace, greatly yearned for, did she come to me'. The usual reading φοιτᾷ is interpreted: 'and ever extolled by me she roams among the gods': implying that Artemis *had* answered her prayer, and that *therefore* 'ever extolled etc.,' the effect for the reason. This surely is unsuited to the meaning of πολυζήλωτος. σὺν θεοῖς too for μετὰ θεῶν is very doubtful Greek. (Brunck I find made the same conjecture.)

170—524. The first episode.

170. **γεραιά**. So Hec. 64, cf. δειλαίας, Phoen. 1287. All such cases arise from the slight change of ἰ to y before a vowel in pronunciation. The occurrence in inscriptions of Ἀθηνάα ἐλάα ποεῖν etc. point to such a pronunciation as common.

172. 'the anxious cloud upon her brow deepens', cf. Med. 107 νέφος οἰμωγῆς, H. F. 1140 νέφος στεναγμῶν, Soph. Ant. 528.

174. **δηλέομαι**, Ionic and Hom. deponent: it is passive however in Her. iv. 198.

175. **ἀλλόχροον**, proleptic. 'What hath marred and changed our lady's form?'

176. Phaedra appears supported by the nurse and her atten-

dants. Her mind wanders deliriously, as her thoughts travel to the various haunts of Hippolytus, till at 239 infr. she 'wakes to weep'.

178. Phaedra had been begging to be brought into the sunlight, infr. 181. ' Here see thou hast the sunlight and clear sky'.

179. νοσεράς κοίτης, see supr. 131.

181. πᾶν ἔπος ἦν σοι, 'your one cry was'.

183. σφάλλει, 'find yourself deceived'. Usener, δ' ἀσχάλλεις. οὐδενί, neuter rarely used thus in oblique cases.

184. σε, cf. supr. 106 n. τὸ δ' ἀπὸν φίλτερον ἡγεῖ, cf. Lucr. iii. 1058 *quid sibi quisque velit nescire et quaerere semper | commutare locum, quasi onus deponere possit.* Pind. Pyth. 3. 20 ἤρατο τῶν ἀπεόντων. So Shelley, 'look before and after, and pine for what is not'.

186. ' Better to be the patient than the nurse'.

187. συνάπτει, intrans. = 'is joined', cf. Soph. O. T. 667 κακὰ κακοῖς προσάψει, fr. 348 μοι ἀγχοῦ προσῆψεν, Eur. Supp. 1013 τύχα δέ μοι συνάπτει ποδός. λύπη τε φρενῶν χερσίν τε πόνος, 'grief of heart and toil for hand'.

189. πᾶς with ὀδυνηρός, 'the life of man is naught but woe'.

191. φίλτερον, 'more to be desired': an irreg. and epic comparative: also in this meaning Il. xi. 162 (of the dead) γύπεσσιν πολὺ φίλτεροι ἢ ἀλόχοισιν, so too supr. 185.

193. 'Fond lovers truly do we show ourselves of this, whate'er this be, that glitters on the earth, through inexperience of another life, and the un-proven nature of the things beneath the earth'. ἡ οὐκ-ἀπόδειξις, cf. Thuc. i. 137 οὐ-διάλυσις, iii. 95: v. 35: Eur. Bacch. 1288 ἐν οὐ-καιρῷ πάρει: cf. Terence's *semper-lenitas.* ἀπόδειξις is 'proof', 'absolute demonstration', which is lacking to our guesses at what is awaiting us below, cf. fr. 813, 9—11 οὕτως ἔρως βροτοῖσιν ἔγκειται βίου · | τὸ ζῆν γὰρ ἴσμεν, τοῦ θανεῖν δ' ἀπειρίᾳ | πᾶς τις φοβεῖται φῶς λιπεῖν τόδ' ἡλίου.

198 sq. imitated by Seneca, Phaedra 375 sq. *nunc ut soluto labitur moriens gradu | et vix labante sustinet collo caput | ...attolli jubet | iterumque poni corpus, et solvi comas | rursusque fingi.*

200. εὔπ. χεῖρας, 'take these fair hands and arms' : lit. 'hands with fair arms'. πῆχυς is from the wrist to the elbow, cf. Bacch. 1206 λευκοπήχεσι χειρῶν ἀκμαῖσι.

201. κεφαλᾶς. Throughout this conversation the nurse uses Attic forms, Phaedra Doric, as expressing deeper emotion, cf. Dindorf on Med. 140.

ἐπίκρανον, a head-dress confining the hair. From I. T. 51 it seems that the hair escaped from beneath it.

203. **χαλεπῶς μεταβάλλειν**, 'toss violently about'. Cf. Med. 121.

205. Cf. Hor. Od. i. 24. 19 *durum, sed levius fit patientia | quidquid corrigere est nefas.*

207. **μοχθεῖν...ἀνάγκη**, cf. fr. 37 μοχθεῖν ἀνάγκη. So fr. 719.

209. **πῶμα.** The true Attic form, not πόμα, cf. Elmsley on Bacch. 279. κρηνίς, a rare dimin. of κρήνη, found also Pind. fr. 136.

210. **κομήτῃ**, cf. Bacch. 1055 θύρσον...κισσῷ κομήτην : 'long-tressed'. Cf. too Verg. Geor. iv. 122 *sera comantem narcissum.*

212. **θροεῖς** of rapid loud speech, Soph. Phil. 1195 οὔτοι νεμεσητὸν ἀλύοντα λύπᾳ παρὰ νοῦν θροεῖν.

213. **οὐ μή...γηρύσει.** Goodwin Gr. Gr. § 257, note.

214. **μανίας ἔποχον**, 'borne on frenzy': only here metaph., cf. Hom. Od. i. 297 νηπιάας ὀχέειν (though Merry explains = 'practise', νηπιάας being accus.). Soph. O. C. 189 εὐσεβίας ἐπιβαίνοντες, Phil. 1463. Jahn's transposition of 213, 4 and 223, 7 (he rejects 224), approved by Nauck, Wecklein, Wilamowitz, certainly makes cry and comment correspond more precisely: but the MSS order is defensible. Phaedra's first ravings the nurse endeavours merely to hush, without referring to the matter of them, which she proceeds to do in her next speech.

215. **πέμπετε**, 'escort', cf. 158. Phaedra's mind travels to the spots where she would meet Hippolytus : the fir-clad slopes, which form the southern boundary of the Troezenian plain, haunt of the deer: or the Taurius flowing through the rich lowlands, on whose banks the young hunter would rest in the alder shade, and gather wreaths of flowers for Artemis: or the hippodrome near the sea-shore, where he tamed to his hand the steeds from distant Italy.

218. **ἐγχριμπτόμεναι**: picturesque epic and Ionic word, once used by Soph. El. 898, where the active voice is used intransitively, as also in Her. 9. 98. βαλ. ἐλ. 'dappled hinds', Hec. 90.

219. Cf. Bacch. 871 θωΰσσων δὲ κυναγέτας συντείνῃ δρόμημα κυνῶν.

220. 'And hurl past my long yellow locks (χαίτη, always 'flowing hair') the Thessalian lance'. She thinks of the whirr of the spear, as it flies past her ear from her back-drawn hand, cf. Verg. Aen. ix. 417 *ecce aliud summa telum librabat ab aure.*

223. **κηραίνεις,** 'art disquieted': so H. F. 518 ποῖ' ὄνειρα κηραίνουσ' ὁρῶ;

226. 'Bounding thy castle is a hillside set with streams'; συνεχὴς with πύργοις, Her. iv. 22. γένοιτ' ἄν 'would be if you chose to take it'.

228. **Λίμνας,** cf. 148 n. There were temples to Ἄρτεμις Λιμναία or Λιμνᾶτις at Troezen and several other places in the Peloponnesus: also in Athens.

230. **δάπεδα**=level places, like ἔδαφος: of the floor of a room etc. Here of large level exercise grounds for horses (γάπεδα is also found), cf. Hel. 206 ἱππόκροτα λέλοιπε δάπεδα γυμνάσιά τε δονακοέντος Εὐρώτα, Anth. Plan. xii. 131.

231. **δαμαλιζομένα,** only here and Pind. Pyth. 5. 112.

Ἐνέτας. The name appears more commonly in the form Veneti. We know of four distinct tribes of this name. Beside the one here referred to, there were (i) a Gallic tribe in Brittany, (ii) a Slav tribe (Wends) on the Baltic, Tac. Germ. 46: (iii) the Ἔνετοι of Hom. Il. ii. 852, a Paphlagonian people, Παφλαγόνων δ' ἡγεῖτο Πυλαιμένεος λάσιον κῆρ | ἐξ Ἐνετῶν, ὅθεν ἡμιόνων γένος ἀγροτεράων. These last are said by tradition to have migrated under Antenor after the Trojan war to the head of the Adriatic, Verg. Aen. i. 242. As no more is known of this Paphlagonian tribe, no argument can be based upon them. The probability is that the Veneti of the Illyrian country were the remains of a wave of Slav incursion, and were kinsfolk of the Venedi or Wends on the Baltic, with whom they seem to have had communication from very early times, by means of the well-known amber route (Mommsen, i. 135, Eng. tr.). The Southern Veneti must have been a commercial people: at any rate that their civilisation was far higher than that of their neighbours the Gauls is attested by Livy (x. 2), who contrasts their habits. They like their Paphlagonian homonyms were celebrated for their breed of horses. It was as exporters of amber however that they were best known to the Greeks. Cf. infr. 737.

232. **παράφρων,** 'beside thyself'. Instances of this well-known force of παρά in compos. are παραβαίνω, παράγω, παρακόπτω, παρακούω ('misunderstand', Plat. Prot. 330 E).

233. **νῦν δὴ μὲν...νῦν δὲ...,** 'a short while ago (ἀρτίως)...but now'. Cobet VL. 233, 4 says that νυνδὴ should be written, relying on this and similar passages, where νῦν δὴ μὲν not νῦν μὲν δὴ is found. **ὅρος,** accus. after βᾶσα.

235. **ψαμάθοις ἀκυμάντοις,** 'the waveless sands' of the hippodrome. Weil compares Aesch. Sept. 64 κῦμα χερσαῖον στρατοῦ. As the hippodrome would be on the level ground near the sea, 1126 and 1173 infr. are not inconsistent with this line.

236. **μαντείας ἄξια πολλῆς,** cf. Plat. Symp. 206 B μαντείας δεῖται ὅτι ποτὲ λέγεις. τάδε, sc. ὅστις σε θεῶν κ.τ.λ.

237. **ἀνασειράζει.** σεῖρα is a rope: σειραῖοι or σειραφόροι ἵπποι (Lat. *funales equi*) were the two trace-horses in a *quadriga*, one on each side of the pair of yoked horses. The trace-horses were connected with the car by ropes which were fastened to the ἄντυξ or rim. The force of ἀνα- here is obscure. The Schol. says it = 'pulled aside' out of the right way.

238. **παρακόπτει,** usually intrans.: here transitive.

240. 'Whither have I strayed from my right (παρ-) senses?' Cf. Pind. Ol. I. 94 εὐφροσύνας ἀλᾶται, 'wandereth from, misseth happiness'.

γνώμας ἀγαθᾶς (cf. Arist. Rhet. i. 15. 5 : ii. 25. 10 τὸ γνώμῃ τῇ ἀρίστῃ κρίνειν, part of the dicast's oath), 'sound judgment'.

243. **μαῖα.** A word of affectionate respect used towards nurses etc. Homer uses it especially in the Odyssey.

κρύψον, of a single act, 'put a covering over'. κρύπτε, **245** 'keep the covering over'.

244. **αἰδούμεθα...μοι,** cf. I. T. 348...ἠγριώμεθα...δοκοῦσα...

245. **κατ' ὄσσων...ὄμμα.** The root in both cases is the same, ὄκϳε having become ὄσσε, and ὄπμα (ὀπ- being the labialized form of ὀκ-, Lat. *oc-ulus*) ὄμμα. In meaning ὄσσε denotes definitely the two eyes: ὄμμα, a more general word, includes expression; 'look', 'face'.

247. **ὀρθοῦσθαι γνώμην,** not 'to recover one's senses', which would require the aorist: but 'to be in one's right mind')(τὸ μαινόμενον, 'frenzy'. For τὸ μαινόμενον = τὸ μαίνεσθαι, cf. Goodw. Gr. Gr. § 139. 2, Madvig Gr. S. § 87. a, rem. 1. This use is not infrequent in Thuc. e.g. τὸ δεδιός i. 36; ἐν τῷ μὴ μελετῶντι i. 142.

248. **κρατεῖ,** absol. 'it is best', cf. Aesch. Ag. 1364 κατθανεῖν κρατεῖ.

249. **μὴ γιγνώσκοντα,** 'without coming to one's senses'. Cf. fr. 204 κέρδος δ' ἐν κακοῖς ἀγνωσία. Phaedra relapses into a stupor, in which she remains till aroused by the nurse at l. 288.

250. **πότε δή;** 'when, O when'.

251. **σῶμα,** cf. 132 n.

252. πολλὰ διδάσκει κ.τ.λ. This remark may be intended as some excuse for the philosophical observations which Euripides here (as elsewhere) puts into the mouth of an uneducated person. Cf. Med. 119 sq.

253 sq. Quoted by Cic. de Am. 54: also by Plutarch Op. Mor. 95 E (who gives ἀνατείνασθαι and θέλγητρα for ἀνακίρνασθαι and στέργηθρα). For φιλίας ἀνακίρνασθαι cf. Her. iv. 152 φιλίαι συνεκρήθησαν, vii. 151. Aesch. Cho. 344 νεοκρᾶτα φίλον, Ag. 771 ὑδαρεῖ φιλότητι. στέργηθρα occurs Aesch. Prom. 492 (with the same variant θέλγητρα), Cho. 233, Eum. 192, in the sense of 'affection'. 'That the loves of our hearts should be easy, easy to thrust from us, easy to knit close'. Plut. loc. cit. says that the metaphor is from the sheets of a sail. Cf. Soph. Aj. 679 sq. ὅ τ' ἐχθρὸς ἡμῖν ἐς τόσονδ' ἐχθαρτέος | ὡς καὶ φιλήσων αὖθις, ἔς τε τὸν φίλον | τοσαῦθ' ὑπουργῶν ὠφελεῖν βουλήσομαι | ὡς αἰὲν οὐ μενοῦντα.

260. Cf. Alc. 883 μία γὰρ ψυχή, τῆς ὑπεραλγεῖν μέτριον ἄχθος.

261. A line of argument adopted again by the nurse in a different connection, infr. 467. Possibly 'dietetic reform' was known in Athens. For Eur.'s medical metaphors cf. n. on infr. 1346.

Entire devotion to a friend is ideally best: but the ideally best does not suit this life of ours, neither in friendship nor food.

264. τὸ λίαν. Cf. Phoen. 584 μέθετον τὸ λίαν μέθετον.

265. μηδὲν ἄγαν. A saying of one of the σοφοί of the next line: of which particular σοφός is doubtful: of the σοφώτατος says an epigram in the Anthology.

269. ἄσημα. Cf. infr. 371, Hec. 1107 συγγνωστά, Med. 491, Andr. 955, Thuc. iii. 88 θέρους δι' ἀνυδρίαν ἀδύνατα ἦν ἐπιστρατεύειν: ἀδύνατα is especially common, Madv. G. S. 1. b. 4.

270. For ἂν repeated cf. infr. 480. Madv. G. S. 139 b.

271. 'Try as I may I know not'.

275. τριταίαν ἡμέραν. For the redundance cf. Hec. 32 τριταῖον ἤδη φέγγος. Thuc. v. 75 προτεραίᾳ ἡμέρᾳ.

276. 'ἄτη *dicitur de calamitate qualibet, sed praesertim de ea quae divinitus immissa sit*'. Monk.

277. εἰς, 'with a view to'.

278. εἰ after θαυμαστόν. Cf. Goodw. Gr. Gr. § 228.
ἐξαρκεῖ πόσει, cf. inf. 702; 'if her husband is content'.

279. οὔ φησιν, 'denies'.

281. γὰρ, 'no, for' etc. ἔκδημος. Theseus had gone to consult the oracle about his purification from bloodguiltiness, cf. 35 n.

283. **πλάνος**, Soph. and Eur.; πλάνη, Aesch. Plato uses both forms.

284. **εἰς πᾶν ἀφῖγμαι.** The usual expression is ἐπὶ πᾶν ἀφικέσθαι, ἐλθεῖν, cf. Soph. O. T. 265 ἐπὶ πάντ᾽ ἀφίξομαι. εἴς τι ἀφικ. generally=to be brought into a condition. Plat. Euth. 292 E εἰς πολλήν γε ἀπορίαν ἀφίκεσθε.

οὐδὲν πλέον εἴργασμαι. Cf. I. A. 1373 ὁρᾶν χρή, μὴ πλέον πράξωμεν οὐδέν. Cf. πλέον ἔχειν, 'to have the advantage', Thuc. vii. 36.

285. **ἀνήσω προθυμίας.** Med. 456 σὺ δ᾽ οὐκ ἀνίεις μωρίας.

287. **δυστυχοῦσι δεσπόταις**: in the 'generalizing plural', the masc. gender is invariable. Cf. infr. 798, Hec. 403 χάλα τοκεῦσιν εἰκότως θυμουμένοις (of Hecuba).

289. **ἡδίων**, 'more pleasant' to me. Cf. Jebb on Soph. O. T. 82.

290. 'And smooth that gloomy brow and path of thought'. Cf. Horace's *explicare frontem.* For the metaphorical use of ὁδός (οἴμη is very common in this sense) cf. Aesch. Eum. 989 γλώσσης ὁδόν, Eur. Hec. 744 βουλευμάτων ὁδόν. The metaphor is preserved in εἰπόμην and εἶμι. It is hard to see how the translation of Prof. Mahaffy and Mr Bury ('and if in any point I did not *speak* to you well on former occasions', etc.) is to be extracted from the text. 'And where'er I did not then go with thee aright (i.e. follow thy γνώμης ὁδόν), quitting that path, I will betake me to other better speech'. If ἕπεσθαι be translated 'go with', the distinction between ἕπεσθαί τινι of an equal and ἕπεσθαι μετά τινος of an inferior (Cobet VL. 22) is intelligible. Cf. n. on infr. 1196.

293. This line is explained by supr. 161 sq.

294. 'Women are here to help in treating thy complaint'. For the infin. after αἴδε Musgrave quotes Hom. Il. ix. 688 εἰσὶ καὶ οἴδε τάδ᾽ εἰπέμεν: xix. 140. With the general sense cf. Andr. 956 κοσμεῖν γυναῖκας τὰς γυναικείας νόσους.

300. **φθέγξαι τι**, 'speak if but a word'.

302. 'I am as far off as before'. οὔτε...τε. This is not uncommon, but τε...οὔτε is never found. Cf. Jebb on O. C. 367, 1397. οὐ-πείθεται coalesces, as οὔ-φησι 279. ἐτέγγεθ᾽ 'was softened'. Aesch. Prom. 1008 τέγγῃ γὰρ οὐδὲν οὐδὲ μαλθάσσῃ λιταῖς.

304. **πρὸς τάδ᾽...θαλάσσης** is parenthetic. For πρὸς τάδε implying obstinacy cf. Aesch. Prom. 1030 πρὸς ταῦτα βούλευε, Soph. O. T. 343 πρὸς τάδ᾽ εἰ θέλεις θυμοῦ. προδοῦσα with ἴσθι. The

argument is: 'Know that if you die you will have betrayed your children, who being defenceless will fall victims to their half-brother Hippolytus'. It would be impertinent to do more than call attention to the consummate art of these lines. Racine has followed them closely, Phèdre i. 3 vous trahissez enfin vos enfants malheureux, | que vous précipitez sous un joug rigoureux. | Songez qu'un même jour leur ravira leur mère | et rendra l'espérance au fils de l'étrangère, | à ce fier ennemi de vous, de votre sang, | ce fils qu'une Amazone a porté dans son flanc, | cet Hippolyte... *Phèdre*. Ah, dieux! *Oenone*. Ce reproche vous touche. | *Ph*. Malheureuse, quel nom est sorti de ta bouche?

306. μὴ, not οὐ μεθ., as putting a contingency. The reference in 307 to a late rival in Theseus' affections was calculated to rouse Phaedra still more.

309. 'A bastard with the ambitions of a lawful child'. Weckl. quotes Plut. Per. 37 μόνους ᾿Αθηναίους εἶναι τοὺς ἐκ δυοῖν ᾿Αθηναίων γεγονότας. Hippolytus' mother was not Athenian; hence he was νόθος.

312. αὖθις, 'for the future', inf. 892, Or. 910.

313. The nurse misunderstands Phaedra's οἴμοι, interpreting it as due to her anxiety for her own children (Acamas and Demophon, says the scholiast). εὖ φρονεῖς)(μαίνει.

315. φιλῶ τέκνα perhaps implies ᾿Ιππολύτου ἐρῶ: 'but other is the hap, wherein I am foundering'. The metaphor of a 'sea of troubles' occurs in many forms.

316. 'μὲν in an interrogative sentence marks a proposition as preliminary, and points to a sequel. It implies therefore that the speaker either wishes or feels bound to assume it true'. Verrall on Med. 676. It generally implies that unless the answer is 'yes', the discussion cannot go on. Cf. Ar. Av. 1214 ὑγιαίνεις μέν; Plat. Meno 82 D ῞Ελλην μέν ἐστι καὶ ῾Ελληνίζει;

318. πημονῆς ἐχθρῶν τινός. The genit. is subjective. ἐπακτὸς πημονή: ἡ ἔξωθεν ἐπαγομένη γοητεία Schol. So πολυπήμων of witchcraft, Hom. Hymn. Herm. 37.

319. οὐχ ἑκ. οὐχ ἑκών, 'unmeaning he as I'.

321. ὀφθείην. Cf. inf. 430.

322. On γὰρ strengthening an interrogative, cf. Hadley Gr. Gr. 1050. 4: Madv. G. S. 262. γὰρ has its original meaning, 'Ah then' (γ' ἄρ').

324. ἑκοῦσα, sc. ἐάσω: suggested by 319. ἐν δὲ σοὶ λελείψομαι,

Sed penes te est ut vincar, Monk. Alc. 278 ἐν σοὶ δ' ἐσμὲν καὶ ζῆν
καὶ μή.

325. Cf. Med. 339 τί οὖν βιάζῃ; of a suppliant. καὶ σῶν γε
γονάτων, sc. ἐξαρτωμένη, 'Aye and thy knees'.

328. **γάρ**, 'no, not evil (by comparison): for what greater evil
can befall me than to fail in obtaining my request from you?' A weak
sense, which Nauck's ἤ σε μὴ εὐτυχεῖν would improve.

330. Following Hirzel I have transposed 330 and 332. γὰρ in
331 thus (as very frequently in στιχομυθίαι) connects with the
speaker's previous words, and not with the immediately preceding
sentence.

κᾆπειτα. 'And yet, such being the case, do you etc.?' Cf.
Alc. 796, inf. 440. It is the ἔπειτα '*indignantis*'.

333. **δεξιὰν** corrected from the MS δεξιᾶς in accordance with
Dawes' canon, μεθιέναι τι, μεθίεσθαι τινός.

334. **δίδως**, 'art not for granting'.

335. 'This hand has given thee a holy claim and I respect it'.

337—352. These wonderful lines are imitated by Racine, as
indeed is the whole scene. Phèdre i. 3 should be read and compared. Cf. too Seneca, Phaedr. 118 sq. *fatale miserae matris agnosco
malum* etc.: 132 *nulla Minoïs levi | defuncta amore est, jungitur
semper nefas.*

μῆτερ, Pasiphae. **ὅμαιμε**, Ariadne.

342. **ἔκ τοι πέπληγμαι.** Goodw. Gr. Gr. § 191. 7, n. 3.

343. **ἐκεῖθεν**, from the curse which prompted their loves.

345. This line is quoted by Ar. Eq. 15 to express the timid
indecision of Nicias.

347. **τί τοῦθ' ὃ δὴ κ.τ.λ.** Cf. supr. 194, inf. 351.

ἀνθρώπους ἐρᾶν. 'What is it, that men talk of—of people being
in love?' It almost=τὸ ἐρᾶν.

349. **κεχρημένοι.** When a speaker uses the plural of him- or
herself ('we' for 'I') the masculine is always found. Cf. Hadley
Gr. Gr. § 637 b, Soph. El. 399 and Jebb's n.

θατέρῳ, sc. ἀλγεινῷ. **εἶμεν ἄν**, potential optative. Cf. Her. i. 2
εἴησαν δ' ἂν οὗτοι Κρῆτες.

352. **σοῦ τάδ'**, a well known phrase. Plat. i. Alcib. 113 C.
The name of Hippolytus opens (310) and closes the στιχομυθίαι.

353. **τί λέξεις**; cf. Med. 1310 οἴμοι τί λέξεις; ὡς μ' ἀπώλεσας,
γύναι. λέξεις in these cases is future because the person speaking
cannot immediately grasp the evil news. **οὐκ ἀνασχετά**, cf. 269 n.

356. **ἀπαλλαχθήσομαι.** Attic prose writers and Aesch. use only the 2 aor. pass.: Soph. and Eur. both the first and second, preferring the first.

359. **οὐκ ἄρ' ἦν.** 'The imperfect is often used instead of the present to denote a present fact, which has been just recognized, although true before'. Hadley, Gr. Gr. § 833. In such cases *ἄρα* is usually added. 'Is not, as now I know'. *θεὸς*, i.e. *θεὸς μόνον*. Cf. Hec. 1111 *ἀπώλεσ', οὐκ ἀπώλεσ', ἀλλὰ μειζόνως*.

362—370. These lines correspond metrically with 668—679. **ἔκλυες ἀνήκουστα.** Cf. Ion 782 *ἄφατον λόγον θροεῖς*. **θρεομένας,** cf. Aesch. Supp. 111 *πάθεα μέλεα θρεόμενα*. *θρέομαι* (like *ὀλολύζω* generally) is used only of women. The rhythm is dochmiac (normal form ⏑–́–⏑–́ e.g. *ἀνήκουστα τᾶς*). This striking rhythm is used to express great mental agitation.

364. I have followed Elmsley's correction of these lines. The MSS give *ὀλοίμαν ἔγωγε πρὶν σὰν φιλίαν* (some *φίλαν*) *καταλῦσαι* (some *κατάνυσαι*) *φρενῶν*. Elmsley compares Soph. El. 1451 *φίλης γὰρ προξένου κατήνυσαν*: where Triclinius notes *κατήνυσαν = ἐπέτυχον*. 'For myself, may I die, before I reach, dear lady, thy state of mind'.

367. **τρέφοντες,** cf. fr. 55. 3 *πενία δὲ δύστηνον μὲν ἀλλ' ὅμως τρέφει | μοχθοῦντ' ἀμείνω τέκνα καὶ δραστήρια*.

369. 'What life awaits thee henceforth (*ὅδε*) each livelong day?'

370. **τελευτάσεται.** The fut. mid. of this verb is always passive in sense.

371. **ἄσημα,** cf. n. on 269. *οἷ φθίνει κ.τ.λ.*, lit. 'whither is setting (i.e. how is ending) the luck of love'. Cf. Plat. Symp. 181 C *οἷ κακίας τελευτᾷ*.

Κύπριδος τύχα, 'the luck sent by Cypris'.

374. **προνώπιον.** Hesych. *τὸ ἔμπροσθεν τῶν πυλῶν*. With *προνώπιον χώρας Πελοπίας* cf. Pind. Ol. 13. 4 *Κόρινθον Ἰσθμίου πρόθυρον Ποτειδᾶνος*.

375. **ἤδη ποτ' κ.τ.λ.** An excuse for the somewhat studied disquisition which follows. Cf. supr. 252 for a similar introduction to the nurse's reflections. The MSS have *ἄλλως*: the uses of which word may be grouped according to two meanings, (i) in another way, (ii) in another way than the right, to no purpose. These meanings are inappropriate here, and of *ἄλλως* = at other times (which is the meaning we should expect in combination with *ἤδη ποτ'*), I can find no instance. Reading *ἄλλων* here, we bring her former general speculations into connection with her present individual case [or we

might read ἄλλα...θνητῶν τ' ἐφρόντισ']. These lines are parodied by Ar. Ran. 931 ἤδη ποτ' ἐν μακρῷ χρόνῳ νυκτὸς διεγρύπνησα κ.τ.λ. Monk reminds us of the proverb ἐν νυκτὶ βουλή.

377. **κατά**, 'by reason of'. Thuc. vi. 89 τὴν προξενίαν ἀπεῖπον κατά τι ἔγκλημα. For κάκιον cf. Madv. G. S. § 93 b.

380. *video meliora proboque, deteriora sequor.* Cf. fr. 576 ἀλλὰ ταῦτα γὰρ λέγειν | ἐπιστάμεσθα, δρᾶν δ' ἀμηχάνως ἔχει: fr. 837 γνώμην δ' ἔχοντα μ' ἡ φύσις βιάζεται: Plat. Prot. 352 D πολλούς φασιν γιγνώσκοντας τὰ βέλτιστα οὐκ ἐθέλειν πράττειν.

381. **ἐκπονοῦμεν**, 'practise'.

382. **προθέντες ἀντὶ κ.τ.λ.** For the pleonasm cf. Heracl. 58 αἱρήσεται τὴν σὴν ἀχρεῖον δύναμιν ἀντ' Εὐρυσθέως.

383. **ἄλλην τινά.** Cf. L. and S. s.v. ἄλλος II. 7. Cf. the French *nous autres.*

383 sq. It is with great hesitation that I have printed this most difficult passage in accordance with my own view of it. In spite of all that has been urged in defence of lines 384—7, to me they seem impossible. That λέσχη, σχολή, αἰδὼς should be selected as the typical pleasures, which interfere with the performance of a known duty: that thereupon a quibbling subdivision of αἰδώς into 'not bad' and 'ruinous to households' should be added: and that too in a speech where 'if any calm a calm despair' should reign, as with merciless plainness Phaedra lays bare her agony and sin, are disfigurements so offensive in their weakness, that I cannot believe Euripides, often as his subtlety outran his judgment, to be chargeable with them. The *pannus* is not even *purpureus.* The ingenious interpolator would find the words εἰσὶ δ' ἡδοναὶ πολλαὶ βίου a suitable and tempting hook, whereon to hang his scraps, whether taken from the first edition, or compiled from sources now unknown. One could find excuse for λέσχη and σχολή, the idle hours which Phaedra had spent watching Hippolytus as he exercised in the palaestra below (cf. Paus. ii. 32. 3 κατὰ δὲ τὸ ἕτερον μέρος στάδιόν ἐστιν Ἱππολύτου καλούμενον, καὶ ναὸς ὑπὲρ αὐτοῦ Ἀφροδίτης Κατασκοπίας. αὐτόθεν γὰρ, ὅποτε γυμνάζοιτο ὁ Ἱππόλυτος, ἀπέβλεπεν ἐς αὐτὸν ὁρῶσα ἡ Φαίδρα); but αἰδώς is incomprehensible: it may have been suggested by fr. 367 αἰδοῦς δὲ καὐτὸς δυσκρίτως ἔχω πέρι· | καὶ δεῖ γὰρ αὐτῆς κάστιν αὖ κακὸν μέγα. Cf. Hom. Il. xxiv. 44 αἰδὼς | ...ῆτ' ἄνδρας μέγα σίνεται ἠδ' ὀνίνησιν. If one were at liberty to change αἰδὼς to ἔρως (to complete the chain of Phaedra's reflections on the ἡδοναὶ fatal to her),

and compare I. A. 547 ὅτι δὴ δίδυμ' ἔρως ὁ χρυσοκόμας τόξ' ἐντείνεται χαρίτων, τὸ μὲν ἐπ' εὐαίωνι πότμῳ, τὸ δ' ἐπὶ συγχύσει βιοτᾶς κ.τ.λ. (cf. too Seneca Ph. 280 *geminus cupido*), the passage might perhaps stand. But the gender of ἔρως would necessitate re-writing the passage thus: ἔρως τε· δισσὸς δ' ἐστί, τῇ μὲν οὐ κακὸς, τῇ δ' ἄχθος οἴκων. This however would savour of Procrustes. That the interpolation is of very long standing is shown by the fact that Plutarch (de virt. mor. 448 F) quotes it as from this play : but Valckenaer (on 253) proves that the recension, from which Plutarch cited, was a faulty one.

One other change I have made, viz. the transposition of 388—390 to follow 402. According to this arrangement, Phaedra follows up her general reflections (reading ἄλλων in 375) on the causes of evil, 375—383, by narrating her own case, 391 sq.: finally declaring her intention to seek deliverance in death, 402 : the three lines 388—390 then follow very appropriately: by φρενῶν is signified her 'purpose' of self-destruction, and διαφθερεῖν gives the exact meaning we want, viz. to spoil a design by want of nerve or the like. Cf. Med. 1055 χεῖρα δ' οὐ διαφθερῶ : φαρμάκῳ too derives significance from the subsequent course of the play : cf. 479 φανήσεταί τι τῆσδε φάρμακον νόσου.

391. γνώμης ὁδόν. Cf. supr. 290.

392. ἔτρωσεν, aorist of a single act: ἐσκόπουν, 'I began to consider'. Cf. 243 n.

395. γλώσσῃ γὰρ οὐδὲν πιστόν. Cf. Soph. fr. 583 βροτῷ δὲ πιστὸν οὐδέν: Hom. Od. xi. 456 οὐκέτι πιστὰ γυναιξίν.

θυραῖα φρονήματ' ἀνδρῶν = φρονήματα θυραίων ἀνδρῶν. Cf. El. 391 θυραῖα πήματα. 'It is all very well', says Phaedra, 'to criticise others, but when you talk of your own affairs, you often suffer for it'. By αὐτή is meant really the owner of the tongue.

397. κέκτηται. A general truth is sometimes expressed by the perfect, e.g. Xen. Mem. iv. 2. 35 πολλοὶ διὰ δόξαν μεγάλα κακὰ πεπόνθασιν. For κακὰ κέκτ. cf. Eur. Hel. 272 τὰ μὴ προσόντα κέκτηται κακά.

398. ἄνοιαν, 'my mad passion'.

401. Notice the alliteration.

388. τυγχάνω φρονοῦσ'. 'In the habitual irony of Attic speech "accidental" frequently means "essential": to say that a thing "happens to be such", may if pronounced suitably be merely a way of saying that the quality predicated is the most important which the thing possesses'. Verrall on Med. 608.

389. **οὐκ ἔσθ' ὁποίῳ κ.τ.λ.**=οὐκ ἐστὶ τοιοῦτον φάρμακον, οἵῳ κ.τ.λ. Though the sentence is in past time, οὐκ ἔσθ' ὁποίῳ is so much a single crystallized expression, that its tense is not affected.

διαφθερεῖν, to spoil by want of nerve or the like. Cf. Med. 1055: Hec. 597 ὁ δ' ἐσθλὸς ἐσθλὸς, οὐδὲ συμφορᾶς ὕπο | φύσιν διέφθειρ', ἀλλὰ χρηστός ἐστ' ἀεί.

403. **καλά,** sc. δρώσῃ.

405. **ἤδη.** The correct Attic form of the pluperfect (contracted from ᾔδεα), not ᾔδειν, which several good MSS have.

407. **μίσημα.** A very strong word. Cf. Heracl. 52, 941: Med. 1323: Aesch. Sept. 186 σωφρόνων μισήματα (of women).

ὡς=*utinam.* Soph. El. 126 ὡς ὁ τάδε πορὼν ὄλοιτο. Cf. Hadley, Gr. Gr. § 870 c.

408—410. **ἤρξατ'...ἦρξε.** This passage is illustrated by Shilleto in a note on Thuc. i. 145. 2, where he points out that ἄρχω=*initium facio,* ἄρχομαι=*initium mihi facio.*

409. **γενναίων—ἐσθλοῖσιν—κακοῖς:** used in the political sense of high and low. Cf. Soph. Ant. 38 εἴτ' εὐγενὴς πέφυκας εἴτ' ἐσθλῶν κακή. Cf. Welcker, pref. to Theognis, p. 21 sq.

413. Racine, Phèdre iii. 3 'Je ne suis point de ces femmes hardies, | qui goûtant dans le crime une tranquille paix, | ont su se faire un front, qui ne rougit jamais.

414. **τόλμας οὐ καλὰς κεκτ.,** 'have acquired the habit (force of plur.) of bold sin': a strained use of κεκτῆσθαι: possibly I. T. 1171 is parallel: οἰκεῖον ἦλθον τὸν φόνον κεκτήμενος.

418. Both τέραμνα and τέρεμνα are found. Cf. infr. 536.

μή ποτε φθ. ἀφῇ, 'lest they should cry out'. Monk compares Aesch. Ag. 37 οἶκος...λέξειεν: Andr. 923 ὡς δοκοῦσί γε | δόμοι τ' ἐλαύνειν φθέγμ' ἔχοντες οἶδε με: Cic. pro Cael. 60 *nonne ipsam domum metuet, ne quam vocem eliciat? non parietes conscios?* Juv. 9. 102—104: infr. 1074.

419. ' 'Tis that, 'tis that which is killing me (i.e. is driving me to suicide), that never may I be found guilty of dishonouring my lord, never of dishonouring the children of my womb'.

422. **παρρησίᾳ,** 'with unfettered lips'. παρρησία and ἐλευθερία were the boasts of the Athenian democrat. With this passage compare Ion 671 sq. ἐκ τῶν Ἀθηνῶν μ' ἡ τεκοῦσ' εἴη γυνὴ, | ὥς μοι γένηται μητρόθεν παρρησία. | καθαρὰν γὰρ ἤν τις ἐς πόλιν πέσῃ ξένος, | κἂν τοῖς λόγοισιν ἀστὸς ᾖ, τό γε στόμα | δοῦλον πέπαται κοὐκ ἔχει παρρησίαν.

423. **μητρὸς οὕνεκα**, 'as far as their mother is concerned'. Cf. Soph. O. C. 22 χρόνου μὲν οὕνεκ': El. 387. In this sense the tragedians frequently use ἔκατι. Aesch. Pers. 337 πλήθους ἔκατι, 'as far as mere numbers went'. Eur. Cyc. 665. ἕνεκα is found in Aristoph. (Ach. 365 ἐμοῦ γ' ἕνεκα) and prose writers.

424. **δουλοῖ**, 'cows'. Cf. Thuc. ii. 61. 3 δουλοῖ γὰρ φρόνημα τὸ αἰφνίδιον. κακά, 'guilt'. Racine, Phèdre iii. 3 le crime d'une mère est un pesant fardeau.

426. **ἁμιλλᾶσθαι βίῳ**, 'stands the brunt of life'. Lit. 'strives with ', ' vies with '.

427. **ὅτῳ παρῇ** : on the omission of ἄν cf. Madv. G. S. § 126 rem. 2.

428. **ἐξέφηνε**, gnomic aorist.

429. **ὥστε = ὡς** : an epic use. Cf. Soph. O. C. 343 οἰκουροῦσιν ὥστε παρθένοι : Ant. 1033 ὥστε τοξόται σκοποῦ | τοξεύετ'.

430. **ὀφθείην**. Cf. supr. 321.

432. Paley on Aesch. Sept. 597 distinguishes καρποῦμαι, 'I enjoy', from καρπίζομαι, 'I produce fruit', and insists on the distinction here: 'bears fruit of good report'.

433. **μὲν** is misplaced: in antithesis to νῦν δὲ should stand ἀρτίως μέν.

435. **φαῦλος**, 'shallow': like μάταιος, γενναῖος, δίκαιος etc., φαῦλος is sometimes of three, sometimes two terminations. For οὖσα cf. Madv. G. S. 178.

436. A proverb was and still is for imperfectly educated persons a firm ground of assurance or justification. Such reflections are far more suited to the nurse than philosophic subtleties (supr. 252). For more proverbs cf. supr. 265. Cicero gives us the same sentiment in Johnsonian Latin—*posteriores cogitationes, ut aiunt, sapientiores solent esse.* Phil. 12. 5.

438. Both ἀπο- and ἐπι-σκήπτω are found in the intransitive sense, 'to fall upon'. Cf. Aeschin. 27. 20: Aesch. Eum. 482. The best MSS here have ἐπέσκηψαν.

θεᾶς, sc. Κύπριδος.

440. The use of εἶτα, ἔπειτα, κἄπειτα to mark an opposition, is more frequent after a participle (Aesch. Eum. 654 τὸ μητρὸς αἷμα ἐκχέας πέδοι ἔπειτα δώματ' οἰκήσεις πατρός;), but is also found after a verbal clause, as here; cf. Ar. Av. 27 οὐ δεινὸν οὖν δῆτ' ἐστὶν ἡμᾶς δεομένους | ἐς κόρακας ἐλθεῖν...ἔπειτα μὴ 'ξευρεῖν δύνασθαι τὴν ὁδόν; Cf. Madv. G. S. § 175 a.

441. The MSS give οὔτ' (or οὐκ) ἄρα γ' οὐ δεῖ τοῖς ἐρῶσι τῶν πέλας, which is unintelligible. Valckenaer proposed οὐ τἄρα λύει (for λυσιτελεῖ), which though good in itself does not help the sentence as a whole, since τῶν πέλας as object of ἐρῶσι is almost grotesque, and there is nothing to prepare the way for ὅσοι τε μέλλουσ'. I have ventured to print a conjecture of my own, which is not far from the MSS, and gives a satisfactory sense: οὐκ ἄρ' ἀγὼν δὴ τοῖς ἐρῶσι νῦν μέγας, | ὅσοι τε μέλλουσ', εἰ θανεῖν αὐτοὺς χρεών; where νῦν makes ὅσοι τε μέλλουσ' natural.

443. **φορητός.** Cf. supr. 393 ἐνέγκαιμ'. πολλή, cf. I. A. 557 μετέχοιμι τᾶς Ἀφροδίτας, πολλὰν δ' ἀποθείμαν.

ῥυῇ. Cf. Hec. 1055 ἀποστήσομαι | θυμῷ ῥέοντι Θρῃκὶ δυσμαχωτάτῳ: also Horace's *tota ruens Venus*.

445. **περισσόν** (supr. 437 and n. on 138). It is used in the same sense infr. 948, 'out of the common', and so 'haughty': very similar to σεμνὸς supr. 93.

446. **πῶς δοκεῖς;** parenthetic. Cf. Hec. 1160 κᾆτ' ἐκ γαληνῶν, πῶς δοκεῖς; προσφθεγμάτων κ.τ.λ.: I. A. 1590 κἂν τῷδε Κάλχας πῶς δοκεῖς; χαίρων ἔφη: Ar. Ach. 24. It is a colloquial phrase, not found in Aesch. or Soph. καθύβρισεν, gnomic aor. 'flouts'. Cf. fr. 341 Κύπρις...ἤν τ' αὖ βιάζῃ, μᾶλλον ἐντείνειν φιλεῖ.

447. **φοιτᾷ,** cf. supr. 148: Soph. fr. 607 ἔρως γὰρ ἄνδρας οὐ μόνους ἐπέρχεται | οὐδ' αὖ γυναῖκας, ἀλλὰ καὶ θεῶν ἄνω | ψυχὰς χαράσσει κἀπὶ πόντον ἔρχεται. Cf. also Lucretius' famous invocation at the beginning of Book I.

449. **ἔρον.** Eur. is the only tragedian who uses the form ἔρος in iambics. Cf. Ion 1127. Weckl. for διδοῦσ', which he calls meaningless, conjectures κἀνιεῖσ'.

451. **γραφὴ** is used twice by Aeschylus, once by Sophocles: with the meaning in each passage of 'picture'. Eur. uses the word eleven times, five times meaning 'picture', six times with reference to a definite document or the like: e.g. inscription of laws on a pillar or writing on a tablet: no example can I find either in tragedy or elsewhere, where 'writings' of a literary character are spoken of as γραφαί. Below (1005) Hippolytus says οὐκ οἶδα πρᾶξιν τήνδε (sc. ἔρωτα) πλὴν λόγῳ κλύων γραφῇ τε λεύσσων: taking that passage with the present, I infer that Euripides (whose interest in painting, as an old student of the art, was great) refers to some well-known paintings, dealing with the subject in question.

452. **ἐν μούσαις,** 'interested in culture' generally, which would

include both painting and literatuŕé. Cf. Alc. 962 διὰ μούσας ἦξα.

457. **κοὐ φεύγουσιν θεούς**, sc. ὡς νῦν σὺ φεύγεις βροτούς, i.e. by suicide.

458. **οἶμαι**, *ironice*, 'they find it easy I fancy to acquiesce in their defeat'. The use of *credo* in Latin is parallel. στέργουσι, as infr. 461 στέρξεις: with this passage cf. H. F. 1314—1321, especially 1318—21: ἀλλ' οἰκοῦσ' ὅμως | Ὄλυμπον ἠνέσχοντό θ' ἡμαρτηκότες· | καίτοι τί φήσεις εἰ σὺ μὲν θνητὸς γεγὼς | φέρεις ὑπέρφευ τὰς τύχας, θεοὶ δὲ μή; Cf. Racine, Phèdre iv. 6 mortelle subissez le sort d'une mortelle etc.

459. 'Your father ought as it seems to have begotten·you conditionally or with other gods as lords'. Notice χρῆν (imperf.) φυτεύειν, not χρὴ πεφυτευκέναι. Cf. Hadley, Gr. Gr. § 834 a.

462. **ἔχοντας εὖ φρενῶν**. Cf. Madv. G. S. § 42 b rem. 2 and examples there quoted. ἥκειν is used similarly.

465. **συνεκκομίζειν**, 'help their erring sons in achieving their love'. Cf. fr. 340 πατέρα τε παισὶν ἡδέως συνεκφέρειν | φίλους ἔρωτας ἐκβαλόντ' αὐθαδίαν, | παῖδάς τε πατρί.

466. **λανθάνειν τὰ μὴ καλά**. Cf. supr. 402, 3. The nurse turns Phaedra's own words against her.

467. For the sentiment cf. supr. 261. The argument is: 'undue scrupulousness in life is a mistake: we must be content often with what is second best, or even faulty (especially if the fault is not easily to be detected). For instance, in building a house, you would not elaborate with minute care the roof, which cannot be inspected closely, and where therefore slight flaws will pass unnoticed'.

ἀκριβώσειαν: the awkward omission of ἄν and the difficult construction of κατηρεφεῖς have led to many conjectures: if we read ἀκριβώσαις ἄν both grammar and sense are satisfactory. The rarer form of the optative would be very likely to be corrupted. For the construction of κατηρεφεῖς Monk quotes a parallel passage of Anacr. τράπεζαι κατηρεφέες παντοίων ἀγαθῶν.

469. The metaphor is the common one of a 'sea of troubles'. Cf. 315, 823. The sense is: 'now that by no fault of your own (πεσοῦσα) you are in this trouble, you must not expect to be able to free yourself: so accept fate and make the best of it'.

470. **ἄν** with ἐκνεῦσαι.

471. Cf. Soph. O. C. 796 κάκ' ἂν λάβοις τὰ πλείον' ἢ σωτήρια.

472. **ἄνθρωπος** of a woman : so *homo*, Cic. Fam. iv. 5. 4 *quoniam homo nata fuerat.*

473. **λῆγε,** 'cease' (as a continued state) : λῆξον, 'cease' (at this particular time).

476. **τόλμα δ' ἐρῶσα,** not 'have the heart to love' : but 'bear up under thy passion'. Lit. 'being in love, bear up'.

477 sq. On this passage cf. Appendix A. νοσοῦσα = ἐρῶσα, νόσον = ἔρωτα. εὖ καταστρ., 'bring to good issue'.

480. **ἄν...ἄν.** For ἄν repeated cf. supr. 270: Porson on Hec. 730.

483. **πρὸς,** 'viewed with reference to'. Cf. Thuc. iii. 44. 3 δικαιότερος γὰρ ὢν αὐτοῦ ὁ λόγος πρὸς τὴν νῦν ὑμετέραν ὀργὴν κ.τ.λ. In 484 I have adopted Weil's ψόγων.

485. **μᾶλλον ἀλγίων,** infr. 1421 μάλιστα φίλτατος. Hec. 377 μᾶλλον εὐτυχέστερος: Aesch. Supp. 673: Hom. Il. xxiv. 243.

486—9. 486, 7 are curiously parallel to a fragment of Sophocles' Phaedra (fr. 606) οὐ γάρ ποτ' ἂν γένοιτ' ἂν ἀσφαλὴς πόλις | ἐν ᾗ τὰ μὲν δίκαια καὶ τὰ σώφρονα | λάγδην πατεῖται, κωτίλος δ' ἀνὴρ λαβὼν | πανοῦργα χερσὶ κέντρα κηδεύει πόλιν: while 488, 9 resemble a fragment of the same play (fr. 605) οὐ γὰρ δίκαιον ἄνδρα γενναῖον φρένας | τέρπειν, ὅπου μὴ καὶ δίκαια τέρψεται. On rhetoric in democracies cf. Cleon's remarks in Thuc. iii. 83. 3 : Eur. Supp. 410 sq., 424—5: fr. 57.

490. **σεμνομυθεῖς.** Our colloquial 'talk fine'. δεῖ σε...λόγων, cf. supr. 23.

491. Some editors punctuate after τἀνδρός : others after διιστέον. The former take τἀνδρὸς = τοῦ ἀνδρός : the latter take it = τὰ ἀνδρὸς (which Nauck asserts, but Wecklein denies), or else regard it as a genitive governed by διιστέον (in the sense 'come to a right judgment about'), to defend which is brought forward Soph. Tr. 387 πιθοῦ μολοῦσα τἀνδρός. The fault lies I think in διιστέον : διειδέναι means to 'distinguish one thing from another' Med. 519, Plat. Phaedr. 262 A, or to 'decide a matter' Soph. O. C. 295, and is therefore inappropriate here. ΔΕΙΠΕΙCΤΕΟΝ might easily become ΔΙΙCΤΕΟΝ, Π and ΙΙ being confused, and the copyist's eye mistaking what should have been the second stroke of Π for the I in the syllable ΠΕΙ. The variant διοιστέον, found in AE Pal. I take to have arisen from ΔΕΙΠCΤΕΟΝ which was the first corruption. Accordingly I propose ἀλλὰ τἀνδρός· ὡς τάχος δὲ πειστέον κ.τ.λ. For πειστέον = 'one must persuade', cf. Plat. Rep. iv. 421 C τοὺς

φύλακας πειστέον, ὅπως ὅτι ἄριστοι δημιουργοὶ ἔσονται. For the accus. of the agent (ἐξειπόντας) cf. Plat. Gorg. 507 C τὸν βουλόμενον εὐδαίμονα εἶναι σωφροσύνην διωκτέον.

494. **οὖσ' ἐτύγχανες**, cf. 388 n. Her σωφροσύνη, the nurse argues, was really lost when her passion for Hippolytus became uncontrollable: from this she proceeds sophistically to urge that, since the desire as well as the sin is guilty, as she gave way to the former, it is but a small matter to commit the latter. 'Had you really been σώφρων, I would never have urged the course'.

496. **προῆγον** is Scaliger's emendation for προσῆγον.

νῦν δὲ, 'but, as matters stand', cf. Thuc. iv. 126 εἰ μὲν ὑπώπτευον, οὐκ ἄν...ἐποιούμην· νῦν δὲ κ.τ.λ.

498. **οὐχὶ συγκλήσεις...καὶ μὴ μεθήσεις**, cf. supr. 213. Hel. 437 οὐκ ἀπαλλάξει δόμων | καὶ μὴ......ὄχλον παρέξεις δεσπόταις ;

501. **τοὔργον**, 'the sin'. εἴπερ=*siquidem*. τοὔνομ', sc. εὐκλεής, supr. 423, 489, infr. 687, 717.

503. The variants in this line are many but unimportant. σε for γε is due to Porson, cf. Phoen. 1665 ναὶ πρός σε τῆσδε μητρὸς Ἰοκάστης, Κρέον, where is a similar ellipse of ἄντομαι.

504. **ὑπείργασμαι μὲν εὖ.** Bothe's correction οὔ (with which ὑπείργ. must = 'am subdued') has been generally received: but if we give to ὑπείργ. its usual meaning ('prepare land for sowing', cf. L. and S. s.v.) we may translate : 'my heart has been well prepared by love', i.e. is already prone to yield. This agrees with my view of the scene as a whole. Dr Verrall (Med. 871) defends εὖ on these same grounds: see his note.

506. **ἀναλωθήσομαι.** Schol. διαφθαρήσομαι ἐγὼ καὶ ἐμπέσω εἰς ὃ φεύγω. If any parallel in sense and construction to εἴς τι ἀναλίσκομαι (of a person) could be brought forward, this passage would be plain: but I can find none. Barthold (led by Schol. δέδοικε μὴ λαθοῦσα ἁλῷ) conjectures λανθάνουσ' ἀλώσομαι: but ἀλώσομαι εἰς is as hard as ἀναλωθήσομαι εἰς. Perhaps ἀναλωθήσομαι is a gloss, which has ousted the original word bodily from the text: such a word for example as διαφθαρήσομαι, found in the schol. quoted above. Eur. uses (Andr. 709, 715) φθείρεσθαι ἀπό..., Demosth. uses φθείρεσθαι εἰς... of rushing headlong into a party or the like, a sense which would certainly suit this passage. The scholiast then, when he adds καὶ ἐμπέσω εἰς ὃ φεύγω, is explaining the somewhat rare construction with εἰς.

507. 'If that is your way of looking at it (or 'may it please

you'), you ought not to have gone astray at first' (cf. 494 n.) says the nurse: 'but if, as you admit, you have, then follow my advice: that is all I ask: gratitude is a secondary consideration' (or perhaps 'comes afterwards'). Translations such as 'this is a second favour' etc. are pointless, and also would require ἥδε or the like. I see no reason to condemn the clause if proper emphasis is laid on πιθοῦ μοι. On εἰ δ' οὖν (sc. ἥμαρτες) cf. Soph. Ant. 722 and Jebb's note.

509. The nurse I think both here and 478 designedly speaks with ambiguity about the φίλτρον, so as to leave her mistress the means of disclaiming all share in her plot, in case of failure; cf. appendix. Supr. 490 she had spoken quite plainly, and from Phaedra's answers had gathered that her mistress understood and approved. Now fortified by this conviction, she again speaks so ambiguously, that it would not even be clear whether the φίλτρον was intended for Hippolytus or Phaedra: though to Phaedra's own ears the nurse doubts not that φίλτρα κατ' οἴκους—ἣν σὺ μὴ γένῃ κακή—ὄνασθαι μὴ μαθεῖν βούλου—are φωνᾶντα συνετοῖσιν. To line 520 (which she would regard as an actual commission) she merely answers ἔασον—'let be'—and with an appeal to the goddess of love for her help, retires to speak with οἱ ἔνδον φίλοι, to wit, Hippolytus. Lines 513—515 may well be interpolations from the first edition, and as destroying the designed ambiguity of the scene, I have followed Nauck in rejecting them. With them may be compared Theocr. 2. 53.

511. ἐπὶ, of the accompanying circumstances: cf. Soph. Ant. 759 οὐ χαίρων ἐπὶ ψόγοισι δεννάσεις ἐμέ. Soph. El. 108, Eur. Hec. 822.

516. Cf. Aesch. Prom. 480 οὐκ ἦν ἀλέξημ' οὐδὲν οὔτε βρώσιμον | οὐ χριστὸν, οὔτε πιστόν. Theocr. 11. 1 οὐδὲν ποττὸν ἔρωτα πεφύκη φάρμακον ἄλλο, | Νικία, οὔτ' ἔγχριστον, ἐμὶν δοκεῖ, οὔτ' ἐπίπαστον, | ἢ ταὶ Πιερίδες.

519. For ἂν with the participle, cf. Madv. G. S. § 184. 'Know that thou would'st fear anything (if thou fear'st aught here)'. Cf. Rhes. 80 πάντ' ἂν φοβηθεὶς ἴσθι, δειμαίνων τόδε, where the protasis is expressed (δειμαίνων).

521. θήσω καλῶς, a formula of reassurance. Hec. 875, Or. 511, 1664, I. A. 401, El. 648.

522. The nurse uses the same invocation as Phaedra had used in 415.

525—564. First stasimon. The chorus sing the might of love,

quoting the fates of Iole and Semele in illustration. The chorus in Seneca Ph. 279 sq. (*diva non miti generata ponto* etc.) may be compared.

525. **ὁ στάζων.** So Wecklein for MSS ὁ στάζεις, which violates the rule that the article may be used for the relative in the oblique cases (cf. Jebb on Soph. O. C. 747), but not in the nominative. 'Thou who distillest yearning from the eyes'.

οὓς ἐπιστρατεύσῃ. The antecedent to οὓς is ἐκείνων understood, depending on ψυχαῖς: on the omission of ἅν, cf. supr. 427. The military metaphor is kept up in βέλος below (possibly too in εἰσάγων), cf. Soph. Ant. 781 ἔρως ἀνίκατε μάχαν: Eur. fr. 433 ἔρωτα δυσμαχώτατον θεόν.

529. **ἄρρυθμος,** 'in undue measure'.

531. **ὑπέρτερον...οἷον,** cf. Theocr. 9. 34 οὔτ' ἔαρ ἐξαπίνας γλυκερώτερον...ὅσσον ἐμὶν Μῶσαι φίλαι. The full construction would be οὔτε γὰρ...ὑπέρτερον βέλος ἢ τοιοῦτον βέλος, οἷον κ.τ.λ. Eur. is the first author to speak of the bow as an attribute of Love.

ἄστρων βέλος. ἄστρον in the sing. (like ἀστήρ) usually means the 'dog-star'—the οὔλιος ἀστὴρ of Il. xi. 62, the star which φέρει πολλὸν πυρετὸν δειλοῖσι βροτοῖσι Il. xxii. 31. Hence ἀστροβολεῖσθαι 'to be blasted', 'palsied', which Hesych. explains by ὑπὸ τοῦ κυνὸς βάλλεσθαι. (The supposed baleful influence of certain stars produced in Lat. the verb *siderari*, which Pliny uses also in connection with the dog-star.) As both ἄστρον (Pind. O. 1. 9) and *sidus* (Tib. ii. 1. 47) are used κατ' ἐξοχὴν of the sun, some think that sun-stroke is referred to in this passage.

534. **Ἔρως ὁ Διὸς παῖς.** The authorities for this paternity of Ἔρως being only the author of the Ciris (134), Lactantius and Apuleius, Valck. conjectured Ἔρως ὀλίγος παῖς, the English equivalent of which is 'Love, the small boy': other emendations are ὁλοός, δόλιος. Kalkmann's theory is that the allusion to a union between Zeus and his daughter Aphrodite is intentionally made, in order to soften the guilt of Phaedra's passion. But in an eulogy of Ἔρως, it is natural to refer to his close relationship with the *divom pater*, and παῖς may be loosely put meaning 'grandson'.

537. **βούταν φόνον,** cf. Tro. 490 γραῦς γυνή: Aesch. Cho. 805 γέρων φόνος: infr. Ἑλλὰς αἶα (where αἶα was inserted by Hermann): Lat. *anus charta*.

δέξει. Homeric word, found here and Soph. Aj. 226: for the phrase cf. Pind. Isth. 3. 80 ἔμπυρα αὔξομεν.

541. Ἔρωτα οὐ σεβίζομεν, cf. Plat. Symp. 177 A οὐ δεινὸν ἄλλοις μέν τισι θεῶν ὕμνους καὶ παιῶνας εἶναι πεποιημένους, τῷ δ' Ἔρωτι, τηλικούτῳ ὄντι καὶ τοσούτῳ θεῷ, μηδὲ ἕνα πώποτε κ.τ.λ. Also 189 C. The conception of Eros as an independent god is not met with till the later poets : Aesch. does not mention him : this conception was first embodied in art by Praxiteles: for his celebrated statue at Thespiae, cf. Cic. in Verr. iv. 2. 4 *idem...Cupidinem fecit illum qui est Thespiis, propter quem Thespiae visuntur : nam alia visendi causa nulla est.*

542. διὰ πάσας ἰόντα συμφορᾶς, cf. L. and S. s.v. διά, A IV, for examples of this common Attic idiom.

545. Iole was offered as a prize of contest by her father Eurytus king of Oechalia. Heracles was victorious, but the prize being withheld, he sacked Oechalia and carried off Iole.

Οἰχαλίᾳ, for the dat. cf. Phoen. 608 Μυκήναις μὴ ἐνθάδ' ἀνακάλει θεούς : Hel. 375 ὦ μάκαρ Ἀρκαδίᾳ ποτὲ παρθένε.

546. πῶλον ἄζυγα λέκτρων, cf. Med. 673 ἄζυγες εὐνῆς: I. A. 805 γάμων: infr. 1425. For the genit. cf. 147 n. πῶλος, either of a boy or a girl : so μόσχος. Lat. *juvenca.*

547. MSS οἴκων ζεύξασ' ἀπειρεσίαν δρομάδα ναΐδα (ναΐδαν, ἀΐδαν, ναΐδ', ἀΐδ') ὅπως τε βάκχαν. The Schol. (ἀποζεύξασα καὶ ἀποχωρίσασα τῶν οἴκων) helps us with the first line. Matthiä restored οἴκων ζεύξασ' ἄπ' εἰρεσίᾳ κ.τ.λ., cf. Phoen. 239 δόμων ἀποζυγεῖσαι: for the anastrophe, cf. Goodwin § 23, 2. εἰρεσίᾳ, = *remigio*, is found (always in dative) in three other lyric passages of Euripides. Heracles carried Iole away over sea to Cenaeum in Euboea. Wecklein and others, not satisfied with this, read Εὐρυτίων, agreeing with οἴκων. The next difficulty is ναΐδα. The metre of the antistrophe is —◡◡—◡—◡——: many conjectures have been made in order to bring this line into metrical agreement. If however we replace the form ναϊάδ' no further alteration is needed', while if we keep εἰρεσίᾳ, the word is certainly appropriate. Wecklein reads μαινάδα τιν' ὥστε βάκχαν. Musgrave δρομάδα τιν' ἄιδος ὥστε βάκχαν, comparing Hec. 1077 βάκχαις αἴδου, H. F. 1121 Ἅιδου βάκχος, which is very ingenious.

552. I have adopted Weil's φονίοις ἐφ' ὕμνοισιν, keeping the MSS κατευνάσεν (which of course is from κατευνάω, cf. Soph. Phil. 699) : see note on 562.

553. ἐξέδωκεν, 'gave in marriage' : the regular word. Cf. I. A. 964 θυγατέρ' ἐκδοῦναι πόσει.

556. **στόμα**, appropriate to συνείπαιτ' ἄν 'ye would in concert tell'. ἔρπει, of misfortunes coming on a man, Soph. Ant. 585 ἄτας οὐδὲν ἐλλείπει γενεᾶς ἐπὶ πλῆθος ἔρπον.

559—562. In this passage I have adopted νυμφευσαμένα (Kirchhoff), kept the MSS κατεύνασεν, and taken βροντᾷ ἀμφιπύρῳ with τοκάδα. 'For Semele, brought by the lightning-girt thunder to travail of Bacchus, seed of Zeus, having linked in wedlock to a deathly fate she laid to sleep'.

ἀμφιπύρῳ. The force of ἀμφι- in composition is 'on both sides': of περι- 'on all sides': e.g. ἀμφίστυλος of a temple is 'with a row of pillars at the two ends': περίστυλος, 'with pillars all round'. Prof. Mahaffy calls attention to the representation in works of art of the thunderbolt with tongues of flame *above and below*. τοκάδα properly means 'that has just brought forth', Lat. *feta*. Now the birth of Bacchus was hurried on by Semele's shock at the sight of the Thunderer in his glory: cf. Bacch. 87: hence I have connected τοκάδα with βροντᾷ.

νυμφευσαμένα, the middle of this verb is used of the person who brings about a marriage, cf. Ἥρα νυμφευομένη=*pronuba*; Paus. ix. 2 ad fin. Thus Aphrodite fulfils the same function for Semele (νυμφευσαμένη, κατεύνασεν) as for Iole (ἐξέδωκεν). Further I was loath to part with so apt and picturesque a word as κατεύνασεν, for Bothe's colourless κατέλυσεν or Paley's κατέπαυσεν, and accordingly accepted Weil's φονίοις ἐφ' ὑμνοισιν in 552 for the MSS φονίοις θ' ὑμεναίοις, which does not correspond metrically: the more readily as ὑμεναίων awkwardly recurs in the next line but one.

563. Of the numerous slightly differing variants I have chosen that (found in Flor.) which corresponds with the antistrophic line.

We may notice in this chorus the following cases of the recurrence of the same or very similar words in corresponding positions. ἔρως ἔρως 525—ἄλλως ἄλλως 535; ἴησιν 533—ἰόντα 543; Βάκχαν 550—Βάκχου 560; φονίοις 552—φονίῳ 562.

565—731. Second episode. Phaedra overhears the nurse's declaration to Hippolytus, and his indignant scorn. For herself she decides on immediate death, though not without vengeance on her proud step-son.

566. Following Wilamowitz I have transposed 566, 568. τὸ φροίμιον then is the exclamation ἐξειργάσμεθα. Cf. Phoen. 1336 ΑΓ. ὦ τάλας ἐγώ....ΚΡ. οὐκ εὐπροσώποις φροιμίοις ἄρχει λόγου.

567. ἐπίσχετ'...ἐκμάθω, cf. Soph. Phil. 539 ἐπίσχετον μάθωμεν: infr. 1354: H. F. 1059 σῖγα πνοὰς μάθω.

τῶν ἔσωθεν, cf. Thuc. I. 62 ὅπως εἴργωσι τοὺς ἐκεῖθεν ἐπιβοηθεῖν, Hec. 731 τἀκεῖθεν γὰρ εὖ | πεπραγμέν' ἐστίν : Her. 142.

571. The iambics of Phaedra, who is deadly calm (cf. her formal description of Hippolytus, infr. 581), contrast with the excited dochmiacs (cf. 362 n.) of the chorus.

573. The rhythm makes it preferable to take φρένας as the accus. after ἐπίσσυτος (cf. ἄπορα πόριμος Aesch. Prom. 904, χοὰς προπομπός Cho. 21) than as a secondary accus. after φοβεῖ (φοβεῖ σε...φρένας).

575. ταῖσδε πύλαις, the doors of the proscenium. The chorus are below in the orchestra. κέλαδος, of the noise of quarrelling, Hom. Il. xviii. 530.

577. πομπίμα : passive, as Soph. Tr. 872 δῶρον Ἡράκλει πομπίμον. The genit. δωμάτων goes closely with it, 'sent from the house'.

585. ἀχάν. So Elmsley for ἰαχάν. Weil (led by schol. ἰωάν) conjectures ἴαν (found in Aesch. Pers. 936).

589. σαφῶς takes up σαφὲς of 585.

τὴν προμνήστριαν κακῶν, 'procuress of wickedness'. For this use of the article, cf. Heracl. 978 πρὸς ταῦτα τὴν θρασεῖαν ὅστις ἂν θέλῃ | καὶ τὴν φρονοῦσαν μεῖζον ἢ γυναῖκα χρὴ | λέξει: I. A. 1354.

597. φίλως καλῶς δ' οὐ.... For φίλως μὲν...καλῶς δ' οὐ, cf. Or. 100 ὀρθῶς ἔλεξας οὐ φίλως δέ. It is noticeable that Phaedra here recognises the goodness of the nurse's motive, though later, when worked up to passion, she has nothing but abuse for her. This confirms the view that Phaedra was aware that the nurse had gone within to work upon Hippolytus in her favour by some means, though perhaps ignorant of the special means she intended to adopt. In ἰωμένη there is bitter reference to the nurse's words (479) φανήσεταί τι τῆσδε φάρμακον νόσου. Weil gives the line to the chorus, but πῶς οὖν; τί δράσεις; must be the words of a fresh speaker.

601. Hippolytus and the nurse come on the stage, Phaedra and the chorus retiring out of view.

ἀναπτυχαὶ ἡλίου, 'unclouded orb', L. and S. Cf. Ion 1445 λαμπρᾶς αἰθέρος ἀμπτυχαί: El. 868 (of the opening of the eye): so perhaps here, 'Oh, open eye of day'.

602. ἄρρητον ὄπα, cf. ἀνήκουστα ἔκλυες supr. 363.

605. πρός σε τῆσδε κ.τ.λ., cf. Latin *per te deos oro.*

τῆσδε, so BC for τῆς σῆς.

δεξιᾶς εὐωλένου, 'right hand and goodly arm', supr. 209.

606. οὐ μὴ προσοίσεις κ.τ.λ., cf. supr. 498. As above 325, 6 the nurse adjures first by the hands and then the knees.

608. τί δὲ κ.τ.λ., 'how shall I be ruining you, if, as you say, you have done no wrong'?

609. κοινός, 'for all ears'.

610. τοι introduces a recognised fact, = 'you know'. The nurse had used the same argument to Phaedra, supr. 332.

611. Beginners should bear in mind that ὅρκος is according to the oldest and strictest sense the object sworn by, e.g. Styx. Cf. Il. xv. 38 Στυγὸς ὕδωρ, ὅς τε μέγιστος ὅρκος κ.τ.λ.

612. Eurip. has been most unjustly assailed for this line spoken in haste by Hippolytus, and contradicted by his subsequent words (657) and actions. The poet however has had to suffer for it from the days of Aristophanes to our own. Aristophanes parodies the line in Ran. 101, 1471, Thesm. 275. Cicero too (de off. iii. 29) has: *scite enim Euripides 'juravi lingua, mentem injuratam gero'.*

614. ἀπέπτυσ'. Hec. 1276, I. A. 874, I. T. 1161. 'The aorist is sometimes used in the 1st singular, to denote a feeling, or act expressive of it, which began to be just before the moment of speaking'. Hadley, Gr. Gr. § 842. So ἐγέλασα, ἐπῄνεσα, etc. This seems to be the oldest meaning of the aorist.

615. With the sentiment cf. Thuc. iii. 40. 1 ἐλπίδα, ὡς ξυγγνώμην ἁμαρτεῖν ἀνθρωπίνως λήψονται.

616. κίβδηλον, properly of alloy in metal. Med. 516 χρυσοῦ... ὃς κίβδηλος ᾖ.

619. Cf. Med. 573 χρῆν γὰρ ἄλλοθέν ποθεν βροτοὺς | παῖδας τεκνοῦσθαι, θῆλυ δ' οὐκ εἶναι γένος· | χοὔτως ἂν οὐκ ἦν οὐδὲν ἀνθρώποις κακόν. So Milton in Paradise Lost ...fill the world at once | with men as angels without feminine: | or find some other way to generate | mankind.

622. '*Verbum* ὠνεῖσθαι *apud veteres habet aoristum* πρίασθαι *certo perpetuoque usu*'. Cobet VL. 137. 'Each child at the assessment of its worth'. For the genit. cf. Goodw. Gr. Gr. § 178.

625, 6. The incongruity between these lines, which describe the marriage customs of early Greece, and lines 628 sq., which refer to a later state of society, has led to their expulsion from the text by most editors. In heroic times brides were bought from their fathers by ἕεδνα or ἔδνα (perhaps √ svad, *suadeo*), 'persuaders' given by the bridegroom. Later the custom of the father giving with his daughter a portion (φερνή) prevailed. Cf. fr. 772 ἐλεύθερος δ' ὢν δοῦλός ἐστι τοῦ λέχους, | πεπραμένον τὸ σῶμα τῆς φερνῆς ἔχων.

629. **ἀπῴκισ'**, gnomic aorist.

631. Aesch. Cho. 772 γηθούσῃ φρενί is the only example in Attic Greek of the use of any part of the verb, except the perf. γέγηθα (in present sense). It is significant as showing the perfection reached in the plastic arts, that **ἄγαλμα** is frequently used to denote extraordinary or divine beauty. Cf. Hec. 560 στέρνα θ' ὡς ἀγάλματος κάλλιστα: Plat. Charm. 154 C πάντες ὥσπερ ἄγαλμα ἐθεῶντο αὐτόν: Phaedr. 251 A θύοι ἂν ὡς ἀγάλματι καὶ θεῷ τοῖς παιδικοῖς: Eur. fr. 284. 10 λαμπροὶ δ' ἐν ἥβῃ καὶ πόλεως ἀγάλματα | φοιτῶσ'. For κόσμον προστιθεὶς cf. Plat. Phaedr. 252 D (τὸν ἔρωτα) οἷον ἄγαλμα τεκταίνεταί τε καὶ κατακοσμεῖ. ἐκπονεῖ, 'decks out': lit. 'finish off', 'perfect': the word preserves the metaphor of ἄγαλμα. πέπλοισι too would suggest to an Athenian the sacred πέπλος, which was carried in procession at the Panathenaea. Cf. Hec. 466 sq.

633. **ὄλβον** in the double sense of wealth and happiness.

634—7. These lines, mainly on the ground that Hippolytus, though including the whole sex in his condemnation, yet (636) allows the possibility of goodness in a wife, have been bracketed by Barthold: while the awkwardness of the expression ἔχει ἀνάγκην ὥστε κ.τ.λ. has led to many conjectures. The first objection is not serious, as the poet in following out his own train of thought might easily fall into so small an illogicality. The second, though better founded (as so far as I can find there is no instance of ἀνάγκη, ἀναγκαῖόν ἐστί, ἀναγκαίως ἔχει, ὥστε), is not fatal. The translation is not 'he is under a necessity of keeping' etc., which would require σώζεσθαι, but 'he is in a strait, so that he keeps': thus ὥστε σώζεται depends on the general sense, and not on the particular words ἔχει ἀνάγκην. These lines are an excellent example of Eur.'s tendency to lapse into prose.

635. **γαμβρὸς** is any relation by marriage, though generally of the man's family)(πενθεροί of the woman's. For the sentiment cf. fr. 499 τίσασθε τήνδε· καὶ γὰρ ἐντεῦθεν νοσεῖ | τὰ τῶν γυναικῶν· οἱ μὲν ἢ παίδων πέρι | ἢ συγγενείας οὕνεκ' οὐκ ἀπώλεσαν | κακὴν λαβόντες.

637. **πιέζει**, 'tries to counterbalance': lit. 'presses down': so *deprimere.*

638. **τὸ μηδέν**, 'a nobody', 'a cipher'. Cf. Soph. Tr. 1107 κἂν τὸ μηδὲν ὦ. ὁ μηδείς, ὁ μηδὲν, τὸ μηδὲν are all found in this sense.

ἀλλά may perhaps be explained on the analogy of οὔτις ἀλλ' ἐγώ and the like: the analogy however being one of sound rather than syntax, as μηδὲν not τὸ μηδὲν would be required. Kirchhoff conjectures (for ἀλλ') οὖσ', Wecklein οὖσα κἀφελής.

639. ἴδρυται preserves the metaphor of ἄγαλμα, superadding the idea of a stupid stockish creature.

640. Cf. Med. 303 σοφὴ γὰρ οὖσα, τοῖς μέν εἰμ' ἐπίφθονος (where perhaps we might read σοφὴ γὰρ οὖσ', ἀστοῖς μὲν κ.τ.λ., comparing line 298 φθόνον πρὸς ἀστῶν ἀλφάνουσι δυσμενῆ). This and the following line are condemned by Barthold, since μὴ γὰρ ἔν γ' ἐμοῖς δόμοις εἴη κ.τ.λ. assumes the possibility that women, if not σοφαί, might be admitted. The same defence applies here as in 634 supr. See n.

644. μωρίαν, *impudicitiam*. Monk compares Ion 545, infr. 966 n. Cf. Verrall on Med. 61. For the accus. cf. Madv. G. S. § 25.

645. Cf. Andr. 945 ἀλλ' οὔποτ'...χρὴ τούς γε νοῦν ἔχοντας οἷς ἐστὶν γυνὴ | πρὸς τὴν ἐν οἴκοις ἄλοχον εἰσφοιτᾶν ἐᾶν | γυναῖκας.

647. ἵν' εἶχον, cf. infr. 930. Goodwin Gr. Gr. § 216, 3.

649. ἐννοοῦσιν. So Wecklein for ἔνδον δρῶσιν of the MSS. δρῶσιν cannot be right, since δρᾶν 'to act')(ποιεῖν 'produce', 'make'. The line is omitted in Pal. and Flor., but it seems needed to complete the sense.

653. ἁγὼ κ.τ.λ. ἃ refers generally to the previous sentence. The efficacy of running water for purification was insisted on by the Levitical law: cf. too Verg. Aen. ii. 719 *donec me flumine vivo* | *abluero*. Plat. Phaedr. 243 D.

657. ὅρκοις θεῶν, supr. 611 n. Cf. Soph. O. T. 647 ὅρκον αἰδεσθεὶς θεῶν: Hom. Od. ii. 377 θεῶν μέγαν ὅρκον ἀπώμνυ. ἄφρακτος with ᾑρέθην, 'taken off my guard'.

658. οὐκ ἄν ποτ' ἔσχον...μὴ οὐ. Goodw. Gr. Gr. § 283, 7.

659. ἔστ' ἄν ἔκδημος (sc. ᾖ). Ellipsis of ἐστὶ is very common: of εἰμὶ or εἶ rare: of ᾖ also rare. Cf. Madv. G. S. § 215, R. 2. Hermann ἐκδημῇ. Dawes ᾖ 'κδημος.

661. σὺν πατρὸς μολὼν ποδί, *quando cum patre reverso huc rediero*, Markland. Cf. Or. 1217 παρθένου δέχου πόδα, *expecta virginis reditum*. (Monk.)

662. πῶς for ὅπως.

663. τῆς σῆς, emphatic, 'of your audacity I have had experience, and shall know what to expect; how your mistress will behave remains to see'.

γεγευμένος, cf. H. F. 1353 πόνων μυρίων ἐγευσάμην: Hec. 375 γεύεσθαι κακῶν. ὅλοισθε, both you and she.

664—668. Valckenaer suspected that these lines had been imported into this play from the first edition, by the actors, as more than enough on the subject of the shortcomings of the sex had already been said: accordingly he condemns them as '*valde frigidi*'. Euripides might have been anticipating this criticism when he wrote 665. The poet however rather than Hippolytus is speaking here. Cf. supr. 634, 640 n. This habit betrays Euripides into many inconsistencies, the subtleties of the nurse, supr. 250, and the cool analysis so often indulged in where the language of passion would be more suitable. The genuineness of these lines is strongly supported by the obvious reference in l. 731 to l. 667.

μισῶν ἐμπλησθήσομαι, cf. Ar. Ach. 236 ὡς ἐγὼ βάλλων ἐκεῖνον οὐκ ἂν ἐμπλήμην λίθοις.

666. κἀκεῖναι, 'for they too are always—bad'.

668. κἄμ', 'me in my turn'. Cf. fr. 36 γυναῖκα δ' ὅστις παύσεται λέγων κακῶς, | δύστηνος ἄρα κοὐ σοφὸς κεκλήσεται.

668—679 correspond metrically with 363—371.

670, 1. Wecklein enumerates 17 conjectures on these lines. I have followed the MSS, with the slight exception of ψόγου, which I have conjectured for λόγου in 671. The confusion is a very common one, and the change seems supported by fr. 496 αἱ γὰρ σφαλεῖσαι ταῖσιν οὐκ ἐσφαλμέναις | αἶσχος γυναιξὶ καὶ κεκοίνωνται ψόγον. Besides, the repetition λόγους λόγου is disagreeable.

τέχναν...λόγους: the two divisions into which a defence in the law courts naturally fell—legal devices or 'moves' and arguments. This would be sure to suggest itself to Euripides. 'What devices now have we' (the nurse and Phaedra), 'what pleas, to unknit the mesh of men's rebuke, now that we have failed?' σφαλέντες (cf. n. on 349) would be required, if Phaedra were speaking of herself alone (Weckl.). Phaedra still admits her share in the responsibility.

675. 'Who of the gods would appear as the helper of my wickedness? who of men to countenance or abet it?' ἀρωγὸς of direct help: πάρεδρος, ξυνεργός, of help by counsel or cooperation. Cf. Ar. Thesm. 715 τίς ἄν σοι, τίς ἂν σύμμαχος ἐκ θεῶν | ἀθανάτων ἔλθοι σὺν ἀδίκοις ἔργοις;

678. I have ventured to write βίῳ for βίου. Phaedra (674) cries: 'How am I to conceal my misery and shame? I have

actually committed (ἔργων) wrong: it is no longer a sin of the
heart, but of the hand. No god, no man can help me. Formerly
death would have delivered me, and left my name still fair: but not
now'. τὸ γὰρ παρ' ἡμῖν πάθος παρὸν δυσεκπέρατον ἔρχεται βίῳ, 'a
disaster from which death offers no escape' (lit. 'hard to be escaped
from at the expense of life'). The emphatic words are κρύψω and
ἔργων. Wecklein connecting the sentence with the immediately
preceding τίς ἂν θεῶν κ.τ.λ. reads πέρας δυσεκπέρατον.

680. **κατώρθωνται.** On this form of the 3rd plural perfect in-
dicative, cf. Hadley, Gr. Gr. § 464.

682. **διαφθορεῦ,** fem. as φονεύς, Hel. 280.

684. **πρόρριζον ἐκτρίψειεν,** cf. Her. vi. 86 ἐκτέτριπται πρόρριζος
(of a man): Ar. Ran. 587 πρόρριζος αὐτός...ἀπολοίμην.

685. **οὐκ εἶπον** (sc. σοι...σιγᾶν), 'bade I you not be silent?' οὐ
σῆς προυν. φρενὸς then is parenthetic: 'did I not provide against
your intention?' For εἶπον = 'bid' cf. Soph. O. C. 933 εἶπον τοὺς
παῖδας δεῦρ' ἄγειν τινά.

686. **κακύνομαι,** 'become vile'. Hec. 251 οὔκουν κακύνει τοῖσδε
τοῖς βουλεύμασι, | ὃς ἐξ ἐμοῦ μὲν ἔπαθες οἷα φῂς παθεῖν, | ὁρᾷς δ' οὐδὲν
ἡμᾶς εὖ;

687. **ἀνέσχου,** sc. σιγῶσα. Cf. supr. 354 οὐκ ἀνέξομαι ζῶσα.

688. 'Need have I in good sooth (δή) of fresh plans'. For δεῖ
με λόγων cf. supr. 23, 490.

691. This line is universally rejected.

695. **κακά,** 'the mischief I have done'.

696. 'For present resentment overpowers your judgment'.
τὸ δάκνον = 'that which is stinging you'.

699. **ζητοῦσα φάρμαχ'** κ.τ.λ., cf. 479.

700. **ἐξέπραξα.** So Cobet for εὖ γ' ἔπραξα.

701. 'For according to the issues does one gain repute for
sound judgment'. Cf. Med. 218 δύσκλειαν ἐκτήσαντο καὶ ῥᾳθυμίαν:
Soph. Ant. 924 τὴν δυσσέβειαν...ἐκτησάμην: Eur. I. T. 676 καὶ δειλίαν
γὰρ καὶ κάκην κεκτήσομαι. On πρὸς cf. n. on 483.

702. **ἢ καί,** *formula indignantis.*
ἐξαρκοῦντά μοι, supr. 278. 'Do you think it a fair satisfaction',
asks Phaedra, 'after you have injured me, merely (λόγοις) to admit
that you have done so?' For εἶτα after a participle and before a
verb 'denoting antithesis, especially in expressions of censure and
surprise', cf. Madv. G. S. § 175 a.

703. **συγχωρεῖν,** sc. σε τρώσασθαι.

706. **παῦσαι**: but in the present παῦε, never παύου. Cf. Cobet VL. 264.

709. **τἀμὰ θήσομαι καλῶς.** θήσω καλῶς is the usual formula: supr. 521 n. The middle here is forcible, 'I shall arrange for myself'. The nurse retires without a word, and is no more heard of.

713. **ὄμνυμι** properly = 'I invoke as witness': hence with ὅρκον (e.g. Il. xix. 108 νῦν μοι ὅρκον...ὅμοσσον) it means 'I invoke as witness a sacred object'. Cf. n. on 611. From this the transition is natural to the meaning 'I swear'.

The invocation of Ἄρτεμις here by the chorus contrasts with the nurse's δέσποινα ποντία Κύπρι (522). The two oaths would be suggested by the statues of the two goddesses on the stage. Cf. n. on 82 supr.

This oath is introduced, as the schol. would say, οἰκονομικῶς, i.e. in the interest of the action of the play: but for it, common humanity would compel the chorus to enlighten Theseus, and save a life, but spoil a περιπέτεια: however they only escape perjury by falsehood. Cf. infr. 804, 5. The chorus must have been a thorn in the side of the constructor of plots.

715. **καλῶς ἔλεξας**, a mere formula, which takes no count of number. Valck. quotes fourteen cases of its use in Euripides.

ἐν δὲ προστρέπουσ' (or προτρέπουσ') **ἐγὼ εὕρημα δή τι** (or δῆτα): so the mss. which baffles the boldest translator. Where the text is so entirely a matter of conjecture, I have been emboldened to print a conjecture of my own: **ἐν δὲ πρόσθ' εἰποῦσ' ἐρῶ. εὕρημα δή τι κ.τ.λ.** This it will be seen involves very little alteration of the mss, while the sense seems satisfactory. Phaedra had mentioned her intention of suicide before in the play, e.g. supr. 400. The meaning thus is, 'I will repeat, though I have mentioned before' etc.

717. Racine, Phèdre iii. 3 Je ne crains que le nom que je laisse après moi: | Pour mes tristes enfants quel affreux héritage.

718. Valck. thinks that in the words πρὸς τὰ νῦν πεπτωκότα there is a reference to dice-playing.

721. **οὕνεκα ψυχῆς μιᾶς**, 'for the sake of one poor life'.

724. **εὔφημος ἴσθι**, cf. Or. 1326 ΗΛ. τί δ'; ἄξι' ἡμῶν τυγχάνει στενάγματα. ΕΡ. εὔφημος ἴσθι.

σύ γ' εὖ με νουθέτει, 'do you at any rate (unlike the nurse) give me good advice'.

728. **χἀτέρῳ**, Hippolytus. Cf. the use of τις in threats, e.g. Ion 1311 λυπήσομέν τιν' ὧν λελυπήμεσθ' ὕπο: Ar. Ran. 552 κακὸν

ἥκει τινί: 554 δώσει τις δίκην: Soph. Aj. 1138 τοῦτ' εἰς ἀνίαν τοῦπος ἔρχεταί τινι.

731. **σωφρονεῖν μαθήσεται.** A bitter reminiscence of Hippolytus' final words (667). For Phaedra's 'love to hatred turned' cf. Racine, Ph. iii. 3 *Oen.* De quel œil voyez-vous ce prince audacieux? *Phèdre.* Je le vois comme un monstre effroyable à mes yeux.

732—775. Second Stasimon. The chorus long for the wings of a bird, that they may flee away to the distant lands of story, and not be present at the scene of horror, which they know is to ensue.

732—734. Literally 'may I come to be beneath the steep hiding-places, and there (ἵνα) may a god make (θείη, Ion. for Attic ποιοῖ, Cobet VL. 302) me a winged bird, and set (θείη, by zeugma) me among the flying bands'. I have kept the MSS reading, only inserting τε after θεὸς ἐν (734), which brings the line into exact correspondence with the antistrophe (744).

ἠλίβατος. An obscure word used both of heights (always in Homer and commonly) and depths (Hes. Th. 483 ἄντρῳ ἐν ἠλιβάτῳ). The translation above takes it in the former sense, 'craggy hiding-places' being 'hiding-places in the crags', where sea-birds or eagles would nest. With the passage cf. Soph. fr. 423 γενοίμαν αἰετὸς ὑψιπέτας, | ὡς ἂν ποταθείην ὑπὲρ ἀτρυγέτου γλαυκᾶς ἐπ' οἶδμα λίμνας. Herwerden's violent alteration of ἵνα με to χθονὸς ἤ, and insertion of με after θεὸς ἐν, has the one merit of affording the alternative commonly offered by Eur., of seclusion *either* in the depths of the earth, *or* in lands beyond seas (infr. 1290, Ion 1238, Med. 1296). It is adopted by Wecklein.

735. 'May I be borne aloft to where the sea waves wash the shore of Adria' (lit. sea wave of the Adr. coast). The correction ἄλμας seems unnecessary. Adria, now 12 or 14 miles from the coast, was in pre-Roman times by far the most flourishing port on the sea to which it gave its name. Probably of Etruscan foundation, it is said to have received Greek colonists from Epidamnus and Syracuse, and its intimate connection with Greece is attested by the number of Greek vases which have been discovered there.

Eridanus, among the early Greeks, was the name of a large river located vaguely in the north of Europe, on whose banks amber was found: cf. Herod. iii. 115: the amber legends became localized at the trade outlet on the Adriatic, and, by the time of Euripides, the Eridanus was the Padus. Cp. supra 231 n.

738. For the legend of the Heliades, cf. Ov. Met. ii. 340—366, Ap. Rh. iv. 601 sq.

739. πατρὸς is most obscure: construed with οἴδμα, it must mean the river Eridanus; but in the passages quoted in illustration (Bacch. 573, Hec. 451), πατὴρ is applied to a river with reference only to its fertilizing qualities, which is quite inconsistent here. Construed with κόραι, it would refer to Helios; but what point is there in describing the Heliades as 'wretched children of their father'? The metre halts too ($- - \smile \smile - \smile \smile - -$ is required). If the text is sound, τάλαιναι πατρὸς might be connected, 'wretched through their father Helios', who by granting Phaethon's request brought about the disaster. Weckl. reads πόρου (=the stream).

740. Φαέθοντος οἴκτῳ, cf. Thuc. vii. 57 Ἀθηναίων εὔνοια, 'affection for the Athenians', and Hadley Gr. Gr. § 729 C.

741. δακρύων ἠλεκτροφαεῖς αὐγάς, 'the amber gleamings of their tears'. The contrast of colour introduced by πορφύρεον (738) is worthy of Pindar.

742. Cf. Hes. Th. 517 sq.

μηλόσπορον refers to the golden apples, guarded by the Hesperides and the serpent Ladon.

743. ἀνύσαιμι (sc. ὁδόν), 'make my way to'; sometimes with the accus. only; cf. Soph. Ant. 805 ὁρῶ θάλαμον τήνδ' ἀνύτουσαν.

ἀοιδῶν, cf. λιγυφώνων in Hesiod quoted above; Eur. H. F. 394 ὑμνῳδῶν κορᾶν. So Milton, in Comus, ' Hesperus and his daughters three | that sing about the golden tree'.

744. λίμνας. Cf. supra 148 n.

746. σεμνὸν τέρμονα κ.τ.λ. Cf. supra 3 n.

The mss vary between ναίων and κυρῶν. Bothe conjectured κύρειν, and translates, 'no further grants a way, whereby to reach etc.' κύρειν = ὥστε κύρειν.

748. ἀμβρόσιαι κρῆναι, here to be taken literally; for from Sappho onwards we not infrequently find ἀμβροσία the drink, and νέκταρ the food, of the gods; cf. Athen. ii. 8 (quoting Anaxandrides) τὸ νέκταρ ἐσθίω πάνυ | μάττων, διαπίνω τ' ἀμβροσίαν: cf. too Ar. Eq. 1095.

749. παρὰ κοίταις. Herm. conjectured παρ' εὐναῖς, Weckl. πάρ' ἀκτᾶς, alii alia, in order to bring the line into metrical correspondence with the strophe: it is however in the strophe that the fault seems to lie: see 739 n.

750. Cf. Pindar's description (Ol. 2, 77 sq.) of the μακάρων νῆσοι.

ἵν' ἆ βιόδωρος. So Brunck (from A), for ὀλβιόδωρος; cf. Soph. Phil. 1161 βιόδωρος αἷα. On the analogy of ὀλβοδότας, ὀλβοφόρος we should have expected ὀλβόδωρος.

751. Brunck read θνατοῖς for θεοῖς, considering the corruption to have arisen from the similarity of the compendia; it would improve the metre. (Strophe 741 αὐγάς. Weil would there read στάγας, retaining θεοῖς here.)

752. λευκόπτερε. Theseus promised his father Aegeus, that, if successful in his endeavour to slay the Minotaur, he would on his homeward voyage from Crete hoist white sails. This he forgot to do, and Aegeus in despair threw himself into the sea, called after him, Aegean. This story probably suggested the epithet λευκόπτερε. Phaedra made the voyage from Crete to Athens with fairseeming omens; the metaphor in λευκόπτερε is kept up in δύσορνις ἔπτατ'.

753. 'Through the salt sea's roaring ocean wave'.

757. κακονυμφοτάταν ὄνασιν. An accus. in apposition to the sentence: cf. Eur. El. 231 εὐδαιμονοίης, μισθὸν ἡδίστων λόγων. Hadley Gr. Gr. § 626. The words are an instance of oxymoron ; 'to bless her with a marriage most unblest'. (Jebb.)

758. If the MSS reading be kept, we must translate, 'for with ill-omen'd flight, either from both lands, or certainly from Crete, she sped to renowned Athens, and on the shores of Munychia they fastened the twisted ends of their cables, and stood upon the mainland of Greece'. ἀπ' ἀμφοτέρων and Κρησίας ἐκ γᾶς must then be taken very closely with δύσορνις; but even so, the expression is extremely harsh, and Weil's restoration is attractive, ἦ γὰρ ἀπ' ἀμφοτέρων ἦν | Κρησίας τ' ἐκ γᾶς δύσορνις, | ἔπταθ' ὡς (when) κλεινὰς 'Αθάνας, | Μουνύχου τ' ἀκτᾶς, ἵν' ἐκδήσαντο κ.τ.λ. 'For of a truth (schol. ὄντως) fraught with ill omens from both shores was she (the ship), both from the Cretan land, when (thence) she sped to renowned Athens, and from the Munychian strand, where etc.' Weckl. adopts this, merely altering ὡς to ᾶς (=from which land).

761. Μουνύχου δ' ἀκταῖσι. ἀκτή (a rugged coast) is appropriately used here, as Munychia (the Acropolis of Piraeus) occupied a hill, which rose 300 feet above the sea. Cf. Smith's Dict. Geog. i. 306.

ἐκδήσαντο. The augment is often omitted by Homer and the lyric poets, and by tragedians in lyric passages, though rarely in senarii; it is also omitted in iterative imperfects and aorists.

762. **πεισμάτων ἀρχάς.** Cf. Herod. iv. 60 ὁ δὲ θύων σπάσας τὴν ἀρχὴν τοῦ στρόφου καταβάλλει μιν.

ἐπ' ἀπείρου γᾶς ἔβασαν. Cf. Hom. Od. v. 399 ἐπειγόμενος ποσὶν ἠπείρου ἐπιβῆναι, ix. 85.

765. **νόσῳ 'Αφροδίτας ἐρώτων,** the sickness sent by Aphrodite (subj. gen.), consisting in passion (obj. gen.).

767. **ὑπέραντλος** means 'water-logged'; the metaphor was suggested by the previous lines.

768. **τεράμνων ἀπὸ νυμφιδίων κρεμαστὸν βρόχον.** Cf. Hom. Od. xi. 277 ἡ δ' ἔβη εἰς 'Αΐδαο...... | ἀψαμένη βρόχον αἰπὺν ἀφ' ὑψηλοῖο μελάθρου. ἄψεται ἀμφὶ = ἀμφιάψεται.

772. **δαίμονα στυγνάν,** Aphrodite. Observe the tenses of the participles; καταιδεσθεῖσα, having come to stand in awe of; in ἀνθαιρουμένα, ἀπαλλάσσουσα the present denotes endeavour, 'essaying to get her heart quit of its weary load of love'.

776—1101. **Third episode.** The discovery of Phaedra's suicide, and the tablets incriminating Hippolytus, lead to Theseus' fatal curses and the banishment of his son.

776. It is uncertain and unimportant whether the nurse or an ἐξάγγελος is heard shouting from within. I have followed Wecklein's distribution of the lines; 782, 783 are spoken by the leader of the chorus, who puts the question, which is then answered in turn by the ἡμιχόρια.

777. **ἀγχόνη,** 'hanging' in the abstract (κρεῖσσον ἀγχόνης, ἀγχόνης πέλας etc.); ἀγχόναι refers to the actual fact, cf. Hel. 200 θάνατον λαβεῖν ἐν ἀγχόναις.

780. **ἀμφιδέξιον,** Lat. *anceps* = ἀμφήκης, two-edged.

781. **ἄμμα λύσομεν** recalls Phaedra's words (671) κάθαμμα λύειν.

782. **τί δρῶμεν;** Paley, on the similar passage Agam. 1317 sq., points out that, as the play demands that its catastrophe should be uninterrupted, the chorus are made to deliberate on the proper action to take, until all action is too late.

783. **ἐπισπαστῶν,** 'self-tightened'. In Hom. Od. xviii. 73, and elsewhere, ἐπισπαστὸς means 'drawn on oneself', e.g. δεσποτεία, κακόν, etc.

785. **τὸ πολλὰ πράσσειν οὐκ ἐν ἀσφαλεῖ βίου.** The chorus are perhaps thinking of the nurse's endeavours: cf. supra 693, where Phaedra says, ὄλοιο καὶ σὺ χὤστις ἄκοντας φίλους | πρόθυμός ἐστι μὴ καλῶς εὐεργετεῖν. There is a political ring in the line too; at this very time the ἀπράγμονες were urging a policy of ἀσφάλεια on

Athens. Cf. Thuc. ii. 40, 2: ii. 63, 2. τὸ πολλὰ πράσσειν here=
'officiousness'.

786. ὀρθώσατ': horizontal, not perpendicular. So Soph.
Phil. 1299, fr. 421, 5. ἐκτείνειν, to lay out (of corpses). Cf. Alc.
366.

787. In Theseus' absence, Phaedra had been οἰκουρός, and her
οἰκούρημα was thus calamitous both for herself and for Theseus
(δεσπόταις ἐμοῖς).

790. Theseus enters, having just returned from consulting the
oracle. θεωροί were representatives sent on solemn occasions (as to
Delos or Delphi or the great games) by the state. The word was
however sometimes used of an individual going to consult an oracle
on his own behalf, as here and Soph. O. T. 114 (of Laius going to
Delphi, to ask Apollo if Oedipus were really dead). Here we may
suppose that Theseus had been consulting the god concerning his
own purification. Cf. supra 35 n.

794. Πιτθέως γῆρας=Πιτθεὺς γεραιὸς ὤν. Cf. Πολυνείκους βία,
Ποσειδῶνος κράτος, *mitis sapientia Laeli*, *Crispi jucunda senectus*
(Juv. 4. 81).

'Naught ill, I trust (μῶν), hath befallen old Pittheus'. νεώτερος
is commoner than νέος in this sense.

ἐργάζεσθαί τινά τι is generally used of 'doing one a harm', cf.
Soph. El. 1206 μὴ δῆτα τοῦτό μ' ἐργάσῃ, Ar. Vesp. 787. In the
passive it is, of course, constructed with one accus. only; so infr.
799 βίος συλᾶται τέκνων τι.

795. 'Far on now are his years, yet still it would grieve
me, should he quit these halls'. For ἄν repeated, cf. supra 480,
961.

797. γέροντας, the generalizing plural; 'the old'. So νέοι in
the next line.

799. μή, interrog. like μῶν (μὴ οὖν)=*num*.

802. βρόχον ἀγχόνης, the noose of (employed in, belonging to)
hanging; not, as L. & S., the noose of a halter.

803. λύπῃ παχνωθεῖσ': cf. Aesch. Cho. 84 πένθεσιν παχνουμένη.
Hom. Il. xvii. 112 τοῦ δ' ἐν φρεσὶν ἄλκιμον ἦτορ | παχνοῦται.

804. τοσοῦτον, sc. μόνον. The chorus cannot help playing a
despicable part.

807. δυστυχής. A θεωρὸς who was the bearer of a favourable
response from an oracle (as presumably Theseus here) wore a wreath
in token thereof. Fabius Pictor returned from Delphi *coronatus*

aurea corona Liv. xxiii. 11 : so Soph. O. T. 82, the priest argues that Creon brings good news from the oracle, οὐ γὰρ ἂν κάρα | πολυστεφὴς ὧδ᾽ εἶρπε παγκάρπου δάφνης.

809, 810. A problem. The MSS give ἐκλύσαθ᾽ ἁρμοὺς ὡς ἴδω δυσδαίμονα (τὸν δαίμονα Pal. and Flor.) | γυναικός, ἥ με κατθανοῦσ᾽ ἀπώλεσεν. Below (825) the palpably spurious line ἐκλύεθ᾽ ἁρμούς, ὡς ἴδω πικρὰν θέαν is found in very inferior MSS and the early books. Nearly all editors replace this latter line here, regarding δυσδαίμονα as the result of a gloss (on πικρὰν θέαν) τὸν δυσδαίμονα νεκρὸν or the like : this seems the least objectionable remedy. (The gloss may have been the work of some one who mistook θέαν for θεάν, imagining Aphrodite to be alluded to.) Barthold condemns both 810 and 825, but, as Weckl. points out, not δυσδαίμονα but τὴν δυσδαίμονα would then be required in 809. The reading of Pal. and Flor., τὸν δαίμονα (=the fate), would strain the usage of δαίμων beyond what the passages quoted in support of it (Soph. O. C. 76 ἐπείπερ εἶ | γενναῖος ὡς ἰδόντι πλὴν τοῦ δαίμονος, fr. 587 μὴ σπεῖρε πολλοῖς τὸν παρόντα δαίμονα) would allow. (In Med. 1314 practically the same lines are found, χαλᾶτε κλῇδας ὡς τάχιστα, πρόσπολοι, | ἐκλύεθ᾽ ἁρμοὺς ὡς ἴδω διπλοῦν κακόν. It is conceivable that a copyist, having these lines in his mind, may have been led to emend, as he thought, a corrupt line here, such as ἐκλύετε, θάλαμον ὡς ἴδω δυσδαίμονα | γυναικὸς κ.τ.λ. (ἐκλύετε being parenthetically addressed to the servants within, who do not obey with sufficient speed) ; 825 would then be a still later correction, in order to find a construction for γυναικὸς, written at the bottom of the page, and finally incorporated in the text as it stood.)

810. **κατθανοῦσ᾽ ἀπώλεσεν.** Cf. infr. 839 ἀπώλεσας γὰρ μᾶλλον ἢ κατέφθισο.

811—855. Kommos.

τάλαινα κακῶν. Cf. Madv. G. S. § 61, f. 2.

815. **πάλαισμα σᾶς χερὸς μελέας.** In apposition to the preceding clause ; cf. supr. 757 n. 'a fall of thine own misguided working'.

816. **τίς,** sc. δαίμων ; so the Schol.

ἀμαυροῖ ζόαν, 'quencheth the light of thy life'. Cf. Soph. fr. 685 χρόνος δ᾽ ἀμαυροῖ πάντα.

818. **μάκιστα** = μέγιστα. Cf. Aesch. Prom. 629 μή μου προκήδου μᾶσσον ὧν ἐμοὶ γλυκύ.

819. **ἐπεστάθης,** 'hast thou fallen upon'. Cf. Soph. O. T. 777

πρίν μοι τύχη | τοιάδ' ἐπέστη. Herod. iv. 203 ἐπὶ τῇ Κυρηναίων πόλι ἐπέστησαν.

820. The doctrine that the curse brought into a family by an unholy deed (ἄτη) visited itself upon generation after generation of the polluted house is familiar to all readers of the Greek tragedians, of Aeschylus particularly. Cf. infr. 831 sq. 1379 sq.

ἀλάστωρ is sometimes the avenging angel (as Soph. O. C. 788 ἐκεῖ | χώρας ἀλάστωρ οὑμὸς ἐνναίων ἀεί), sometimes the criminal, who is pursued, as here. Later it became a mere term of abuse.

821. κατακονά, 'destruction', from κατακαίνω; a ἅπαξ λεγόμενον. 'Nay rather, 'tis a destruction of my life, which makes life life no longer'.

822. κακῶν πέλαγος. Cf. supr. 469 n.

825. Cf. on 809.

827. τύχω. Cf. Goodw. Gr. Gr. § 256. Lit. 'what hap calling it, shall I be right in calling it, I wonder?' Cf. Aesch. Cho. 14 ἢ πατρὶ τῶμῷ τάσδ' ἐπεικάσας τύχω | χοὰς φερούσας νερτέροις μειλίγματα;

828. 'For even as a bird flown from the hand, thou art no more seen, having cast thyself with sheer leap, woe is me (μοι), into the halls of Death'.

831. 'For from some far-off time I am bringing back upon myself the stroke of heaven, by reason of the transgressions of one of them of old days'.

834. Cf. Alc. 417 οὐ γάρ τι πρῶτος οὐδὲ λοίσθιος βροτῶν | γυναικὸς ἐσθλῆς ἤμπλακες.

836. τὸ κατὰ γᾶς κνέφας μετοικεῖν, 'to change my abode and descend to the nether gloom'. Reiske's conjecture of συνὼν for θανὼν is probable.

839. 'More the destruction thou hast wrought than suffered'. Cf. Soph. El. 808 ὥς μ' ἀπώλεσας θανών.

840. τίνα κλύω; is Kirchhoff's emendation for the MS τίνος κλύω; which violates the metre (cf. 362 n.); the meaning is 'why does no one answer me?' Enger τοῦ δὲ κλύω;

841. The MS order of words is unmetrical; the order in the text is Elmsley's.

843. τύραννον, adject. as often. Soph. Ant. 1169 σχῆμα τ. Eur. Med. 1125 κόρη τ. There are some words missing in the next line; Weckl. suggests ὤμοι ἐγὼ τάλας ὤμοι ἐγὼ σέθεν.

845. οἷον εἶδον ἄλγος explains μέλεος. οἷον = ὅτι τοῖον.

847. '*Tragicis* ἔρημος οἶκος *dicitur quando principalis aliqua persona ex familia moritur*'. Markland on Eur. Supp. 1132.

848—852 are metrically unsatisfactory; the text of the MSS has been however retained, but Wecklein's restoration is subjoined: αἰαῖ αἰαῖ ἔλιπες ἔλιπες ὦ φίλα | γυναικῶν ἀρίστα θ' ὁπόσας ὁρᾷ | πέμφιξ ἀλίου | τε καὶ νυκτὸς ἀστερωπὸν σέλας. | ΧΟ. ὅσον, ἰὼ τάλας, κακὸν ἔχει δόμος. Following Weckl. I have assigned 848—851 to Theseus: line 849 is very natural in his mouth, but unsuited to the fuller knowledge of the chorus.

848. φίλα γυναικῶν. Cf. Alc. 460 ὦ φίλα γυναικῶν. Theocr. 15. 74 φίλ' ἀνδρῶν. Eur. Hec. 716 κατάρατ' ἀνδρῶν.

855. φρίσσω πάλαι. Cf. Hadley Gr. Gr. § 826. So in Latin, the present with *jamdudum* etc. By τὸ ἐπὶ τῷδε πῆμα the chorus mean the vengeance threatened by Phaedra (728).

856. By some the mark of interrogation is put after δέλτος, and a full stop after νέον.

858. ἀλλ' ἦ, '*admirantis est*'. Madv. G. S. 279. λέχους and τέκνων are objective genitives, depending on ἐπιστολάς. This latter word is always found in the plural in tragedy; it is used especially of the injunctions of the dying.

ἐξαιτουμένη, absolute: 'making a request of me'. Cf. Alc. 305 μὴ ἐπιγήμῃς τοῖσδε μητρυιὰν τέκνοις.

862. 'Aye, see, the imprints of her golden bezel, hers, who lies dead here, give me friendly greeting'. For the σφενδόνη (which held the stone) cf. Plat. Repub. ii. 359 E, of the man who became invisible τὴν σφενδόνην τοῦ δακτυλίου περιαγαγόντα εἰς τὸ εἴσω τῆς χειρός.

προσσαίνουσι. The metaphorical use of σαίνειν (properly of a dog fawning) is very common. Ion 697 οὐ γάρ με σαίνει θέσφατα. Soph. Ant. 1214 παιδός με σαίνει φθόγγος. O. C. 320 φαιδρὰ γοῦν ἀπ' ὀμμάτων | σαίνει με προσστείχουσα. Rhes. 55 σαίνει μ' ἔννυχος φρυκτωρία.

864. φέρ'...ἴδω. Cf. supr. 567 n.

866. ἐκδοχαῖς, 'in succession'. διαδοχή is far commoner in this sense. *Metri gratia* Weckl. reads φεῦ φεῦ· ὡς τόδ' αὖ κ.τ.λ. Nauck τοῦτο δ' αὖ κ.τ.λ.

867. μὲν οὖν...βίου, a sad echo of Theseus' words above (821). The sense is, 'an evil (κακὸν), said I? nay indeed, to me the lot of life would be an unliveable one to have (τυχεῖν), in the face of what has happened'. The omission of ἂν with εἴη is certainly harsh, and ἐμοὶ μὲν ἂν has been proposed. The conjectures ἐστὶν (Weckl.), ἔσται (Wheeler), for εἴη, would imply that the chorus regard themselves as personally involved in the calamity of the house: it is more natural to consider them as stating the view they would take, were they in their lord's position. For τυχεῖν, cf. Madv. G. S. § 153.

871—873. The Schol. and most editors reject these lines as spurious.

875. The alteration of λεκτὸν to στεκτὸν (Weckl.) seems unnecessary; the slight awkwardness of λέξον (876), referring to κακὸν αὖ λεκτὸν, would be more neatly avoided by transposing 875 and 876 (Weil). Cf. supr. 846.

877. 'It shouts aloud, aloud, the tablet, things unforgetable; where may I escape the burden of this woe?' The meaning is not 'whither am I to flee?', but 'in what place am I to try to escape from my sorrows?', so that Elmsley's ποῖ is not needed.

φύγω. Cf. τύχω 827 n.

879. οἷον, as supr. 845 = ὅτι τοῖον, and is to be taken closely with ἀπολόμενος οἴχομαι.

μέλος, 'song of woe': so infr. 1178 δακρύων μέλος. Hec. 84 μέλος γοερόν. I. A. 1279. γραφαῖς. Cf. supr. 451 n. Weckl. reads φθεγγομέναν, sc. τὴν δέλτον: so Paley.

881. Cf. supr. 568 τὸ μέντοι φροίμιον κακὸν τόδε.

882. τόδε, what follows, namely the curse.

στόματος ἐν πύλαις, an imitation of Homer's ἕρκος ὀδόντων.

883. δυσεκπέρατον should be connected with κακὸν, as, if taken with καθέξω, we should require the sense, 'though it is hard to let it pass my lips', which the word will not bear. Cf. supr. 678, 824.

884. ἰὼ πόλις. He summons all to hear. Dindorf, thinking this inappropriate, reads ἰὼ τάλας. If any change be made, ἰὼ πάτερ would suit the context. Theseus would thus be invoking his father Poseidon. For ἰὼ, invoking divine aid, cf. Aesch. Theb. 96 ἰὼ μάκαρες. Soph. Tr. 221 ἰὼ Παιάν. Phil. 736.

886. Ζηνὸς ὄμμα. Cf. Aesch. Supp. 381 τὸν ὑψόθεν σκοπὸν ἐπισκόπει | ......μένει τοι Ζηνὸς Ἰκταίου κότος.

887. The construction is μιᾷ τούτων (ἀρῶν) ἃς ὑπέσχου. The Schol. enumerates τὸ ἀνελθεῖν ἐξ ᾄδου, τὸ ἀποστρέψαι ἀπὸ τοῦ Λαβυρίνθου, τὸ πεμφθῆναι τῷ υἱῷ αὐτοῦ θάνατον. So too Cic. off. i. 10 *ex tribus enim optatis, ut scribitur, hoc erat tertium, quod de Hippolyti interitu iratus optavit.* Of the two former wishes we have no traces in Eur. Cf. supr. 46.

890. **σαφεῖς**, 'unfailing'. So infr. 1315. Soph. O. C. 623 εἰ Ζεὺς ἔτι Ζεὺς χώ Διὸς Φοῖβος σαφής.

891. Valck. proposed ἀνεύχου: he quotes Plat. Legg. iii. 687 D ὧν γ' ὁ παῖς εὔχεται...πολλὰ ὁ πατὴρ ἀπεύξαιτ' ἄν with the remark, 'alteri optata si quis evenire nolit, illa quidem dicitur quis ἀπεύξασθαι: qui sua ipsius optata revocat, is dicitur ἀνεύξασθαι'. Cf. too for this force of ἀνα-, Soph. Aj. 476 προσθεῖσα κἀναθεῖσα τοῦ γε κατθανεῖν. According to Suidas, ἀναθέσθαι is to recall a move at draughts.

892. **γνώσει ἀμπλακών.** Cf. Madv. G. S. § 178.

893. **καὶ πρός γε.** Cf. Med. 704 ὄλωλα· καὶ πρός γ' ἐξελαύνομαι χθονός. Heracl. 641.

σφε for αὐτόν, αὐτὴν only in poets.

898. **ἀντλήσει βίον.** Cf. fr. 456 ἀλλὰ μυρίαι | τὸν αὐτὸν ἐξήντλησαν ὡς ἐγὼ βίον. So exanclare, in Latin is used by Enn., Att., Lucil., cf. Cic. Tusc. i. 118 *cum exanclavisset omnes labores.*

899. **καὶ μήν**, introducing the fresh character; in this sense γε cannot follow. Cf. Eur. El. 339 καὶ μὴν δέδορκα τόνδε, σὸν λέγω πόσιν. Soph. O. C. 549, 1249. Ant. 526. El. 78.

903. An intelligible confusion of οὐκ οἶδα τὸ πρᾶγμα ἐφ' ᾧ and οὐκ οἶδα ἐφ' ᾧτινι πράγματι. Elmsley says that ᾧτινι for ὅτῳ never occurs elsewhere in tragedy; certainly ὅτου, ὅτῳ are far commoner than οὕτινος ᾧτινι (in older Attic the former are exclusively used. Cf. Hadley Gr. Gr. § 280). The compiler of the Christus Patiens seems to have had ἐφ' ᾧ τὰ νῦν in his copy. Altogether the case against ἐφ' ᾧτινι is strong, though not unanswerable. Monk, Nauck and others read ἐφ' ᾧ τὰ νῦν.

905. Hippolytus' agitation, which Theseus interprets as cleverly acted pretence, is manifested by the short sentences and somewhat confused construction of these lines.

907. For the antecedent to ἦν, ἤ we go back to δάμαρτα (905). οὔπω χρόνον παλαιὸν = οὔπω χρόνος παλαιὸς ἀφ' οὗ.

910. **πάτερ.** 'It is to you, as my father (emphatic position of the vocat.), that I look for an explanation. You give me none? you surely cannot resent my question as over-curious; were I a stranger, that might be, but one, who is so near and dear as I, has a right to ask your troubles'. There is surely no necessity for excision or transposition of lines, even though 911 is not found in the parallel passage of the Christus Patiens. The emphatic πάτερ in

910 is the key to the thought. 'If I were not your son, my inquiry might be resented and unanswered'.

γάρ (912) introduces the argument of all the four lines 912—915.

913. λίχνος. An experiment of Euripides, not repeated till the time of Plato and Xenophon. The former uses it thrice in the Republic: it seems to mean 'hankering after new sensations'; cf. the English 'lickerish'.

915. κρύπτειν φίλους δυσπραξίας. Cf. Goodw. Gr. Gr. § 164.

916. MSS πόλλ' ἁμαρτάνοντες. Weil (following the Schol. πολλὰ ἐπιστάμενοι καὶ διδάσκοντες, and comparing Hec. 814 τί δῆτα θνητοὶ τἄλλα μὲν μαθήματα | μοχθοῦμεν ὡς χρὴ πάντα καὶ ματεύομεν κ.τ.λ.) reads πολλὰ μαστεύοντες. Markland, πολλὰ μανθάνοντες. Assuming the drift to be, 'among the many errors of men is this, that they teach everything, except the one thing needful', we may regard the Schol. as referring to the general sense, and (comparing with μάτην ἁμαρτάνοντες supr. 197 ἄλλως φερόμεσθα) keep the reading of the MSS. That Eur. did not sympathise with the dogma of Socrates, that virtue was knowledge, and could be instilled by teaching, is probable from supr. 79, 376, where the assailable point in Socrates' theory is brought out, viz. that it took no account of the weakness of man's will. Lines 921, 922 seem a bitter mock at the δεινὸς σοφιστής, who then, in the streets of Athens, was endeavouring to convince men of ignorance, hoping by conviction to drive them into virtue (εὖ φρονεῖν ἀναγκάσαι). That Socrates is meant is rendered more probable by the fact, that he was unique among Sophists, in making moral advance his aim, not worldly wisdom. σοφιστὴς seems here to be used in the ironical sense (cf. Aesch. Prom. 62 and Blomfield's Glossary), which was intermediate between its early honourable, and its later (from Plato onwards) invidious signification. Cf. Grote, Hist. viii. 151 sq.

923. λεπτουργεῖς, 'art refining'.

924. 'I fear lest thy tongue be wandering by reason of thy sorrows'.

ὑπερβάλῃ, 'be overstepping due bounds': absol., as Alc. 1077 μὴ νῦν ὑπέρβαλλ' ἀλλ' ἐναισίμως φέρε. Bacch. 785 οὐ γὰρ ἀλλ' ὑπερβάλλει τάδε | εἰ πρὸς γυναικῶν πεισόμεσθ' ἁ πάσχομεν.

925. Cf. Med. 516 sq. In the H. F. 655 sq. the solution proposed is that the good should have a double youth (φανερὸν χαρακτῆρ' ἀρετᾶς), others but one, καὶ τῷδ' ἦν τούς τε κακοὺς ἂν | γνῶναι καὶ τοὺς ἀγαθούς κ.τ.λ.

927. **ἀληθὴς φίλος.** Cf. Supp. 867 (of Capaneus) φίλοις τ᾽ ἀληθὴς ἦν φίλος.

928. Cf. Hec. 1187 sq. ἀνθρώποισιν οὐκ ἐχρῆν ποτὲ | τῶν πραγμάτων τὴν γλῶσσαν ἰσχύειν πλέον· | ἀλλ᾽ εἴ τε χρήστ᾽ ἔδρασε, χρήστ᾽ ἔδει λέγειν· | εἴτ᾽ αὖ πονηρὰ τοὺς λόγους εἶναι σαθρούς.

929. **ὅπως ἐτύγχανεν,** 'as it happened', a sort of euphemism for ἄδικον.

930. **ὡς...ἐξηλέγχετο.** Cf. Goodw. Gr. Gr. § 216. 3.

931. **κοὐκ ἂν ἠπατώμεθα,** 'and in that case (ἄν, cf. Monro Hom. Gr. § 362) we should not have been deceived'.

932. From the last lines of Theseus' speech, and especially the last word, it suddenly dawns upon Hippolytus, that he is himself in some way concerned, and he breaks out with a wondering ἀλλ᾽ ἦ (cf. 858, n.). Barthold's transposition of 932, 933 to follow 935 is mischievous.

διαβαλὼν ἔχει. Cf. Goodw. Gr. Gr. § 279. 1, n. 2. Cobet VL. 115 warns us that διαβαλὼν εἶχον or ἔξω is solecistic.

933. The emphatic position of φίλων shows that Hippolytus is bitterly applying his father's words, supr. 925 sq. ἔκ τοι πέπληγμαι. Cf. supr. 342.

935. **παραλλάσσοντες,** 'deviating from the straight course'. L. and S. Cf. Plat. Tim. εἰ μὴ παντάπασι παραλλάττομεν.

ἔξεδροι φρενῶν, as I. T. 80 ἔξεδροι χθονός.

938. **ἐξογκώσεται κατ᾽ ἀνδρὸς βίοτον,** 'shall swell generation by generation'. For the fut. mid. thus intr. cf. Ar. Ran. 703 εἰ δὲ τοῦτ᾽ ὀγκωσόμεσθα κἀποσεμνυνούμεθα.

939. **τοῦ πρόσθεν εἰς ὑπερβολήν.** Cf. fr. 284. 4 πῶς γὰρ ὅστις ἔστ᾽ ἀνὴρ | ...κτήσαιτ᾽ ἂν ὄλβον εἰς ὑπερβολὴν πατρός; Hor. Od. iii. 6, 46 *aetas parentum pejor avis tulit* | *nos nequiores mox daturos* | *progeniem vitiosiorem.*

942. Weckl. regards this weak line as spurious.

943. 'who, my son though he be, essayed (imperf.) to dishonour my bed'.

946. **δεῖξον δ᾽.** Hippolytus (943) had hidden his face in horror.

948. **σὺ δή,** intense irony. δή = *scilicet :* ' and so thou of all men, thou art the chosen companion of gods (cf. supr. 85), as being one beyond the mark of others!' For περισσός, cf. supra 445 n., where it is used with a different shade of meaning; σεμνὸς has precisely the same variations, '*nunc in bonam nunc in malam partem pro mente loquentis accipiendum*'.

949. **κακῶν**, 'sin'; so too supr. 425.

950. It is perhaps preferable to take κακῶς φρονεῖν as depending on πιθοίμην κόμποις, though examples of πείθεσθαι τινὶ with the infin. are very rare. 'Listen to your vauntings so as to think foolishly', viz. in imputing ignorance of your real character to the gods. Others regard it as epexegetic of ἀμαθίαν.

952. **ἤδη**, 'after this'. ἤδη marks a definite point or crisis. Cf. Cope's n. on Arist. Rhet. i. 1. 7.

953 sq. **σίτοις**. There is no variation in the MSS, and the Schol. seems to have read σίτοις (with possibly an alternative λόγοις). καπήλευε then is used absolutely, ='play the charlatan': it is found with the accus. Aesch. Theb. 545 μάχην καπηλεύειν (cf. Ennius in Cic. Off. i. 12 *bellum cauponantes*), and Plat. Prot. 219 C speaks of the Sophists οἱ τὰ μαθήματα περιαγαγόντες κατὰ τὰς πόλεις καὶ καπηλεύοντες κ.τ.λ. 'By eating food, wherein was never life, impose on men with your loaves'. δι' ἀψύχου βορᾶς thus signifies the general means as it were of the fraud, σίτοις the particular sphere. βορὰ is used especially of the food of carnivorous animals, so there may be a touch of irony here: however supra 109, 112 σίτων, βορᾶς are used by Hippolytus himself, when ordering food after hunting. Emendations on the part of editors who resent σίτοις (which is certainly awkward), are as unconvincing as numerous, though σέβας is attractive.

καπνούς. Cf. Ar. Nub. 319 περὶ καπνοῦ στενολεσχεῖν.

On these lines cf. Appendix B.

955. **ἐπεί γε**, 'since in truth', stronger than ἐπεί. τοὺς τοιούτους is governed by φεύγειν.

956. **θηρεύουσι**. θηρεύω and θηράω are both found in tragedy, but the latter is preferred. Cf. supr. 919.

961. **τῆσδ' ἂν γένοιντ' ἂν**. Cf. Soph. fr. 606 οὐ γάρ ποτ' ἂν γένοιτ' ἂν ἀσφαλὴς πόλις, | ἐν ᾗ τὰ μὲν δίκαια καὶ τὰ σώφρονα | λάγδην πατεῖται. Eur. Supp. 447 πῶς οὖν ἔτ' ἂν γένοιτ' ἂν ἰσχυρὰ πόλις; Ar. Av. 829 καὶ πῶς ἂν ἔτι γένοιτ' ἂν εὔτακτος πόλις;

962. Cf. Alc. 309 ἐχθρὰ γὰρ ἡ 'πιοῦσα μητρυιὰ τέκνοις.

τὸ δὴ νόθον. A class, 'the bastard'. τοῖς γνησίοισι refers to Phaedra's own children. Cf. supr. 306 n.

963. **πολέμιον πεφυκέναι**. Cf. supr. 13 n.

964. **ἔμπορον**, suggested by καπήλευε, supr. 953: cf. supr. 131 n. ad init.: 'a foolish barterer of life', i.e. in giving up her life to gain so worthless a gratification as bringing suspicion upon you.

966. A Greek valued self-control (σωφροσύνη) as the most precious virtue, a feeling illustrated by Arist., when he placed virtue in the 'mean'. Hence many words, which to us would seem to convey a general meaning of 'good' or 'bad', 'wise' or 'foolish', have in Greek a reference to this fact: e.g. τὸ μῶρον here = 'uncontrollable passion'. Cf. supr. 644 n. The same is true of εὖ φρονεῖν, νοῦς etc. Before ὡς understand φήσεις from 962.

968. **ἀσφαλής**, from ἀ- σφαλῆναι, 'not liable to fall', 'stable'.

970. This line may mean that man's greater strength enables him to keep his passions more concealed, or that, if he gives way, less disgrace attaches to him than to a woman similarly placed.

971. 'Why do I bring these arguments against your pleas?' For the construction, cf. Hec. 271 τῷ μὲν δικαίῳ τόνδ' ἁμιλλῶμαι λόγον. It is noticeable that the λόγοι of 971 are not yet spoken: it was the practice of the Athenian bar to bring up and demolish the possible arguments of an opponent.

977. **οὐ μαρτυρήσει...κτανεῖν...ἀλλὰ κομπάζειν**, 'he will not bear me witness that I slew him, but he will bear witness that I am vainly boasting'.

Sinis was a robber, who infested the Isthmus, and was killed by Theseus: cf. Ov. Met. vii. 440 sq., Her. ii. 70 sq. Sciron was a similar character, living in Megara, also killed by Theseus: cf. Ov. Met. vii. 443. ἑαυτὸν, indirect reflexive, cf. Hadley Gr. Gr. § 683. θαλάσσῃ σύννομοι, metaphor from cattle herding together: for the dat., cf. πύργοις συνεχὴς supr. 226.

983 sq. The obedience paid by Eur. to the rules of forensic rhetoric in the construction of his speeches is remarkable. If we take this speech as an instance, we may subdivide it as follows: 983—993, προοίμιον, to conciliate feeling in his favour; there is no need for διήγησις, so he passes on, 993—1006, to the confirmatory πίστις, drawn from his known character; 1007—1020, the refutatory πίστις; (cf. Theseus' speech, 962 sq.): 1021—end, ἐπίλογος, containing amplification, and the endeavour to rouse feeling in his favour by oaths etc.: (cf. Cope's Introd. to Ar. Rhet. p. 330 sq.). Aristoph. frequently ridicules Eur. for this propensity, e.g. Pax 534 he calls him ποιητὴς ῥηματίων δικανικῶν: Ran. 771 ὅτε δὴ κατῆλθ' Εὐριπίδης, ἐπεδείκνυτο ('made a rhetorical display') | τοῖς λωποδύταις...οἱ δ' ἀκροώμενοι | τῶν ἀντιλογιῶν καὶ λυγισμῶν καὶ στροφῶν | ὑπερεμάνησαν κἀνόμισαν σοφώτατον. Quint. Inst. x. i. 68 *namque is* (*Euripides*) *et in sermone magis accedit oratorio generi, et sententiis densus, et*

in iis quae à sapientibus tradita sunt pene ipsis par, et in dicendo ac respondendo cuilibet eorum, qui fuerunt in foro diserti, comparandus.

983. ξύστασις is the MS reading, but Alc. 797 τὸ ξυνεστὸς φρενῶν, which is brought forward to explain it, means 'sullenness', a signification inapplicable here. I have adopted Herwerden's ξύντασις, 'tension', 'excitement'. These opening lines might be an extract from one of Antiphon's pattern pleadings. 'Your passionate arguments are overwhelming (thus asking for sympathy for the difficulty of his position as respondent); but the case, though it admits of (ἔχον, cf. Thuc. ii. 41 ἀγανάκτησιν ἔχει, gives ground for indignation: so id. ib. οὐκ ἔχει κατάμεμψιν) specious pleadings, if you sift it, is unsound'.

986, 987. An apology for Hippolytus' unexpected oratory, cf. supr. 252 n., 374 n. ἄκομψος, 'unskilled'. κομψὸς is used of sophistic refinements, Eur. fr. 188, 4 τὰ κομψὰ ταῦτ᾽ ἀφεὶς σοφίσματα. Rhes. 625 τρίβων γὰρ εἶ τὰ κομψά. Eur. fr. 16, 2 μή μοι τὰ κομψὰ ποικίλοι γενοίατο.

988. ἔχει δὲ μοῖραν καὶ τόδ᾽, 'there is a due share of influence for this capacity also', sc. εἰς ὀλίγους δοῦναι λόγον. For μοῖρα, cf. Jebb on Soph. O.C. 277 (in appendix).

990. ὅμως δέ. The transition is inexact; there is no ὄχλος before him now; his defence however has to be conducted on the lines which would be effective in a public court.

992. ἄρξομαι ὅθεν κ.τ.λ., 'I will begin from that point, where etc.', cf. Med. 475 ἐκ τῶν δὲ πρώτων πρῶτον ἄρξομαι λέγειν. ὑπῆλθες does not seem the compound required. There had been no secrecy or strategy in Theseus' charge. Should not ἐπῆλθες be read? infr. 1089 ἐπέρχεται ὑπέρχεται are confused in the MSS.

993. οὐκ ἀντιλέξοντ᾽, i.e. thinking I should have no possible defence. It should be remembered that only in the compounds with ἀντι- ἐπι- προ- does λέγω bear the meaning 'speak'. (Also διαλέγεσθαι) cf. Cobet VL. p. 35.

995. οὐδ᾽ ἦν σὺ μὴ φῇς. Cf. supr. 949.

996. The connection between σωφροσύνη and τὸ θεοὺς σέβειν was taught by Socrates: cf. Xen. Mem. iv. 3, 17 οὐ γὰρ παρ᾽ ἄλλων γ᾽ ἄν τις μείζω ἐλπίζων σωφρονοίη ἢ παρὰ τῶν τὰ μέγιστα ὠφελεῖν δυναμένων, οὐδ᾽ ἂν ἄλλως μᾶλλον ἢ εἰ τούτοις ἀρέσκοι. With these lines cf. a fr. probably of the earlier play, quoted by Stobaeus, τὸν σὸν δὲ παῖδα σωφρονοῦντ᾽ ἐπίσταμαι | χρηστοῖς θ᾽ ὁμιλοῦντ᾽, εὐσεβεῖν τ᾽ ἠσκηκότα· | πῶς οὖν ἂν ἐκ τοιοῦδε σώματος κακὸς | γένοιτ᾽ ἄν;

998. **ἐπαγγέλλειν**, Milton's correction for the MSS ἀπαγγέλλειν, 'to require', 'levy': a military metaphor, cf. Thuc. vii. 17. 1 ὁ δὲ Δημοσθένης παρεσκευάζετο τὸν ἐκπλοῦν...στρατιάν τε ἐπαγγέλλων ἐς τοὺς ξυμμάχους κ.τ.λ. So Latin *imperare*, Cic. Fl. § 32 *pecuniam*, Caes. B. G. vii. 64. 1.

999. **τοῖσι χρωμένοις,** 'their associates'. Weckl. τοῖς κεχρημένοις, 'those who need (such services)'.

1000. **οὐκ ἐγγελαστής,** sc. ὤν, in apposition to the subject of ἐπίσταμαι, 996.

1001. Cf. Supp. 867 φίλος τ' ἀληθὴς ἦν φίλοις παροῦσί τε | καὶ μὴ παροῦσιν. Epicurus ap. Diog. Laert. x. 118 μόνον τε χάριν ἕξειν τὸν σοφὸν φίλοις καὶ παροῦσι καὶ ἀποῦσιν ὁμοίως.

1002. **ἐνὸς δ' ἄθικτος.** For the genit. cf. Hadley Gr. Gr. 753 c. **ἄθικτος** : passive, as always in Attic.

ἑλεῖν. Cf. ἁλῶ 420, ἁλίσκεται 913, ἁλίσκει 959, ἐλήφθης 955, and Antiph. 111 ad fin. ληφθεῖσαν τὸν θάνατον μηχανωμένην. Dem. c. Mid. 359 § 260 ἐπειδήπερ εἴληπται πᾶσιν ἐστὶ τιμωρητέος.

1004. **οὐκ οἶδα κ.τ.λ.** Cf. Tro. 681 αὐτὴ μὲν οὔπω ναὸς εἰσέβην σκάφος, | γραφῇ δ' ἰδοῦσα καὶ κλύουσ' ἐπίσταμαι. Cf. supr. 451 n.

1005. **οὐδὲ ταῦτα γὰρ κ.τ.λ.** Understand, 'and very little do I know even then, for etc.'

1007. **καὶ δὴ** puts a case. Cf. Hel. 1059 καὶ δὴ παρεῖκεν, 'suppose he has allowed it'. Med. 386 καὶ δὴ τεθνᾶσι. Madv. G. S. § 236.

1009. **ἐκαλλιστεύετο πασῶν γυναικῶν.** Cf. Her. vi. 61 τὴν δὲ εἶπαι ὡς καλλιστεύσει πασέων τῶν ἐν Σπάρτῃ γυναικῶν. Med. 947 δῶρ' ἃ καλλιστεύεται | τῶν νῦν ἐν ἀνθρώποισιν.

1010. By Attic law a νόθος had no right of inheritance, nor could the father make a provision exceeding 1000 drachmas for an illegitimate child. **ἔγκληρον εὐνὴν** is 'an union bringing inheritance'. Cf. I. T. 682 ῥάψας μόρον σοι τῆς τυραννίδος χάριν | ἔγκληρον ὡς δὴ σὴν κασιγνήτην γαμῶν.

1012. **οὐδαμοῦ μὲν οὖν φρονῶν** MSS, but from the Schol. (συνέσεως) the reading φρενῶν is deduced, which is more idiomatic. Cf. Soph. Ant. 42 ποῦ γνώμης ποτ' εἶ; El. 390 ποῦ ποτ' εἶ φρενῶν; Aesch. Eum. 289.

μὲν οὖν, *immo vero.* Aesch. Eum. 38 δείσασα γὰρ γραῦς οὐδὲν, ἀντίπαις μὲν οὖν.

1013. Another possible **reason** for desiring an union with

Phaedra. Following Markland, I have put the mark of interrogation after ἡδύ, reading in the next line (with Fecht) ἥκιστά γ', εἰ δή. 'But would'st thou say, to reign is sweet? Ah no, not to wise men, since (εἰ δή=εἴπερ) sole rule destroyeth (perfect, of a general truth, cf. Hadley Gr. Gr. § 824 b) the balance of all mortals whom it delighteth'. For φρένας, cf. supr. 966 n.

1016. **ἀγῶνας κρατεῖν.** Cf. Hadley Gr. Gr. § 716 a.

1018. **φίλοις** is in apposition to ἀρίστοις, which=foremost in rank, cf. supr. 409 n.

1019. **πράσσειν,** 'live an active life'. κίνδυνος ἀπών, 'absence of danger', cf. the Latin idiom, e.g. Sall. Cat. 48 *Catilinae nuntiavit, ne eum Lentulus et Cethegus deprehensi terrerent.* Roby L. G. 1406—1411. With 1013—1020 should be compared Soph. O. T. 584—593, where Creon uses the same arguments in defending himself against a like charge.

1021. **ἐν οὐ λέλεκται.** The asyndeton calls attention to what follows.

1022. **μάρτυς οἷός εἰμ' ἐγώ,** 'a witness to my real character', meaning the nurse. For the clause depending on the noun, cf. supr. 998 οἷσιν αἰδὼς μήτ' ἐπαγγέλλειν κ.τ.λ.

1023. **ἠγωνιζόμην,** a word of the courts: cf. Antiph. 130. 7 ὁρῶ γὰρ ἔγωγε καὶ τοὺς πάνυ ἐμπείρους τοῦ ἀγωνίζεσθαι πολλῷ χεῖρον ἑαυτῶν λέγοντας, ὅταν ἔν τινι κινδύνῳ ὦσιν.

1025. **ὅρκιον Ζῆνα...ὄμνυμι.** Cf. supr. 713 n. 'I swear that I never offered violence to thy bed, I swear that never even could I have desired (ἄν) or thought of it'.

1028. **ἢ τἄρ'=ἦ τοί ἄρα.** ἤτοι (=ἦ τοι), though a common formula of asseveration in epic Greek, is extremely rare in Attic, cf. Soph. O. C. 1366 ἦ τᾶν οὐκ ἂν ἦ τὸ σὸν μέρος.

1029. Cf. infr. 1046 n.

1030. **καὶ μήτε πόντος κ.τ.λ.,** a wretch so accursed that land nor sea would suffer the pollution of his corpse, cf. Jebb on Soph. O. T. 1427.

1032—1035. This somewhat riddling allusion to the real facts of the case is all that Hipp. can, by reason of his oath, permit himself.

1034. **ἐσωφρόνησεν οὐκ ἔχουσα σωφρονεῖν,** 'unchastely chaste was she'. ἐσωφρόνησε refers to her actions, σωφρονεῖν to her desires. Similar cases of oxymoron are Ion 1444 ὁ κατθανών τε κοὐ θανὼν φαντάζομαι, Phoen. 357 φρονῶν εὖ κοὐ φρονῶν ἀφικόμην.

Euripides' fondness for the figure is parodied by Aristoph. Ach. 396. ΔΙ. ἔνδον ἔστ' Εὐριπίδης; ΚΗ. οὐκ ἔνδον ἔνδον τ' ἐστίν, εἰ γνώμην ἔχεις. (Valck.)

1035. ἔχοντες, sc. σωφρονεῖν. οὐ καλῶς ἐχρώμεθα, 'exercised that virtue to my hurt'.

1036. αἰτίας ἀποστροφήν. The genit. after ἀποστροφή, in other passages, signifies that *from* which one turns away, or escapes: cf. Med. 799 κακῶν, 1223 ζημίας: here it seems better to translate, 'thou hast spoken a sufficing disprover of the charge'.

1037. ὅρκους θεῶν, cf. supr. 657 n. πίστιν οὐ σμικράν, cf. Med. 21 βοᾷ μὲν ὅρκους, ἀνακαλεῖ δὲ δεξιᾶς, | πίστιν μεγίστην.

1038. ἆρ' οὐκ=*nonne.* ἐπῳδὸς καὶ γόης, cf. supr. 953 n. and Appendix B.

1039. εὐοργησίᾳ, 'calmness'. Eur. uses the word again Bacch. 641 πρὸς σοφοῦ γὰρ ἀνδρὸς ἀσκεῖν σώφρον' εὐοργησίαν.

1041. ταῦτα, i.e. εὐοργησίαν, 'in you of all men, in you, my father, I marvel greatly at it'.

1045. ἄξιον. Theseus bitterly catches up the ἠξίους of the preceding line. 'How worthy of thyself is this thou sayest'.

1046. I have followed Weil in transposing 1047 to follow 1045, and 1046 to follow 1048. There is then no need to omit 1029, as it is to that line that 1046 refers. 1049, 1050 are omitted by most editors, following a hint of the Scholiast. 1049 has crept in from 898. With the general sense, cf. Hor. Epod. 17. 62 *sed tardiora fata te votis manent:* | *ingrata misero vita ducenda est in hoc,* | *novis ut usque suppetas laboribus.* Senec. Med. 19 *vivat: per urbes erret ignotas egens,* | *exul pavens invisus incerti laris.*

1051. μηνυτήν. A favourite word with Antiphon, 117, 16: 132, 17: 119, 31.

1053. τόπων Ἀτλαντικῶν. Cf. supr. 3 n.

1054. εἴ πως δυναίμην, 'I will, if haply I may be able', not 'I would if I were able', which would require the indic.

1055. οὐδ'...οὐδὲ...οὐδέ. A stronger opposition is marked by the use of οὐδὲ with successive words 'no, not'...'nor even', than would have been the case had the more usual οὔτε been employed. Cf. Soph. O. T. 1378 οὐδ' ἄστυ γ' οὐδὲ πύργος οὐδὲ δαιμόνων | ἀγάλμαθ' ἱερά κ.τ.λ.

1057. κλῆρον. Cf. Phoen. 838, where Tiresias says, κλήρους τέ μοι φύλασσε παρθένῳ χερί, | οὓς ἔλαβον, οἰωνίσματ' ὀρνίθων μαθὼν | θάκοισιν ἐν ἱεροῖσιν, οὗ μαντεύομαι. Eust. on Hom. Il. iii. (317, 52)

Εὐριπίδης μαντικάς τινας ψήφους κλήρους καλεῖ, ἃς φασὶ δέλτοις παρεσημειοῦντο ἕν τε ταῖς πτήσεσιν ὀρνίθων κ.τ.λ. ' These tablets contain charges clear and definite, unlike the obscure and ambiguous notes on the augurs' tablets '. That κλῆροι had special reference to augury, is shown both by the passages quoted above, and by Theseus' next words.

1059. **πόλλ' ἐγὼ χαίρειν λέγω.** Cf. supr. 113, and with this whole passage Hel. 744 sq.

1060. **λύω στόμα,** 'unlock my lips '.

1061. **ὅστις γε** = *quippe qui.*

1062. **πάντως** is, in Homer, always followed by οὐ, nor is it found in affirmative sentences till Herodotus. With this passage, cf. Aesch. Prom. 333 πάντως γὰρ οὐ πείσεις νιν.

1064. **ἀποκτείνειν** (*enecare*) is a prose word, never occurring in Soph., and only once in Aesch., though Eur. uses it frequently. For the metaph. meaning, cf. Or. 1027.

1068. **ὅστις,** i.e. ἐς δόμους ἐκείνου, ὅστις κ.τ.λ.

1069. **κομίζων,** in the old sense of entertaining, caring for, cf. Aesch. Cho. 260 κόμιζε (of a tree) = ' take care of it '. Hom. Il. viii. 283 ὅ σ' ἔτρεφε τυτθὸν ἐόντα | καί σε νόθον περ ἐόντα κομίσσατο ᾧ ἐνὶ οἴκῳ.

1070. Weckl. reads αἰαῖ· (*extra metrum*) χρίμπτει πρὸς ἧπαρ. Hartung, παίει πρὸς ἧπαρ. Valck. χωρεῖ πρὸς ἧπαρ.

1071. **φαίνομαι δοκῶ τε,** ' seem to eye and mind '.

1074. Cf. supr. 418, Aesch. Ag. 37 οἶκος δ' αὐτὸς εἰ φθογγὴν λάβοι | σαφέστατ' ἂν λέξειεν.

1075. **εἰ κακὸς πέφυκ' ἀνήρ.** Cf. supr. 1031, infr. 1191.

1077. **οὐ λέγον.** 'The facts are ἄφωνοι μάρτυρες: yet they condemn you '.

1079. **ὡς ἐδάκρυσ'.** Cf. supr. 930 n.

1080. Theseus' comment on Hippolytus' last words. ' Aye, much more hast thou made it thy practice to pay honour to thyself, than etc. '

1081. **δίκαιος ὤν** = δίκαιός τε εἶναι, cf. supr. 105 n.

1082. For Eur.'s views on νοθεία, cf. fr. 345 ὁ μὲν γὰρ ἐσθλὸς εὐγενὴς ἔμοιγ' ἀνὴρ | ὁ δ' οὐ δίκαιος...δυσγενὴς εἶναι δοκεῖ. fr. 168 ὀνόματι μεμπτὸν τὸ νόθον, ἡ φύσις δ' ἴση. Andr. 638 νόθοι τε πολλοὶ γνησίων ἀμείνονες.

1084. As Hippolytus' allusion to his νοθεία reflects on his father, Theseus' anger becomes still more violent: a much finer touch than Racine's, who makes Hippolytus exasperate his father by an allusion to Phaedra's antecedents. Phèdre iv. 2 ad fin.

1085. **ξενοῦσθαι,** 'go into exile'. ἀποξενοῦσθαι is more usual in this sense; cf. Hec. **1221,** Soph. El. 777. The simple verb is found in Ion 819 νυμφεύσας λάθρα | τὸν παῖδ' ἔφυσεν, ἐξενωμένον δέ τῳ | Δελφῶν δίδωσιν ἐκτρέφειν. Soph. Tr. 65.

1086. **κλαίων,** *haud impune,* 'to his cost'. Cf. I. A. 306 κλαίοις ἂν, εἰ πράσσοις ἃ μὴ πράσσειν σε δεῖ. Andr. 758 τίς ὑμῶν ἅψεται; κλαίων ἄρα | ψαύσει. Heracl. 271 κλαίων ἄρ' ἄψει τῶνδε. κλαίων)(χαίρων.

ἄρα sometimes, in poetry, in expressions of indignation or surprise=ἆρα. Cf. Soph. El. 1179 οἴμοι ταλαίνης ἆρα τῆσδε συμφορᾶς. Ellendt lex. Soph. s. v. ἆρα, sub fin. Madv. G. S. § 263.

θίξεται. Heracl. 647 is the only other instance of this future: the verb is very rare in Attic, except in the second aorist.

1093. **συγκύναγε.** '*Attici dicunt* 'Aθάνα δαρὸς ἔκατι κυναγὸς ποδαγὸς λοχαγὸς ξεναγὸς ὀπαδὸς *per a non per* η'. Pors. on Or. 26.

φευξούμεσθα. φευξοῦμαι and φεύξομαι both are used by Eur. and Ar., the latter only by Aesch. Soph. Thuc. Hom. Hes. Herod. Cf. Veitch Irreg. Verbs, p. 597.

1096. 'O blessed home, wherein to pass one's youth'. With ἐγκαθηβᾶν, cf. Thuc. ii. 44. 1 τὸ δ' εὐτυχὲς...οἷς ἐνευδαιμονῆσαί τε ὁ βίος ὁμοίως καὶ ἐντελευτῆσαι ξυνεμετρήθη, Bacch. 508 ἐνδυστυχῆσαι τοὔνομ' ἐπιτήδειος εἶ, and examples quoted by Sandys.

1099. **προσείπαθ',** 'bid farewell'. Cf. Med. 1069 παῖδας προσειπεῖν βούλομαι.

1102—1150. Third Stasimon. The chorus, now left alone on the stage, lament that their belief in the care of the gods for men, which has so often comforted them in the past, receives a shock, when they consider cases of such cruel injustice as that now passing before their eyes.

1102. The connection is as follows: 'Greatly in truth does the thought of the gods' care for men relieve my sorrows. Yet though having within me (κεύθων), as I hope (ἐλπίδι), an understanding of the ways of heaven to man, I am at fault, when I consider how little a man's lot (τύχαι) corresponds with his life (ἔργματα)', i.e. as in the case of Hippolytus, a man's ἔργματα may be good, his τύχαι bad. Cf. Sen. Ph. 995 *castos sequitur mala paupertas, vitioque potens regnat adulter.*

θεῶν, subj. genit.

1105. **κεύθων.** Here and in the next strophe (λεύσσων, 1120), the masc. gender, in the antistrophes, the femin. is used (εὐξαμένᾳ, μεταβαλλομένᾳ). The masc. is used in the more general statement, as though the construction were λείπεταί τις λεύσσων, the femin. in the expression of the personal wishes of the chorus as individuals. The Schol. accounts for the gender by the remark, that Eur. is himself speaking in the strophes.

1106. **λεύσσων,** absolute, or rather we must supply τύχας and ἔρυματα as objects.

1108. 'For fresh haps succeed from fresh quarters, and life for men is ever shifting, ever wandering'.

1112. **τύχαν μετ' ὄλβου**=ὀλβίαν τύχαν.

1115. 'And may my judgment be neither rigid, unbending, unable to make allowances, nor on the other hand over-pliant and insincere (παράσημος, metaphor from false coin); but, easily adjusting my ways on the morrow, may I be happy my life long'. I am by no means sure of the interpretation of these lines.

1120. **καθαράν,** 'clear from doubt'. This strophe continues the reflections of the strophe preceding.

1122. **ἀστέρ' Ἀθάνας.** φέγγος is used thus of persons, Aesch. Ag. 602, Ar. Pl. 640, Eq. 1319 ὦ ταῖς ἱεραῖς φέγγος Ἀθήναις. φάος also Hec. 841, but for examples of ἀστήρ so used, Valck. has to go to the Anthology: cf. however Hom. Il. vi. 401 (of Astyanax) ἀλίγκιον ἀστέρι καλῷ. One version of the death of Hippolytus translated him to heaven as the star ἡνίοχος, Paus. ii. 32. 1.

1126. **ψάμαθοι πολιήτιδος ἀκτᾶς,** cf. supr. 229.

δρυμός τ' ὄρειος, cf. supr. 215.

1129. The MSS give ὅθι κυνῶν ὠκυπόδων ἐπέβας θεᾶς μέτα θήρας ἐναίρων κ.τ.λ. ἐπέβας was introduced from 1131, and θεᾶς is due to the influence of μέτα. The corrections of Brunck and Blomfield bring the lines into correspondence with the antistrophe.

1131. **οὐκέτι** repeats the οὐκέτι at the beginning of the strophe, 1120.

συζυγίαν πώλων ἐπιβάσει. Since συζυγίαν πώλων=πώλους, on the analogy of ἵπποι=chariot (cf. ἵππων ἐπεβήσετο Hom. Il. x. 513, ἐπιβησόμενος v. 46), συζυγία πώλων is here used for the car drawn by a pair of horses. As the accus. is very rare after ἐπιβαίνειν (Hes. Sc. 286 νῶθ' ἵππων ἐπιβάντες), it might be well to read συζυγίας here.

Ἐνετᾶν, cf. supr. 231 n.

1133. **Ἀίμνας**, cf. supr. 228 n. The occurrence of the word ἱπποκρότων in the very similar lines 228—231 supports Weckl.'s rendering of ποδὶ = *quadrupedante sonitu*: κατέχων then = 'filling'. Cf. Hom. Il. xvi. 79 ἀλαλητῷ πᾶν πεδίον κατέχουσι. Soph. Phil. 10 ἀλλ' ἀγρίαις | κατεῖχ' ἀεὶ πᾶν στρατόπεδον δυσφημίαις.

1135. 'And Melody, erst sleepless 'neath the lyre-strings' bridge, will cease throughout his father's palace'. The Troezenians offered joint sacrifices to Sleep and the Muses on a special altar, λέγοντες τὸν ὕπνον θεῶν μάλιστα εἶναι φίλον ταῖς Μούσαις. Paus. ii. 31. 5.

1137. **ἀστέφανοι δὲ κόρας κ.τ.λ.** Cf. the opening scene, 73 sq.

1140. **φυγᾷ**, 'banishment'. νυμφίδια ἄμιλλα λέκτρων, lit. 'bridal-rivalry for thy couch', cf. Hec. 352 ζῆλον οὐ σμικρὸν γάμων | ἔχουσ', ὅτου δῶμ' ἐστίαν τ' ἀφίξομαι.

1143. **πότμον ἄποτμον διοίσω**, cf. ἀβίοτος βίου τύχα, supr. 868.

1145. **ἔτεκες ἀνόνατα**, cf. Hec. 765 ἦ γάρ τιν' ἄλλον ἔτεκες ἢ κείνους, γύναι; | ἀνόνητά γ' ὡς ἔοικε τόνδ' ὃν εἰσορᾷς. Alc. 412.

1147. **συζύγιαι Χάριτες**, cf. H. F. 673 οὐ παύσομαι τὰς Χάριτας | Μούσαις συγκαταμιγνὺς | ἀδίσταν συζυγίαν. συζύγιος as an adj. is only found here: the reference may be to some known work of art, where the Charites were represented linked hand in hand. The Schol. however says ἔφοροι τῆς συζυγίας, in support of which it should be remembered, that in Pindar the Χάριτες are the goddesses of the victory-song, cf. e.g. Pyth. 8. 21. At any rate the word seems to have been suggested by συζυγίαν, supr. 1131.

1151—1267. Fourth episode.

1158. 'To you, and to the citizens both of Athens and of Troezen'. (πολίταις, οἵ τε Ἀθηναίων πόλιν καὶ οἳ γῆς τερμ. Τρ. ναίουσι).

1162. **ὡς εἰπεῖν** is used to modify πᾶς and οὐδεὶς (and words compounded with them), ἔμβραχυ being employed for the same purpose with ὅστις, ὅς ἄν, and the like. Cobet VL. p. 208.

1163. 'His life however is still in him, albeit trembling in the balance'.

1164. **δι' ἔχθρας μῶν τις ἦν ἀφιγμένος**; cf. supr. 542 n. Monk quotes a large number of examples of this idiom.

1167. Notice the frequent recurrence of the letter σ; cf. Med. 476 ἔσωσά σ' ὡς ἴσασιν Ἑλλήνων ὅσοι, and Porson's note. Eur.'s '*sigmatismus*' was ridiculed by the comic poets.

1169. **ὡς ἄρ' ἦσθ' ἐμὸς πατήρ,** cf. supr. 359 n. By one account Aethra was mother of Theseus by Poseidon, cf. Paus. ii. 33. 1.

1171. **πῶς καὶ διώλετ';** cf. supr. 92 n.

1172. **ῥόπτρον.** Properly the piece of wood in a trap, which falls and secures the victim. The Schol. explains by ῥόπαλον, while Suidas has ῥόπτρον· ῥόπαλον ἢ παγὶς ἢ τιμωρία. Weckl. compares Aesch. Ag. 531 τοῦ δικηφόρου | Διὸς μακέλλῃ τῇ κατείρ-γασται πέδον.

1173. The **ψάμαθοι ἀκύμαντοι** of supr. 235 were ἀκτῆς κυμο-δέγμονος πέλας.

1176. **ἀναστρέψοι.** It should be borne in mind that the only use of the fut. opt. is to represent in orat. obliq. a fut. indic. of orat. rect. Cf. Goodw. Gr. Gr. § 203, n. 3.

1178. **μέλος δακρύων,** 'a strain of tears'. Cf. Hec. 84 μέλος γοερόν, supr. 879.

1182. **τί ταῦτ' ἀλύω;** cf. Or. 277 τί χρῆμ' ἀλύω; ἀλύειν is to lose control over oneself from frenzy, fear, grief or the like.

1186. The potential optative without **ἄν** is very rare, even in poetry. Cf. Aesch. Prom. 291 οὐκ ἔστιν ὅτῳ μείζονα μοῖραν | νείμαιμ' ἢ σοί: Bacch. 747 θᾶσσον... | ἢ σὺ ξυνάψαις βλέφαρα βασιλείοις κόραις (accepted by most editors; but Weckl. ἢ σὲ ξυνάψαι), I. A. 418 ὥστε τερφθείης ἰδών. Cf. supr. 469 n. Hadley, Gr. Gr. § 872 e. Weckl. here reads θᾶσσον ἢ λόγοισιν, and compares I. T. 836 ὦ κρεῖσσον ἢ λόγοισιν εὐτυχῶν ἐμοῦ (where however Hartung reads λέγοι τις).

1188. **ἀπ' ἄντυγος.** ἄντυξ in its most general sense means an encircling rim, e. g. of a shield. Applied to a chariot, it denotes the rail which ran round the front; an example may be seen in Rich's Dict. of Ant. s. v. *currus* 2. To it commonly the reins were attached; cf. Hom. Il. v. 262 ἐξ ἄντυγος ἡνία τείνας. The use of the word supr. 1135, to denote the bridge over which the lyre-strings were stretched, may have been suggested by a resemblance to the reins lying over the ἄντυξ of a chariot.

1189. **αὐταῖσιν ἀρβύλαισιν ἁρμόσας πόδας,** lit. 'having fixed his feet in the car, hunting-boots and all'. Weckl. follows Schol. Eust. and Valck. in thinking that by ἄρβυλαι is meant a part of the chariot, in which the driver might firmly fix his feet ('foot-holes' apparently); but this meaning is unsupported; besides, αὐταῖσιν would be at least unnecessary, while the idiom, of which it is an example, if we take ἀρβύλαις in its usual sense, is so common as hardly to require illustration. Cf. Hadley, Gr. § 744 a; Bacch. 1133 ἔφερε δ' ἡ μὲν ὠλένην | ἡ δ' ἴχνος αὐταῖς ἀρβύλαις. The reason for the introduction of the words αὐτ. ἀρβ. I imagine to be, that, since in ordinary cases it would be unusual to wear heavy hunting-boots when driving, so by mentioning them here, the poet emphasizes the suddenness of Hippolytus' departure.

1190. ἀναπτύξας χέρας. Cf. Hor. Od. iii. 23. 1 *caelo supinas si tuleris manus*, Hom. Il. vii. 177 λαοὶ δ' ἠρήσαντο θεοῖσι δὲ χεῖρας ἀνέσχον. The well-known statue of the 'Praying Boy' illustrates these passages.

1193. ἤτοι...ἤ. Special emphasis is placed on the first alternative, cf. Hadley Gr. § 1045, 1. a.

1195. The reading is uncertain; the MSS have πώλοις ὁμαρτῇ πρόσπολοι δ' ἐφ' ἄρματι, with variants ἐφ' ἄρματος, ὑφ' ἄρματος and in A, the oldest MS, ἐφασκομ corrected to ἐφαρμοτμ.

ὁμαρτῇ = ὁμοῦ (Hesych.) occurs also Hec. 839, Heracl. 138. I have followed Markland in punctuating after πώλοις. For the position of δέ, cf. Aesch. Ag. 606 γυναῖκα πιστὴν δ' ἐν δόμοις εὕροι μολών. The difficulty of the last four syllables is insoluble; they evidently were corrupted very early, and we can but guess at the words they have supplanted. Weckl. reads πώλοις ὁμοκλῇ· πρόσπολοι δ' ἄκασχ' ὁμοῦ, the last two words being due to Nauck: ἄκασκα means 'gently', and occurs once, in Cratinus (L. and S.). Perhaps ἀφάρτεροι (Hom. Il. xxiii. 311), 'fleeter', may have been in the original. 'The fleeter of foot among us ran with our master'. It is a rare word and would easily be corrupted.

1196. εἱπόμεσθα δεσπότῃ. If we regard the origin of the distinction between ἕπεσθαι τινὶ and ἕπεσθαι μετά τινος to have been, that the former meant 'to go along with' a person, the latter 'to go in a person's train', the dictum of Cobet, referred to supr. 290 n., that ἕπ. τινὶ is used of equals, ἕπ. μετά τινος of inferiors, still holds good, and at the same time, the use of the dative in cases like the present, where the servants are described as running *alongside of* their master, is no longer anomalous.

1197. τὴν εὐθὺς Ἄργους κἀπιδαυρίας ὁδόν. The breach of the rule, that εὐθύ is of place, and εὐθύς of time, has led to the correction τὴν εὐθύ τ' Ἄργους κ.τ.λ. It is not to be doubted, that the common Attic idiom, in cases like the present, was εὐθὺ with the genit. Cf. Thuc. viii. 88 εὐθὺ τῆς Φασήλιδος, Ar. Av. 1421 εὐθὺ Πελλήνης, but since Homer uses ἰθὺς in this sense with the genit.

(cf. Il. xii. 106 βάν ῥ' ἰθὺς Δαναῶν), and εὐθὺς for εὐθὺ became frequent in later Greek, there is no need to disturb the text.

1198. **εἰσεβάλλομεν**, cf. Bacch. 1045 λέπας Κιθαιρώνειον εἰσεβάλλομεν. The word implies violent motion, and is very commonly used of hostile raids, cf. Herod. i. 15: Thuc. vi. 70.

1199. **ἀκτή τις ἔστι**, 'there is as you know'. τοὐπέκεινα τῆσδε γῆς means beyond the boundary of Troezenia.

1201, 2. Notice the intentional repetition of β and ρ. Racine has imitated this description, Phèdre v. 6.

χθόνιος βροντή, cf. El. 748 ὥστε νερτέρα βροντὴ Διός, Aesch. Prom. 1025 βροντήμασι χθονίοις κυκάτω πάντα.

1204. Eur.'s contemporary Hippocrates speaks of νεανικὸν ῥῖγος, αἱμορραγία νεανική.

1205. **πόθεν** for ὁπόθεν. Cf. Soph. Aj. 794 ὥστε μ' ὠδίνειν τί φής, Aesch. Cho. 84 οὐδ' ἔχω τί φῶ.

1206. **ἱερόν**, 'mighty', cf. Cycl. 265 ἱερὰ κύματα, Hom. Il. xvi. 407 ἱερὸν ἰχθύν.

1207. **στηρίζον**, 'rising solid', cf. Hom. Il. iv. 443 (of Ἔρις) ἥ τ' ὀλίγη μὲν πρῶτα κορύσσεται, αὐτὰρ ἔπειτα | οὐρανῷ ἐστήριξε κάρη καὶ ἐπὶ χθονὶ βαίνει, Eur. Bacch. 972 ὥστ' οὐρανῷ στηρίζον εὑρήσεις κλέος. The construction is ὥστ' ὄμμα τοὐμὸν ἀφῃρέθη Σκ. ἄκραν, εἰσορᾶν αὐτήν. Hadley Gr. § 724 a: so Soph. Phil. 1303 τί μ' ἄνδρα πολέμιον | ἐχθρόν τ' ἀφείλου μὴ κτανεῖν τόξοις ἐμοῖς;

1208. **Σκιρωνίδ' ἄκραν.** So Kirchhoff from Σκίρωνος δ' ἀκτᾶς of A. Compare Sen. Ph. 1031 *latuere rupes, limen Epidauri dei | et scelere petrae nobiles Scironides | et quae duobus terra comprimitur fretis.* Aesculapius was specially worshipped at Epidaurus. In the precincts of his temple there is laid the opening scene of Plautus' Curculio.

1210. **ἀφρόν**, cogn. acc. after καχλάζον: the latter word is onomatop. according to the Etym. M. ὁ γὰρ ἦχος τοῦ κύματος ἐν τοῖς κοιλώμασι τῶν πετρῶν γινόμενος δοκεῖ μιμεῖσθαι τὸ κάχλα κάχλα.

1213. 'at the very moment of the breaking of the mighty surge, the wave shot forth a bull, a monster wondrous fierce'.

1216. **φρικῶδες**, supr. 1202, 138 n.

1217. **κρεῖσσον δεργμάτων** is translated 'too fearful for our eyes to look upon'. Musgrave proposed φθεγμάτων.

1220. **πολὺς ξυνοικῶν**, 'being familiar with'.

1222. He not only pulled with his arms, but fastening the reins round his waist at the back, threw his whole weight on to

them, as a rower does on to his oar.   This was a regular practice
with chariot drivers, and was, as here, a fertile source of disaster.
Homer always uses the form τὰ ἡνία.

1223. **ἐνδακοῦσαι στόμια,** 'getting the bit between their
teeth'. Cf. Aesch. Prom. 1010 δακὼν δὲ στόμιον ὡς νεοζυγὴς | πῶλος
βιάζῃ.

1224. **βίᾳ φέρουσιν,** 'run away'. Cf. the similar passage in
Soph. El. 725 ἔπειτα δ' Αἰνιᾶνος ἀνδρὸς ἄστομοι | πῶλοι βίᾳ φέρουσιν.
The metaphor, commenced in κώπην 1221, is sustained in ναυκλήρου
1224, οἴακας 1227.

1226. **μεταστρέφουσαι** for the more usual ἐπιστρέφουσαι, 'regarding', 'obeying', or perhaps the force of μετα- is, 'changing
their course' out of regard for.

1228. **ἔμπροσθεν** is a purely prose word.   I have adopted
Wecklein's ἐκ τοῦ πρόσθεν.

1229. **τέτρωρον ὄχον,** the team: so infr. 1355.   Alc. 483 ἅρμα
τέτρωρον, of the horses of Diomed.

1232. **ἀνεχαίτισεν,** 'he overturned' (the car).   The metaphor
is from a horse throwing its rider.

1233. **ἁψῖδα,** the wheel.   σύριγγες, the axle boxes.   ἐνήλατα,
the linch-pins.   Our oldest MS A stops here.

1236. **ἡνίαισιν ἐμπλακείς,** 'entangled in the ruins'.   Cf. 1222 n.
δεσμὸν δεθείς, cf. Hadley Gr. § 715 a.   With these lines compare
Ov. Met. xv. 500—529.

1242. Comparing the previous line, and infr. 1362, and Aesch.
Theb. 898, possibly ἀραῖον might be read for ἄριστον.

1245. **τμητῶν ἱμάντων.**   τμητ. is an *epitheton constans,*
'shapely'. Cf. Hom. Il. x. 567 ἵππους μὲν κατέδησαν εὐτμήτοισιν
ἱμᾶσιν, Soph. El. 747 (a passage which should be compared
with this).

1246. Weckl. for πίπτει reads τείνει, which he connects with
βίοτον.

1247. **ἔκρυφθεν** for ἐκρύφθησαν.   This form of the 3rd plur.
though very common in epic (cf. Goodwin Gr. § 119. 9) is extremely rare in Attic, cf. Ar. Vesp. 662 κατένασθεν.   Much license
is allowed in the long ῥήσεις of ἄγγελοι.   Paley thinks 1247, 1248
may be spurious, and calls attention to the inappropriate epithet
δύστηνον, and the feeble iteration in οὐ κάτοιδ' ὅπου.   The latter
may well be intentional, and meant to show the excited state of the
messenger.

1253. It is not unnatural to suppose that Ida in Crete is referred to, considering that Crete was Phaedra's birth-place. Ida however was a generic term for any wooded hill. Herod. constantly uses ἴδη=timber. The reference is of course to the incriminating tablets found upon Phaedra's body. For πεύκη= δέλτος, cf. I. A. 39 ῥίπτεις τε πέδῳ πεύκην.

1255. 'the hap of fresh disasters has been fulfilled, nor is there means of escape from destiny and the inevitable'. For τοῦ χρεών (which is indeclinable, and in Eur. is always accompanied by the article), cf. H. F. 21 τοῦ χρεών μέτα.

1258. ἤσθην. 'My first emotion was one of joy; but now I recognise the heaven-sanctioned ties of blood, and forbear to rejoice, as I forbear to grieve'.

1261. τί δράσαντας τὸν ἄθλιον. For the double accus. cf. Hadley Gr. § 725 a.

1265. ἰδὼν ἐν ὄμμασι, cf. Hom. Il. i. 587 μή σε φίλην περ ἐοῦσαν ἐν ὀφθαλμοῖσιν ἴδωμαι | θεινομένην, Eur. Or. 1020 ὥς σ' ἰδοῦσ' ἐν ὄμμασι | πανυστάτην πρόσοψιν ἐξέστην φρενῶν.

1268—1282. Fourth Stasimon. A short ode on the might of Love. 'The unbending heart of gods and men thou leadest captive, Cypris; and with thee, he with the wing of shifting hue, circling on swiftest wing around them: he flieth over land and tuneful waters of the seas: Eros doth bind with spells him, whoe'er he be, on whose frenzied heart winged he swoopeth, with golden gleam: bindeth too the brood of mountain whelps: of whate'er is in the waters: of whate'er earth nurtures, earth, that warms beneath the gaze of Helios; men too he bindeth: over all, all, thou Cypris wieldest queenly sway, and thou alone'.

1268. The power of love has been celebrated already in this play, 445 sq., 525 sq.

1270. ποικιλόπτερος. The jarring repetition of πτερῷ in the next line has many parallels in this and other plays of Eur., cf. supr. 138 n.

1274. The MSS vary between φλέγει and θέλγει. Weckl. reads φλέγει and infr. 1275 πανὸν ἐφορμάσῃ | χρυσοφαῆ. This seems unnecessary. Both ᾧ and κραδίᾳ follow ἐφορμάσῃ.

1275. ἐφορμάσῃ. For the subj. without ἄν, cf. supr. 427.

1277. φύσιν σκυλάκων, cf. Soph. Ant. 345 πόντου δ' εἰναλίαν φύσιν.

1279. αἰθομέναν is proleptic: as also is μαινομένᾳ, supr. 1274.

1280. **ἄνδρας τε.** Notice the emphatic position of the climax.

1281. **τιμὰν κρατύνεις,** cf. Aesch. Ag. 1471 κράτος κρατύνεις. **τιμὴ βασιληΐς** is Homeric. Il. vi. 193 δῶκε δέ οἱ τιμῆς βασιληΐδος ἥμισυ πάσης.

1282. The final words μόνα κρατύνεις would still be echoing in the theatre, as the rival goddess Artemis appears.

1283. A *deus* or *dea ex machina* solves eight other of Eur.'s extant plays, viz. Or. Andr. Supp. I. T. Bacch. Hel. Ion, El. The doubt as to the parentage of Theseus, whether Aegeus or Poseidon was to be regarded as his father, may be paralleled by the similar obscurity in the case of Heracles, where the rival claimants were Zeus and Amphitryon. Theseus himself recognises the difficulty, supr. 1169. Supr. 152 Theseus is addressed as εὐπατρίδης.

1288. I have followed Weckl.'s transposition of δὲ to follow μύθοις instead of φανερὰν, placing a comma at ἀφανῆ, 'having persuaded thyself of dark (i.e. unproven) things, thou hast gotten manifest ruin'.

1289. **ἔσχεθες.** For a discussion of this and similar aorists, cf. Ellendt Lex. Soph. s.v. εἰκαθεῖν.

1290. **ὑπὸ γῆς τάρταρα.** Cf. Hes. Theog. 871 τάρταρα γαίης. In the sing. τάρταρος is both masc. and fem., in the plural generally neut. Compare with this passage supr. 732 sq.

1292. **ἄνω μεταβὰς βίοτον,** 'removing to a life in upper air'.

1293. Cf. Aesch. Prom. 263 ὅστις πημάτων ἔξω πόδα | ἔχει, Heracl. 109 καλὸν δέ γ᾽ ἔξω πραγμάτων ἔχειν πόδα.

1297. 'Yet will I not make thy path easy'.

1299. **ὑπ᾽ εὐκλείας,** 'with honour'. ὑπὸ with the genit. is used to denote accompaniment (e.g. of music, πίνειν ὑπὸ σάλπιγγος, Ar. Ach. 1001). Monk quotes Hec. 351 ἔπειτ᾽ ἐθρέφθην ἐλπίδων καλῶν ὕπο, Soph. El. 630 οὔκουν ἐάσεις οὐδ᾽ ὑπ᾽ εὐφήμου βοῆς | θῦσαί με, H. F. 289 ὥστ᾽ οὐκ ἀνεκτὸν δειλίας θανεῖν σ᾽ ὕπο.

ὡς θάνοι, the reading of Pal. and Flor., would mean 'I came that he might die'.

1302. 'To all of us, who have pleasure in a maiden life'. Weil's ὅσαις τε may be right.

1304. Cf. 398, 399, where τῷ σωφρονεῖν corresponds to γνώμῃ here.

1306. **νόσον.** Cf. supr. 40 n.

1307. **ὥσπερ οὖν δίκαιον,** 'as indeed was right'. ὥσπερ οὖν is a favourite expression with Aesch., from whom Weckl. quotes

Cho. 95 ἀτίμως, ὥσπερ οὖν ἀπώλετο: ib. 887: Ag. 612: so too Ag. 1171, 1427.

1312. ἀλλ' ὅμως emphasizes ψευδεῖς: 'false as was her accusation, yet etc.'

1315. τρεῖς ἀρὰς σαφεῖς. Cf. supr. 44, 890.

1316. παρεῖλες, 'wasted', 'used for a wrong (παρ-) purpose'. From παρεῖλες we must supply the idea of 'employ', to follow ἐξὸν in the next line.

1319. χρῆν, imperfect: 'so much as he was bound to give, in that he had promised'. Cf. supr. 41 n. For this sense of αἰνεῖν, cf. Alc. 12 ᾔνεσαν δέ μοι θεαὶ | Ἄδμητον ᾅδην τὸν παραυτίκ' ἐκφυγεῖν.

1320. ἐν τ' ἐκείνῳ κἂν ἐμοί, 'in his judgment and in mine'. ἐν of the court or persons by whom one is judged; cf. supr. 988 οἱ γὰρ ἐν σοφοῖς φαῦλοι, Soph. Ant. 459 ἐν θεοῖσι τὴν δίκην | δώσειν, Plat. Gorg. 464 D εἰ δέοι ἐν παισὶ διαγωνίζεσθαι.

1321. Cf. supr. 1055 n.

1325. ἀλλ' ὅμως, cf. supr. 47 n.

1327. ἤθελ' ὥστε γίγνεσθαι. ὥστε is redundant. Cf. Soph. O. C. 1350 δικαιῶν ὥστ' ἐμοῦ κλύειν λόγους, Thuc. i. 119 δεηθέντες ὥστε ψηφίσασθαι, Eur. Or. 52 ἐλπίδα δὲ δή τιν' ἔχομεν ὥστε μὴ θανεῖν.

1328. πληροῦσα θυμόν. Cf. Soph. Phil. 324 θυμὸν γένοιτο χειρὶ πληρῶσαί ποτε, Verg. Aen. ii. 586 *animumque explesse juvabit | ultricis flammae.*

1329. ἀπαντᾶν, 'to meet' (in hostile fashion), 'resist', 'cross'. Valck. quotes Ov. Met. iii. 336 *neque enim licet irrita cuiquam | facta dei fecisse deo,* xiv. 784 *nisi quod rescindere nunquam | dis licet acta deum.*

1330. ἀφιστάμεσθ', 'we refrain'. Cf. Pind. Ol. i. 84 ἀφίσταμαι, P. 4. 259.

1331. ἐπεὶ σάφ' ἴσθι, 'else (if this were not so) be sure'. Cf. Soph. O. C. 969 ἐπεὶ δίδαξον, El. 352, Plat. Gorg. 473 D ἃ οὐδεὶς ἂν φήσειεν ἀνθρώπων, ἐπεὶ ἐροῦ τινὰ τουτωνί.

1335. τὸ μὴ εἰδέναι, a very common synizesis: cf. Soph. O. C. 1155: Ant. 263, 535. Eur. Ion 313.

ἐκλύει, 'acquits'. The forensic tone is observable here, as earlier in the play.

1336. ἀνάλωσεν λόγων ἐλέγχους, 'destroyed the opportunity of testing her words'. Weil's conjecture κατθανοῦσ' for δ' ἡ θανοῦσ' would be an improvement. The rendering given above is not

certain. For ἀνάλωσεν one might conjecture ἀνήστωσεν, 'has destroyed'.

1340. **θνήσκοντας οὐ χαίρουσι.** Cf. Soph. Aj. 136 σέ μὲν εὖ
πράσσοντ' ἐπιχαίρω, Phil. 1314 ἤσθην πατέρα τὸν ἀμὸν εὐλογοῦν-
τά σε. According to the Etym. M. the construction was a peculiarity
of Oropus.

'γὲ μὴν expresses an opposition more strongly than δὲ but with
transition to something new'. Madv. G. S. § 250.

1341. **αὐτοῖς τέκνοισι.** Cf. supr. 1189 n.

1342. **καὶ μήν** (without γε), introducing a fresh character.

1344. **διαλυμανθείς,** used especially to denote personal dis-
figurement: cf. Herod. v. 33 ὅτε τὸν ξεῖνον δήσας λυμαίνοιτο.

1346. **καταληπτόν** seems here to be transitive, a use paralleled
in Hippocrates 380 E. Cf. supr. 1204 νεανικός. From the frequency
of medical metaphors and the not uncommon verbal correspondence
between Eur. and the contemporary founder of medical science, we
may infer Eur.'s interest in the study and intimacy with its expounder.

1349. **χρησμοῖς,** the answer of heaven to the unjust curse of his
father.

1352. **πηδᾷ,** 'throbs'. σφάκελος, 'a spasm of pain'. Cf.
Aesch. Prom. 877 ὑπό μ' αὖ σφάκελος καὶ φρενοπληγεῖς | μανίαι
θάλπουσ'.

1353. **σχές...ἀναπαύσω.** Cf. ἐπίσχετ'...ἐκμάθω supr. 567 n.

The hiatus after ἀναπαύσω, which is contrary to rule in anapaests,
is to be explained by the long pause, during which Hipp. is
prevented by his sufferings from speaking.

1355. **ὄχημα.** Cf. supr. 1229 n. Ar. Pax 866 ὄχημα καν-
θάρου.

1360. **δεξιά,** adverbial. Some MSS have τίς ἐφέστηκ' ἐνδέξια ;

1361. **σύντονα,** 'smoothly', 'without jarring', a metaphor from
music.

1365. **ὑπερσχών.** So Valck. for ὑπερέχων, as an anapaest
following a dactyl is a position carefully avoided by the tragedians.

1366. Cf. Soph. O. C. 1440 ὁρμώμενον εἰς προῦπτον ᾅδην.

The MSS vary between κατὰ γᾶς and κατάκρας. Weil reads
κατάραις.

1372. The reading is uncertain, and the line incomplete.

1373. **Θάνατος Παιάν,** 'death the healer'. Cf. Aesch. fr. 244
ὦ θάνατε παιάν, μή μ' ἀτιμάσῃς μολεῖν· | μόνος γὰρ εἶ σὺ τῶν ἀνη-
κέστων κακῶν | ἰατρός, ἄλγος δ' οὐδὲν ἅπτεται νεκροῦ, Soph. O. C. 955

θανόντων δ' οὐδὲν ἄλγος ἅπτεται, Eur. Alc. 937 τῆς μὲν γὰρ οὐδὲν ἄλγος ἅψεταί ποτε.

1374. **προσαπόλλυτέ μ' ὄλλυτε.** The simple verb only is repeated, by a common Greek idiom. Cf. Bacch. 1065 κατῆγεν ἦγεν ἦγεν, Hec. 168 ἀπωλέσατ' ὠλέσατε, Med. 1252 κατίδετ' ἴδετε. Some words have fallen out here also.

1375. Porson, comparing Med. 1399 φιλίου χρῄζω στόματος | παίδων ὁ τάλας προσπτύξασθαι, shows that the construction is ἔραμαι ἀμφιτόμου λόγχας, διαμοιρᾶσαι: for the last word, cf. Hec. 716.

1379. With Weckl. I have read τι for τε: συγγόνων then depends on κακόν τι. The σύγγονοι were Atreus and Thyestes, Theseus' great-uncles.

1381. **ἐξορίζεται** is explained '*terminatur in me*'. εἰς ἐμὲ ὁρίζεται Schol. 'finds its issue in me'. Cf. supr. 831 πρόσωθεν δέ ποθεν ἀνακομίζομαι | τύχαν δαιμόνων | ἀμπλακίαισι τῶν πάροιθέν τινος.

1386. **ἀναλγήτου,** 'cruel', Monk. Taken with πάθους, it may be proleptic, 'relieve my life of this misery, then felt no more'.

1387. 'Would that the black night of death's necessity would lull me from my misery to rest'.

1389. **οἵαις συμφοραῖς συνεζύγης.** Cf. Andr. 98 δαίμον' ᾧ συνεζύγην, Hel. 262 τίνι πότμῳ συνεζύγην;

1391. Prometheus recognises the presence of the Oceanides (Aesch. Prom. 115) with the words, τίς ἀχώ, τίς ὀδμὰ προσέπτα μ' ἀφεγγής; cf. Verg. Aen. i. 507 *ambrosiaeque comae divinum vertice odorem* | *spiravere,* Ov. Fast. v. 375 *tenues secessit in auras:* | *mansit odor: posses scire fuisse deam.*

1394. **φιλτάτη,** active: 'most well-disposed'.

1396. Cf. Ov. Met. ii. 621 *neque enim caelestia tingi* | *ora decet lacrimis.*

1401. **φρονῶ,** 'I recognise'. Cf. Soph. O. C. 791 ἆρ' οὐκ ἄμεινον ἢ σὺ τὰν Θήβαις φρονῶ;

1402. **τιμή** is here put for lack of τιμή. Cf. Hom. Il. i. 93 οὔτ' ἄρ' ὅ γ' εὐχωλῆς ἐπιμέμφεται οὔθ' ἑκατόμβης. For the gen. cf. Hadley Gr. § 744.

1403. Most MSS have ᾔσθημαι Κύπρις. The text is due to Valck., who adduces many examples of similar antithesis, e.g. I. T. 1065 τρεῖς μία τύχη ἔχει, Or. 1244 τρισσοῖς φίλοις γὰρ εἷς ἀγών, δίκη μία.

1405. **ᾤμωξα,** cf. supr. 614 n.

1409. **'μέ** for ἐμαυτόν. Cf. Andr. 256 ἀλλ' οὐδ' ἐγὼ μὴν ἐκδώσω μέ σοι.

1411. **δῶρα σοῦ πατρὸς πικρά.** 'Bitter as my father's are to me' is implied by the emphatic σοῦ.

1412. **ὡς μήποτ' ὤφελ'.** Cf. Hadley Gr. § 871 a.

1415. **ἀραῖον**, active: 'would that mortal man could bring curses upon gods'. **δαίμοσιν**, the generalizing plural, refers as the context shows to Aphrodite specially. For ἀραῖον, cf. Soph. O. T. 1291 οὐδ' ἔτι | μενῶν δόμοις ἀραῖος, Eur. Med. 608 καὶ σοῖς ἀραία γ' οὖσα τυγχάνω δόμοις, I. T. 778 ἀραία δώμασιν γενήσομαι.

1416. **γάρ.** Both here and in 1420 γὰρ follows ἔασον: 'let be, for otherwise it will be the worse for you', and 'let be, for I will avenge you'.

οὐ γὰρ οὐδέ. Cf. Soph. Tr. 280 ὕβριν γὰρ οὐ στέργουσιν οὐδὲ δαίμονες.

1417. **ἄτιμοι**, 'unhonoured', i.e. without effect.

1418. Both κατα- and ἀπο-σκήπτω are used of the rushing down of a storm, sudden attacks of sickness, and the like. Here and supr. 438 of the divine anger falling upon its victim.

1419. A spurious line imported from infr. 1454.

1420. **αὐτῆς**, 'belonging to her', i.e. dear to her. The Schol. points out that the reference is to Adonis, who was slain by Artemis, when hunting. The honours paid to Hipp. in Troezen after his death are so similar to those with which Adonis was worshipped, as to suggest intimate connection between the two myths.

1421. **μάλιστα φίλτατος**, cf. supr. 485 n.

1423. In Med. 1381 and I. T. 1449 wronged innocence is, as here, in a way recompensed by the promise of posthumous honours.

1425. Cf. Paus. ii. 32, where, after giving an account of the general cult of Hippolytus he adds, δρῶσι δὲ καὶ ἄλλο τοιόνδε· ἑκάστη παρθένος πλόκαμον ἀποκείρεται οἱ πρὸ γάμου, κειραμένη δὲ ἀνέθηκεν ἐς τὸν ναὸν φέρουσα.

1427. **καρπουμένῳ.** Valck.'s correction of the MSS καρπούμεναι, which destroys the sense: 'receiving as thy reward through length of days the deep sorrowings of their tears'. For the meaning of καρποῦσθαι, cf. supr. 432 n.

1429. **μέριμνα μουσοποιός**, 'tuneful care', 'a care which prompts to song'. If there were singing contests at the anniversary celebration of Hipp.'s death, μέριμνα could bear its usual Pindaric sense of anxious care or striving for victory.

κοὐκ ἀνώνυμος, cf. supr. 1 n.

1432. προσέλκυσαι, 'strain him to thy breast'. Cf. I. A. 1452 προσέλκυσαί νιν ὕστατον θεωμένη.

1434. θεῶν διδόντων, 'when gods prompt'.

1436. ἔχεις, 'thou knowest the fate, by which thou art undone, and that not thy father, but Cypris, is its author; therefore be reconciled'.

1437. Cf. Alc. 22, where Apollo says τῆδε γάρ σφ' ἐν ἡμέρᾳ | θανεῖν πέπρωται καὶ μεταστῆναι βίου. | ἐγὼ δὲ μὴ μίασμά μ' ἐν δόμοις κίχῃ | λείπω μελάθρων τῶνδε φιλτάτην στέγην.

1440. χαίρουσα καὶ σὺ στεῖχε, i.e. καὶ σὺ χαῖρε στείχουσα. For the mood-sense of the finite verb continued in the participle, cf. supr. 105 n.

ὀλβία contrasts with his own misery: notice how this sense of contrast is brought out in the next line.

1441. In spite of some critics, who seek to justify the excision of this line on the ground of its feebleness, it seems to me the most beautiful in this most beautiful scene. The half-tender reproach, which brings into contrast the lofty calm of the goddess and the yearning for sympathy and help of the mortal in his agony, is unsurpassable.

1444. Cf. fr. 803 πρὶν ἂν κατ' ὄσσων κιγχάνῃ μέλας σκότος.

1447. νερτέρων πύλας, cf. supr. 56.

1448. ἄναγνον, 'with the stain of blood upon it'.

1450. Theseus can hardly credit his son's magnanimity.

1453. Wilamowitz, with much probability, transposes 1453 and 1455.

1455. γνησίων. In its pathos, this word is comparable to the ῥᾳδίως of 1441 ; the thought, that he, the type of purity, should be νόθος seems ever present to the mind of Hippolytus: cf. supr. 1083.

1457. κεκαρτέρηται τἀμά, 'my time for bearing up is done'.

1458. Cf. Hec. 432 κόμιζ' Ὀδυσσεῦ μ' ἀμφιθεὶς κάρα πέπλοις, Soph. Aj. 915 ἀλλά νιν περιπτυχεῖ | φάρει καλύψω, Tro. 626 εἶδόν νιν αὐτὴ κἀποβᾶσα τῶνδ' ὄχων | ἔκρυψα πέπλοις.

1462. Weckl. quotes Callinus fr. i. 18 λαῷ γὰρ σύμπαντι πόθος κρατερόφρονος ἀνδρὸς | θνήσκοντος. It is generally supposed that these verses contain a reference to the death of Pericles, which took place the year before the production of this play. Stobaeus preserves for us the concluding lines of the earlier Hippolytus: ὦ μάκαρ οἵας ἔλαχες τιμὰς | Ἱππόλυθ' ἥρως διὰ σωφροσύνην· | οὔποτε θνητοῖς ἀρετῆς ἄλλη | δύναμις μείζων· | ἦλθε γὰρ ἢ πρόσθ' ἢ μετόπισθεν | τῆς εὐσεβίας χάρις ἐσθλή.

1464. **πίτυλος**, 'plash'. The word denotes any quick repeated movement, e.g. of the hands, Tro. 1236, Aesch. Theb. 856: of oars, I. T. 1050: of wine poured into a cup, Alc. 798: metaphorically, of madness, I. T. 307.

1465. **τῶν μεγάλων φῆμαι**, like φάτις δεσποίνας, supr. 130: 'for the sorrowing talk of men concerning the illustrious prevaileth more widely' (than concerning the obscure).

κατέχουσιν, intrans. Cf. Thuc. i. 10 ὁ λόγος κατέχει.

APPENDICES.

A.

477 sq.

The difficulties of the scene begin here : nor has any entirely satisfactory solution of them been discovered. Free excision has been recommended by some : by others dismemberment and re-construction on kaleidoscopic principles. The first edition is apt to exercise a will-o'-the-wisp-like influence on the ingenuity of editors. Here however the important question of the intentions and character of Phaedra and the nurse has to be discussed. My reading is as follows. 'You have fallen in love by no fault of your own : love is too strong for gods, much more for men and women (and therefore you must yield)'. Next the nurse alludes to what she imagines must be one of the causes of Phaedra's despair, namely the thought of Theseus. She urges (462 sq.) that wise men do not allow domestic scandals to get abroad : that they pretend not to see, or even abet, the guilty passions, which they cannot fail to notice. Lastly (476 sq.), she hints obscurely at possible means of gaining the compliance of the icy Hippolytus himself, thus, as she imagines, having dealt with all the questions, which are distracting her beloved mistress. Had she spoken plainly, she would have said : 'the world will not know, so your honour will be safe : for Theseus will do anything to avoid scandal : and as for your doubt, whether Hippolytus himself will consent, you must remember that there are such things as charms and potions'. Necessarily however she speaks obscurely, and hopes to be able to judge from her mistress' replies, what Phaedra in her inmost heart desires. The latter, in her answer, contents herself with a general remark on the abuse of eloquence. The nurse, emboldened, speaks out more plainly. Phaedra replies with (as the nurse believes) affected horror. On the latter pressing her case still more strongly, Phaedra can but answer, 'Hush, I implore, or I may yield to your terrible promptings'. The nurse, now satisfied that she has followed her mistress' mind, speaks again of her love-philtres, but in such a way, as to make it possible for Phaedra, in case of failure, to disclaim all knowledge of her real intention. All that Phaedra can say is weakly to ask about the manner of application, whether it is a plaster or a draught, and finally (a triumph of the poet's ingenuity), actually to suggest, under guise of warning, the very course the nurse has resolved upon, who naturally goes away fully convinced that she has Phaedra's secret approbation, while with entire self-devotion she has left it possible for her mistress to disclaim all complicity in case of failure. That this is so, line 700 seems to show. 'If I had succeeded' says the nurse 'you would have had a very different name for me'. She acquiesces in her mistress' repudiation, and silently disappears. Phaedra I believe to have understood the nurse's reference to the φίλτρα and ἐπῳδαί literally, and to have imagined that her faithful attendant was intending to try to win for her Hippolytus' affection by their means. That for the moment, at any rate, her passion (under the suggestions of the nurse) gained supremacy over her, I have no doubt. My reading of the scene has one merit at least—it involves no surgery.

B.

953.

Orpheus was unknown to the authors of the Homeric and Hesiodic poems, though from the lyric period onwards reference to him is continual. About no personage is wrapped a greater obscurity; but it was this very obscurity, together with the tradition which ascribed to him the authorship of a large body of mystic hymns, which pointed to him as a suitable person for the association, thenceforth known as Orphic, to claim as founder. About the time of Pisistratus, one Onomacritus collected a large body of writings assigned to Orpheus (the composition of a large part of which was attributed to Onomacritus himself), and this became the nucleus of a very considerable Orphic literature (cf. πολλῶν γραμμάτων τιμῶν καπνούς).

Orphism seems to have been an attempt at religious and moral reform. Closely allied to the mysteries, it endeavoured to bring to a more extended circle the influence of their teaching, which was confined to the few initiated, and felt only at recurring periods, and to make that influence constant in its operation, by insisting on a prescribed method of daily life. In Theology, it taught that the many deities were the expression of the many attributes and powers of the one universal Life, ruler of the world: in morals, the necessity of purity of thought and act, for the attainment of final happiness through an upward series of unspotted lives. Its god was the mystic Dionysus Zagreus (cf. βάκχευε 954): its prophet the equally mystic Orpheus. Abstention (after the initiatory banquet of the raw bull's-flesh, the symbolic ὠμοφαγία) from all food, which had contained the principle of life (Plato Laws vi. 782 c), and white dress (Herod. ii. 81), were its outward marks to the half-respecting, wholly suspecting public, who resented the claims of its professors to superior purity of life, while they pointed with scorn to the abuses of the so-called Ὀρφεοτελεσταί, wandering charlatans described by Plato (Rep. ii. 364). Cf. too Theophr. Char. 28 sub fin. Still the influence of Orphism, in many points analogous to the Indian asceticism, may be traced on several of the highest minds of Greece, on Pindar, on Aeschylus, on Euripides, on Plato. Theseus seems to give expression to the views of an average Athenian citizen. On Orphism generally, cf. Girard, Sentiment Religieux, pp. 207—290, 337 sq. The following fragment from the Κρῆτες of Euripides is worth quoting in connection with the subject (fr. 475 a, 9—19).

> ἁγνὸν δὲ βίον τείνομεν ἐξ οὗ
> Διὸς Ἰδαίου μύστης γενόμην,
> καὶ νυκτιπόλου Ζαγρέως βροντὰς
> τάς τ' ὠμοφάγους δαῖτας τελέσας
> μητρί τ' ὀρείᾳ δᾷδας ἀνασχὼν
> καὶ Κουρήτων
> βάκχος ἐκλήθην ὁσιωθείς·
> πάλλευκα δ' ἔχων εἵματα φεύγω
> γένεσίν τε βροτῶν καὶ νεκροθήκης.
> οὐ χριμπτόμενος τήν τ' ἐμψύχων
> βρῶσιν ἐδεστῶν πεφύλαγμαι.

GREEK INDEX.

9

ENGLISH INDEX.

www.ingramcontent.com/pod-product-compliance
Ingram Content Group UK Ltd.
Pitfield, Milton Keynes, MK11 3LW, UK
UKHW042146280225
455719UK00001B/131